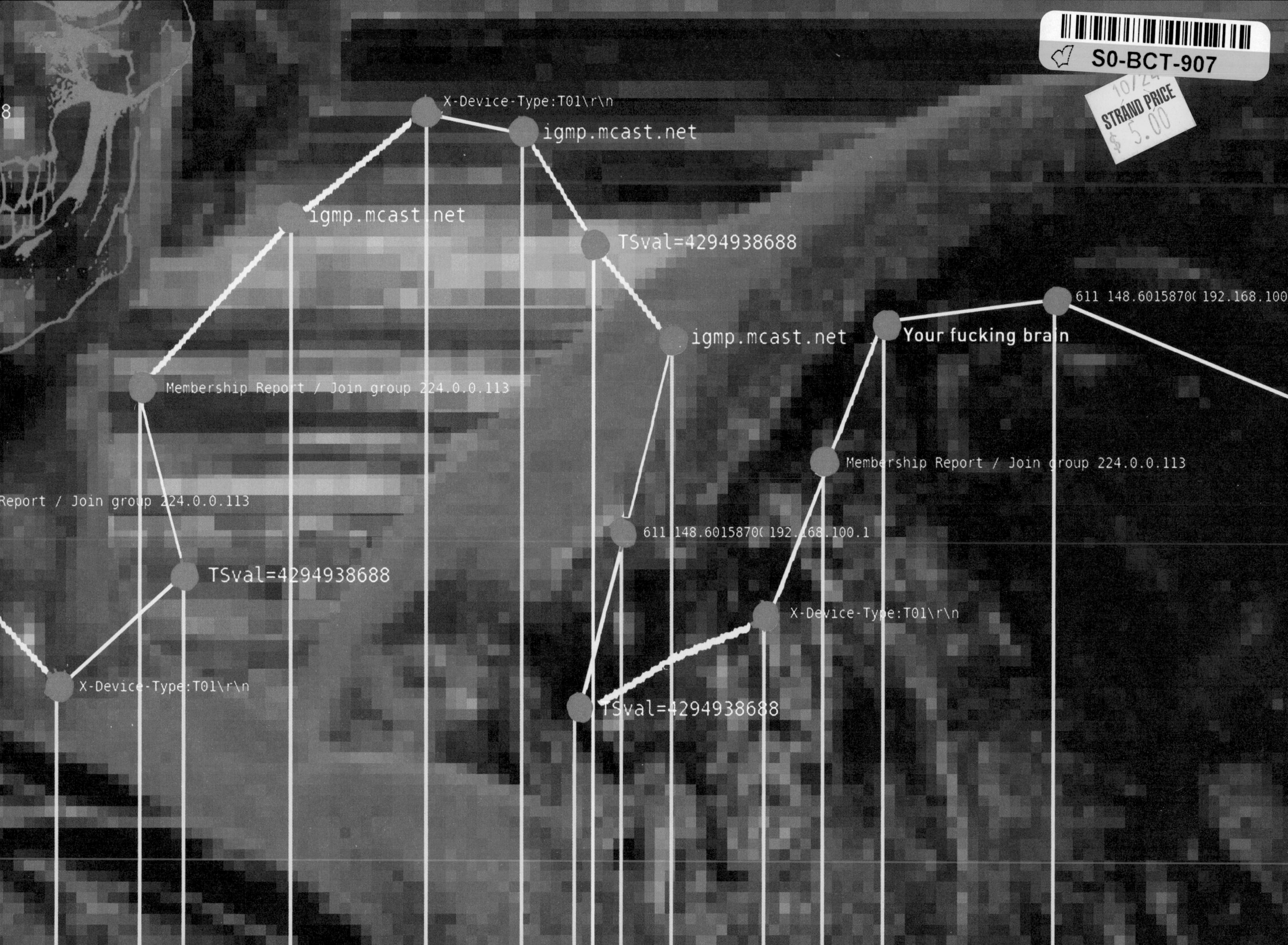
X-Device-Type:T01\r\n
igmp.mcast.net
igmp.mcast.net
TSval=4294938688
igmp.mcast.net
611 148.6015870(192.168.100
Your fucking brain
Membership Report / Join group 224.0.0.113
Membership Report / Join group 224.0.0.113
Report / Join group 224.0.0.113
611 148.6015870(192.168.100.1
TSval=4294938688
X-Device-Type:T01\r\n
X-Device-Type:T01\r\n
TSval=4294938688

Written by **Marcos Prior**   Illustrated by **David Rubín**

GRAND ABYSS HOTEL™

Translated by **Andrea Rosenberg**   Lettered by **Deron Bennett**

Published by
ARCHAIA™

Los Angeles, California

Cover by **David Rubín**

ENGLISH EDITION
Designer **Scott Newman**
Assistant Editor **Gavin Gronenthal**
Editor **Sierra Hahn**

Ross Richie CEO & Founder
Joy Huffman CFO
Matt Gagnon Editor-in-Chief
Filip Sablik President, Publishing & Marketing
Stephen Christy President, Development
Lance Kreiter Vice President, Licensing & Merchandising
Phil Barbaro Vice President, Finance & Human Resources
Arune Singh Vice President, Marketing
Bryce Carlson Vice President, Editorial & Creative Strategy
Scott Newman Manager, Production Design
Kate Henning Manager, Operations
Spencer Simpson Manager, Sales
Sierra Hahn Executive Editor
Jeanine Schaefer Executive Editor
Dafna Pleban Senior Editor
Shannon Watters Senior Editor
Eric Harburn Senior Editor
Chris Rosa Editor
Matthew Levine Editor
Sophie Philips-Roberts Assistant Editor
Gavin Gronenthal Assistant Editor

Michael Moccio Assistant Editor
Gwen Waller Assistant Editor
Amanda LaFranco Executive Assistant
Jillian Crab Design Coordinator
Michelle Ankley Design Coordinator
Kara Leopard Production Designer
Marie Krupina Production Designer
Grace Park Production Design Assistant
Chelsea Roberts Production Design Assistant
Samantha Knapp Production Design Assistant
Elizabeth Loughridge Accounting Coordinator
Stephanie Hocutt Social Media Coordinator
José Meza Event Coordinator
Holly Aitchison Digital Sales Coordinator
Esther Kim Marketing Coordinator
Megan Christopher Operations Assistant
Rodrigo Hernandez Mailroom Assistant
Morgan Perry Direct Market Representative
Cat O'Grady Marketing Assistant
Breanna Sarpy Executive Assistant

ARCHAIA™

BOOM! Studios, 5670 Wilshire Boulevard, Suite 400, Los Angeles, CA 90036-5679. Printed in China. First Printing.

ISBN: 978-1-68415-410-4, eISBN: 978-1-64144-463-7

Originally published in Spanish by Astiberri.

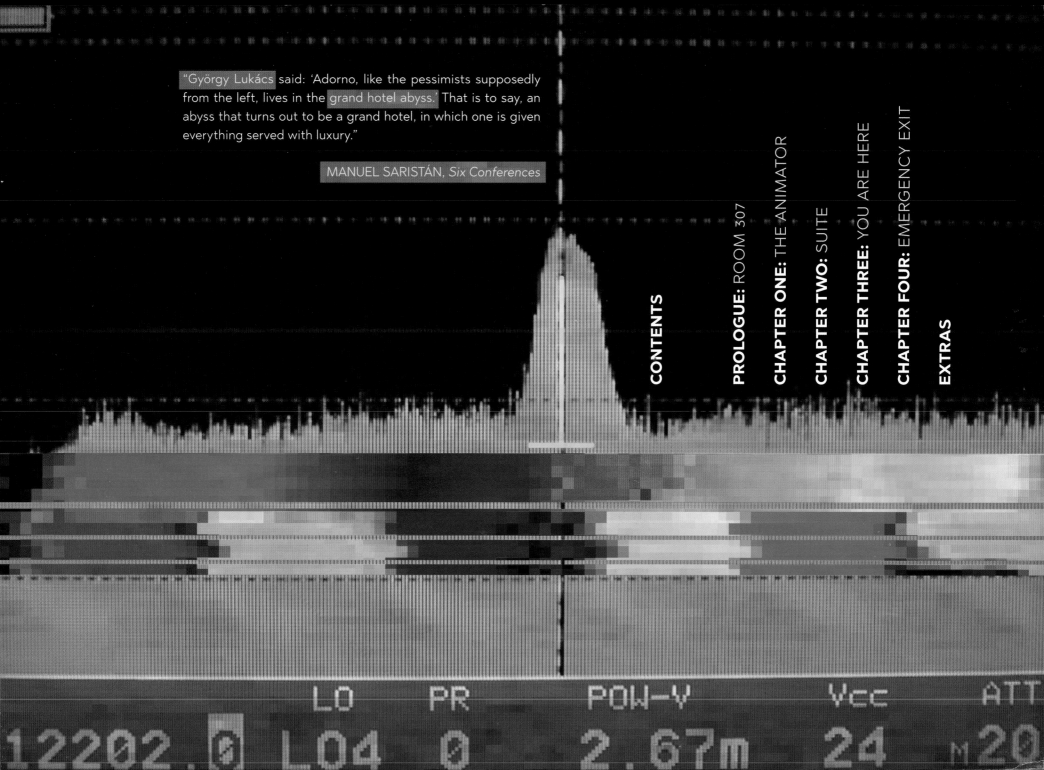

"György Lukács said: 'Adorno, like the pessimists supposedly from the left, lives in the grand hotel abyss.' That is to say, an abyss that turns out to be a grand hotel, in which one is given everything served with luxury."

MANUEL SARISTÁN, *Six Conferences*

CONTENTS

LO   PR   POW-V   Vcc   ATT

12202.0   L04 0   2.67m   24   M20

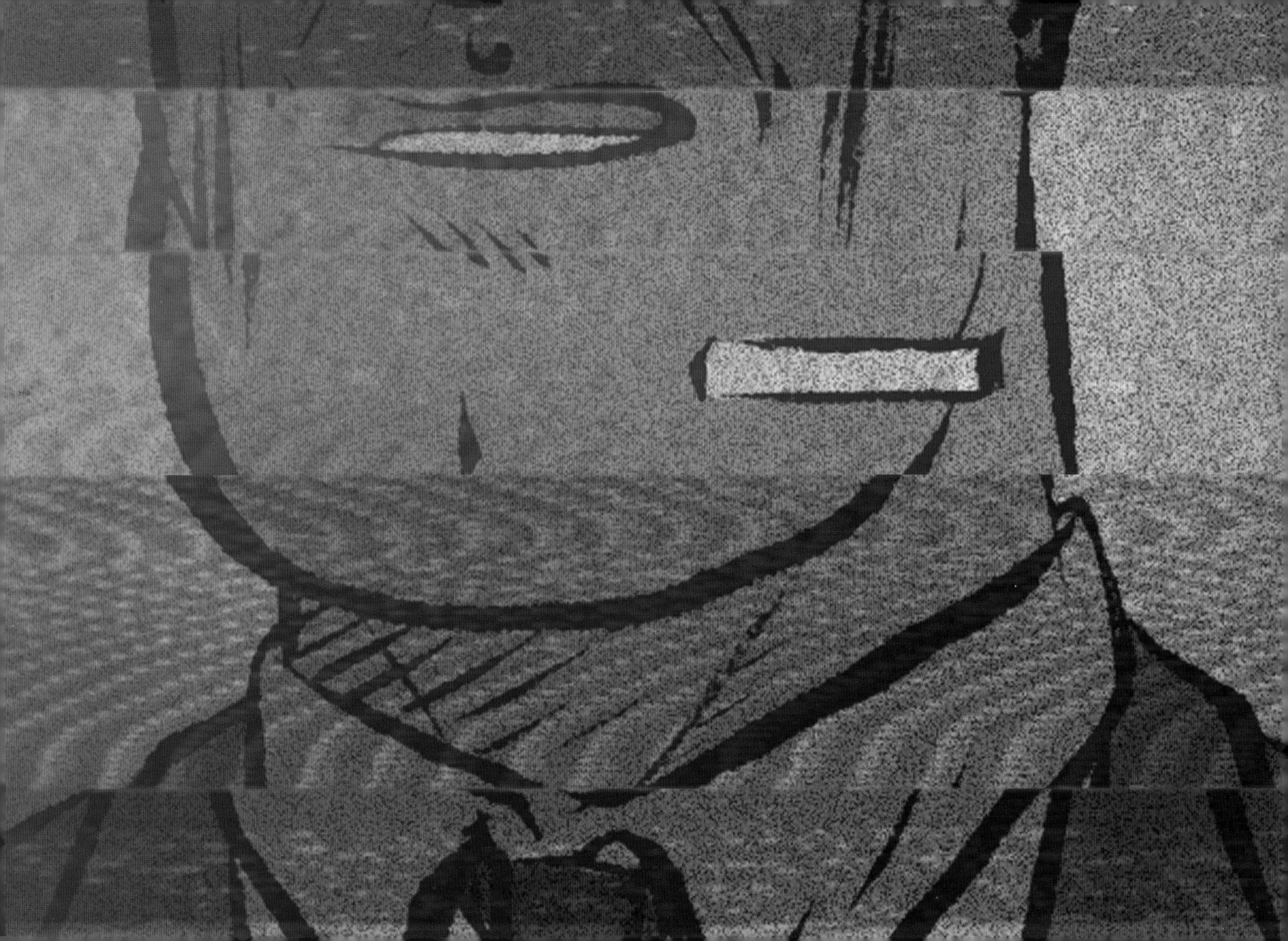

PROLOGUE: ROOM 307

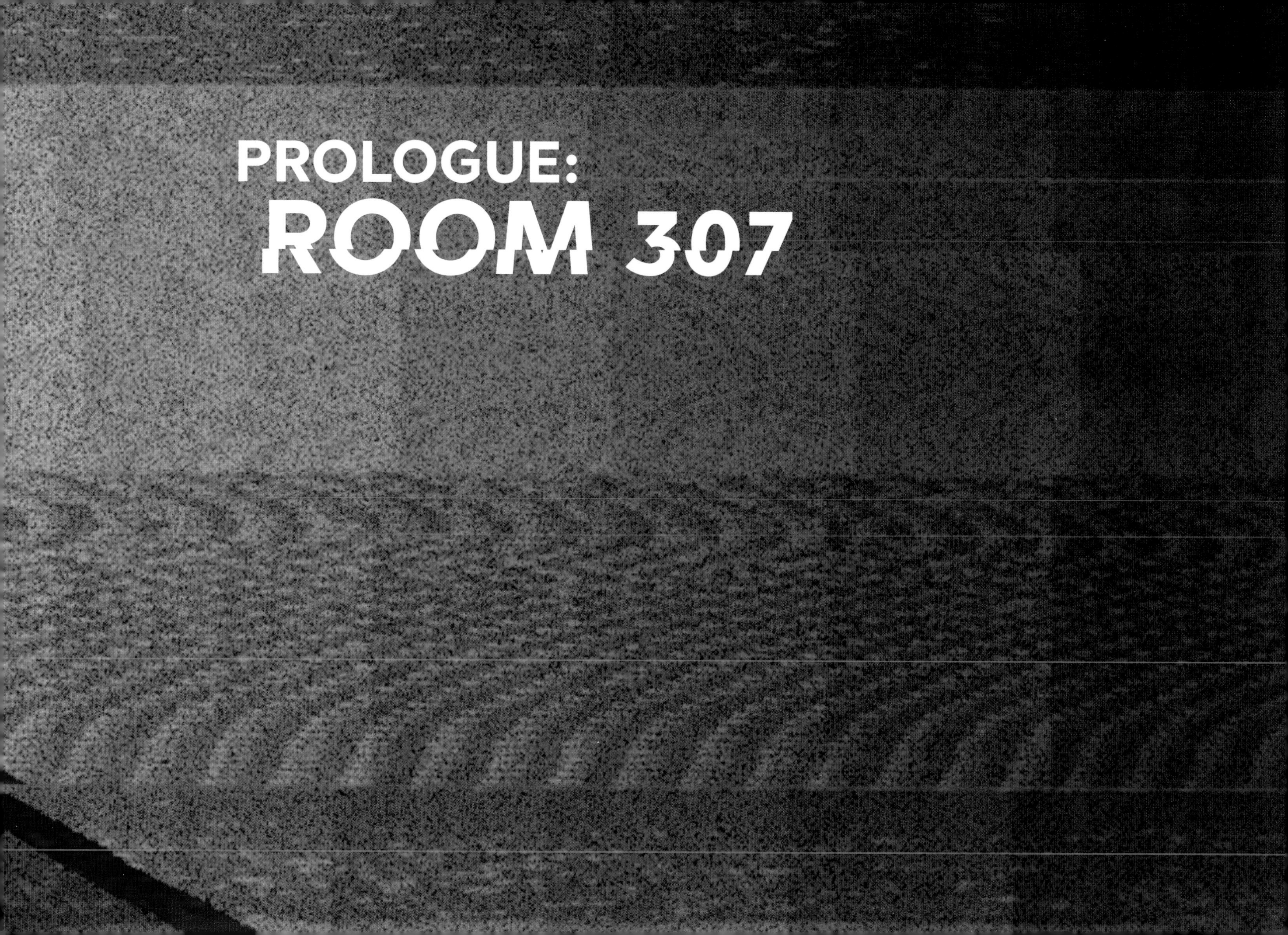

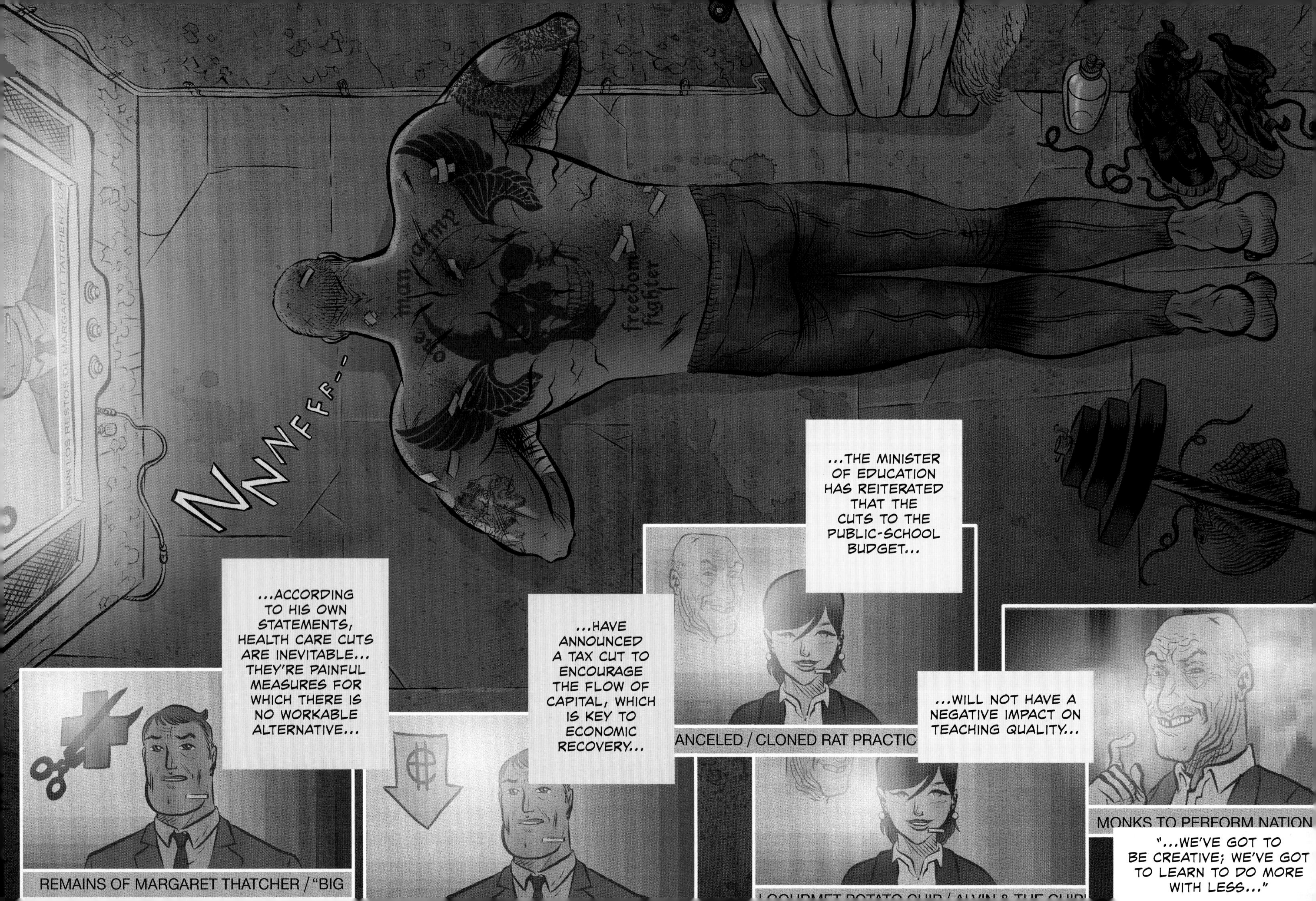

OBAN LOS RESTOS DE MARGARET TATCHER // CA
one man army
freedom fighter
NnnNFFf--
...ACCORDING TO HIS OWN STATEMENTS, HEALTH CARE CUTS ARE INEVITABLE... THEY'RE PAINFUL MEASURES FOR WHICH THERE IS NO WORKABLE ALTERNATIVE...
REMAINS OF MARGARET THATCHER / "BIG
...HAVE ANNOUNCED A TAX CUT TO ENCOURAGE THE FLOW OF CAPITAL, WHICH IS KEY TO ECONOMIC RECOVERY...
...THE MINISTER OF EDUCATION HAS REITERATED THAT THE CUTS TO THE PUBLIC-SCHOOL BUDGET...
ANCELED / CLONED RAT PRACTIC
...WILL NOT HAVE A NEGATIVE IMPACT ON TEACHING QUALITY...
MONKS TO PERFORM NATION
"...WE'VE GOT TO BE CREATIVE; WE'VE GOT TO LEARN TO DO MORE WITH LESS..."

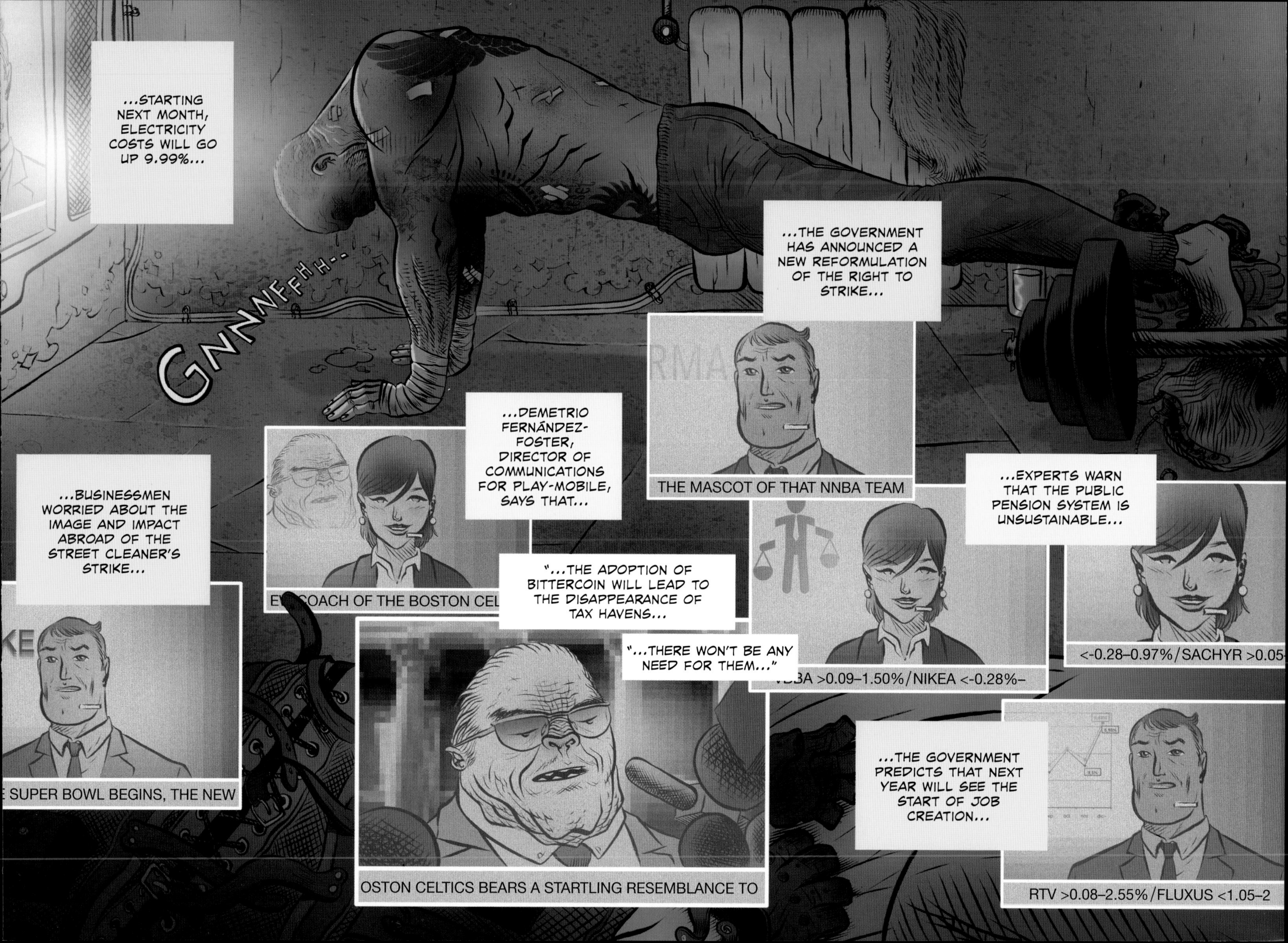
...STARTING NEXT MONTH, ELECTRICITY COSTS WILL GO UP 9.99%...
GNNNFFHH..
...THE GOVERNMENT HAS ANNOUNCED A NEW REFORMULATION OF THE RIGHT TO STRIKE...
THE MASCOT OF THAT NNBA TEAM
...DEMETRIO FERNÁNDEZ-FOSTER, DIRECTOR OF COMMUNICATIONS FOR PLAY-MOBILE, SAYS THAT...
COACH OF THE BOSTON CEL
...BUSINESSMEN WORRIED ABOUT THE IMAGE AND IMPACT ABROAD OF THE STREET CLEANER'S STRIKE...
SUPER BOWL BEGINS, THE NEW
"...THE ADOPTION OF BITTERCOIN WILL LEAD TO THE DISAPPEARANCE OF TAX HAVENS...
"...THERE WON'T BE ANY NEED FOR THEM..."
OSTON CELTICS BEARS A STARTLING RESEMBLANCE TO
...EXPERTS WARN THAT THE PUBLIC PENSION SYSTEM IS UNSUSTAINABLE...
BA >0.09–1.50%/NIKEA <-0.28%–
<-0.28–0.97%/SACHYR >0.05
...THE GOVERNMENT PREDICTS THAT NEXT YEAR WILL SEE THE START OF JOB CREATION...
RTV >0.08–2.55%/FLUXUS <1.05–2

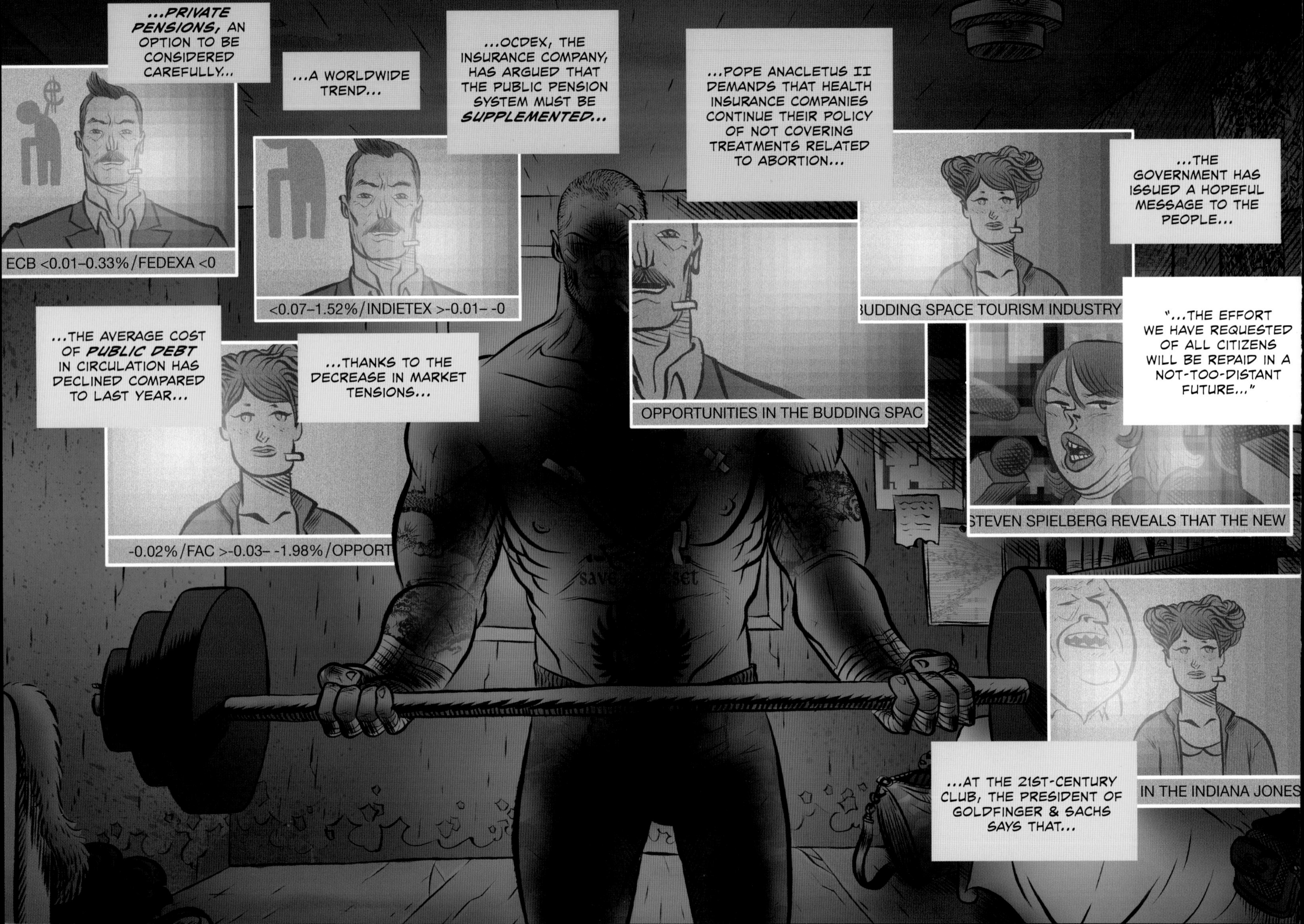

...PRIVATE PENSIONS, AN OPTION TO BE CONSIDERED CAREFULLY...
ECB <0.01–0.33%/FEDEXA <0
...A WORLDWIDE TREND...
<0.07–1.52%/INDIETEX >-0.01– -0
...OCDEX, THE INSURANCE COMPANY, HAS ARGUED THAT THE PUBLIC PENSION SYSTEM MUST BE SUPPLEMENTED...
...POPE ANACLETUS II DEMANDS THAT HEALTH INSURANCE COMPANIES CONTINUE THEIR POLICY OF NOT COVERING TREATMENTS RELATED TO ABORTION...
OPPORTUNITIES IN THE BUDDING SPAC
BUDDING SPACE TOURISM INDUSTRY
...THE GOVERNMENT HAS ISSUED A HOPEFUL MESSAGE TO THE PEOPLE...
...THE AVERAGE COST OF PUBLIC DEBT IN CIRCULATION HAS DECLINED COMPARED TO LAST YEAR...
...THANKS TO THE DECREASE IN MARKET TENSIONS...
-0.02%/FAC >-0.03– -1.98%/OPPORT
"...THE EFFORT WE HAVE REQUESTED OF ALL CITIZENS WILL BE REPAID IN A NOT-TOO-DISTANT FUTURE..."
STEVEN SPIELBERG REVEALS THAT THE NEW
IN THE INDIANA JONES
...AT THE 21ST-CENTURY CLUB, THE PRESIDENT OF GOLDFINGER & SACHS SAYS THAT...

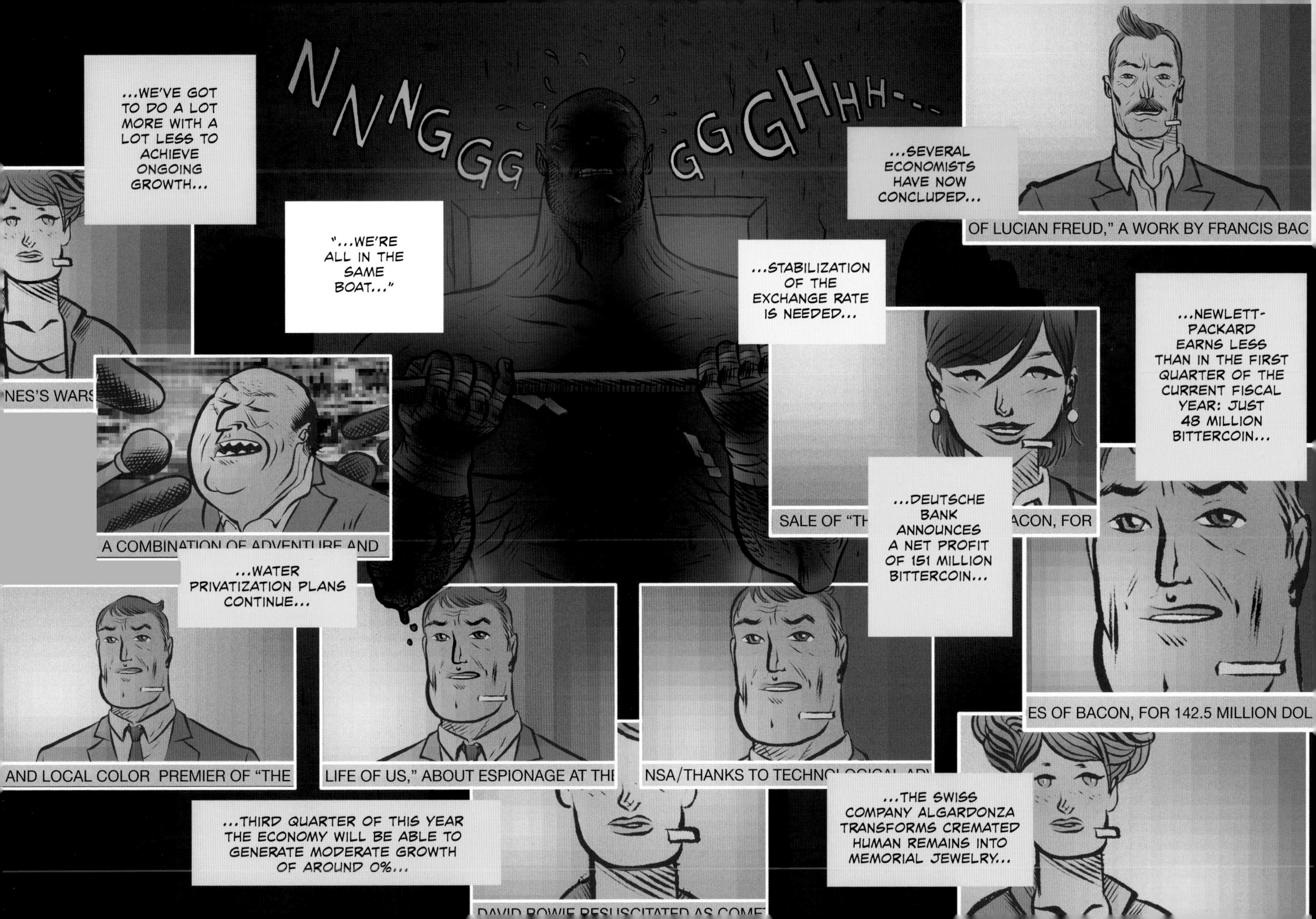
...WE'VE GOT TO DO A LOT MORE WITH A LOT LESS TO ACHIEVE ONGOING GROWTH...
NNNGGG GGGHHH-...
"...WE'RE ALL IN THE SAME BOAT..."
...SEVERAL ECONOMISTS HAVE NOW CONCLUDED...
OF LUCIAN FREUD," A WORK BY FRANCIS BAC
...STABILIZATION OF THE EXCHANGE RATE IS NEEDED...
NES'S WARS
A COMBINATION OF ADVENTURE AND
SALE OF "TH
ACON, FOR
...NEWLETT-PACKARD EARNS LESS THAN IN THE FIRST QUARTER OF THE CURRENT FISCAL YEAR: JUST 48 MILLION BITTERCOIN...
...DEUTSCHE BANK ANNOUNCES A NET PROFIT OF 151 MILLION BITTERCOIN...
...WATER PRIVATIZATION PLANS CONTINUE...
ES OF BACON, FOR 142.5 MILLION DOL
AND LOCAL COLOR PREMIER OF "THE
LIFE OF US," ABOUT ESPIONAGE AT THE
NSA/THANKS TO TECHNO
...THIRD QUARTER OF THIS YEAR THE ECONOMY WILL BE ABLE TO GENERATE MODERATE GROWTH OF AROUND 0%...
...THE SWISS COMPANY ALGARDONZA TRANSFORMS CREMATED HUMAN REMAINS INTO MEMORIAL JEWELRY...
DAVID BOWIE RESUSCITATED AS COMET

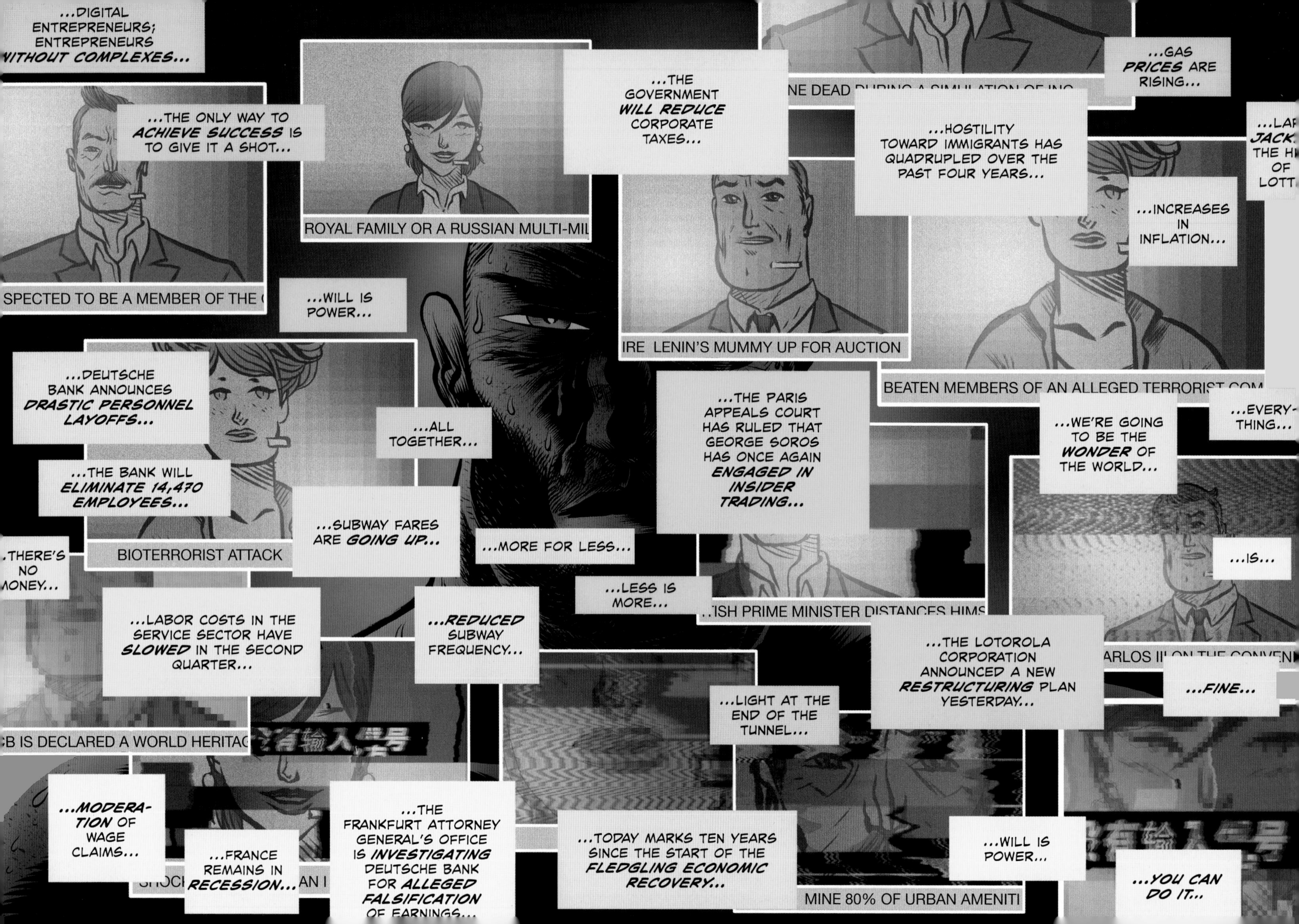

...DIGITAL ENTREPRENEURS; ENTREPRENEURS ITHOUT COMPLEXES...
...THE ONLY WAY TO ACHIEVE SUCCESS IS TO GIVE IT A SHOT...
ROYAL FAMILY OR A RUSSIAN MULTI-MIL
...THE GOVERNMENT WILL REDUCE CORPORATE TAXES...
NE DEAD
...GAS PRICES ARE RISING...
...HOSTILITY TOWARD IMMIGRANTS HAS QUADRUPLED OVER THE PAST FOUR YEARS...
...INCREASES IN INFLATION...
SPECTED TO BE A MEMBER OF THE
...WILL IS POWER...
IRE LENIN'S MUMMY UP FOR AUCTION
BEATEN MEMBERS OF AN ALLEGED TERRORIST
...DEUTSCHE BANK ANNOUNCES DRASTIC PERSONNEL LAYOFFS...
...ALL TOGETHER...
...THE PARIS APPEALS COURT HAS RULED THAT GEORGE SOROS HAS ONCE AGAIN ENGAGED IN INSIDER TRADING...
...WE'RE GOING TO BE THE WONDER OF THE WORLD...
...EVERY-THING...
...THE BANK WILL ELIMINATE 14,470 EMPLOYEES...
...SUBWAY FARES ARE GOING UP...
...MORE FOR LESS...
THERE'S NO ONEY...
BIOTERRORIST ATTACK
...IS...
...LESS IS MORE...
ISH PRIME MINISTER DISTANCES HIMS
...LABOR COSTS IN THE SERVICE SECTOR HAVE SLOWED IN THE SECOND QUARTER...
...REDUCED SUBWAY FREQUENCY...
...THE LOTOROLA CORPORATION ANNOUNCED A NEW RESTRUCTURING PLAN YESTERDAY...
ARLOS II
...FINE...
...LIGHT AT THE END OF THE TUNNEL...
B IS DECLARED A WORLD HERITAG
...MODERA-TION OF WAGE CLAIMS...
...FRANCE REMAINS IN RECESSION...
...THE FRANKFURT ATTORNEY GENERAL'S OFFICE IS INVESTIGATING DEUTSCHE BANK FOR ALLEGED FALSIFICATION OF EARNINGS...
...TODAY MARKS TEN YEARS SINCE THE START OF THE FLEDGLING ECONOMIC RECOVERY...
MINE 80% OF URBAN AMENITI
...WILL IS POWER...
...YOU CAN DO IT...

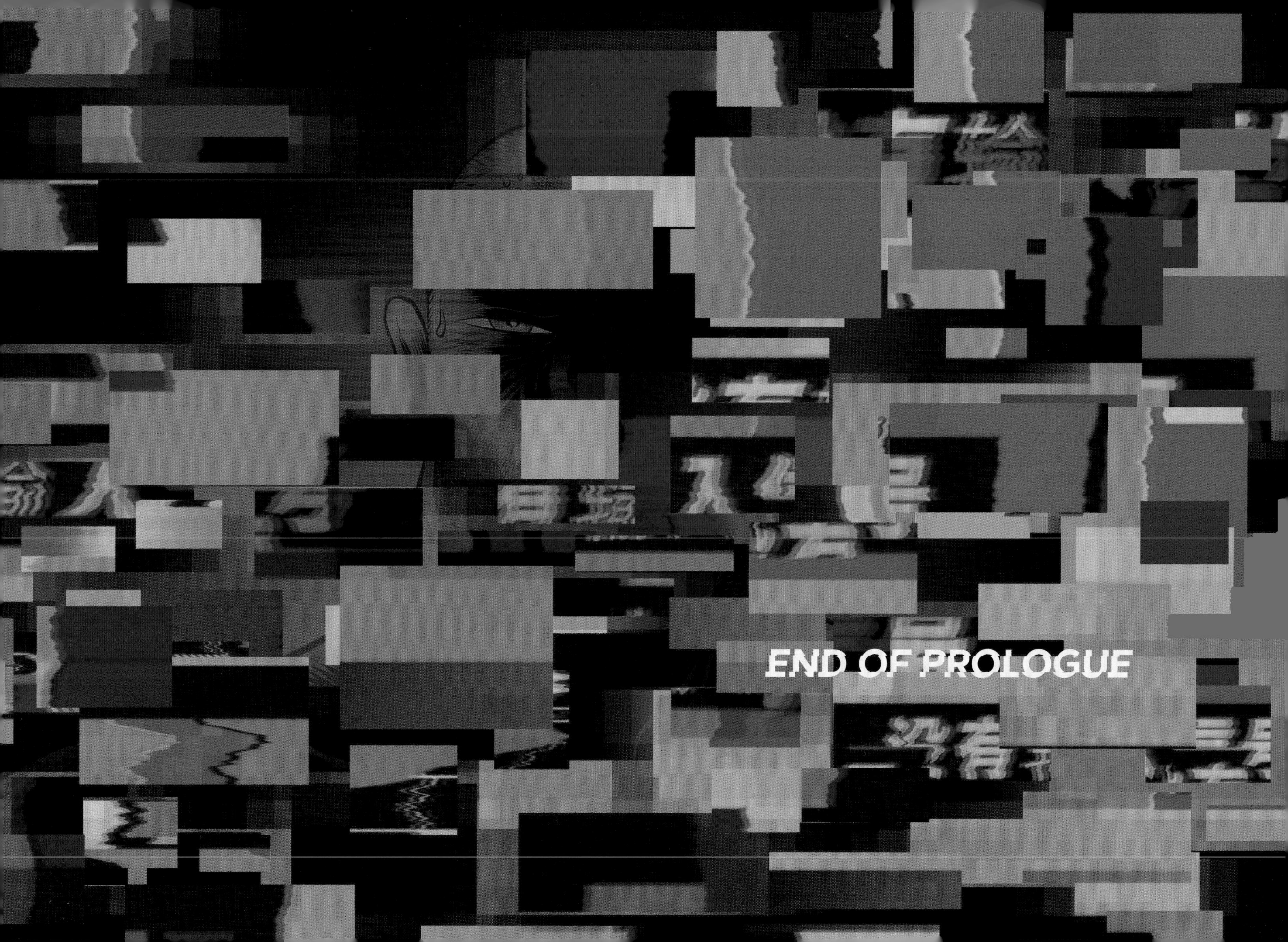
END OF PROLOGUE

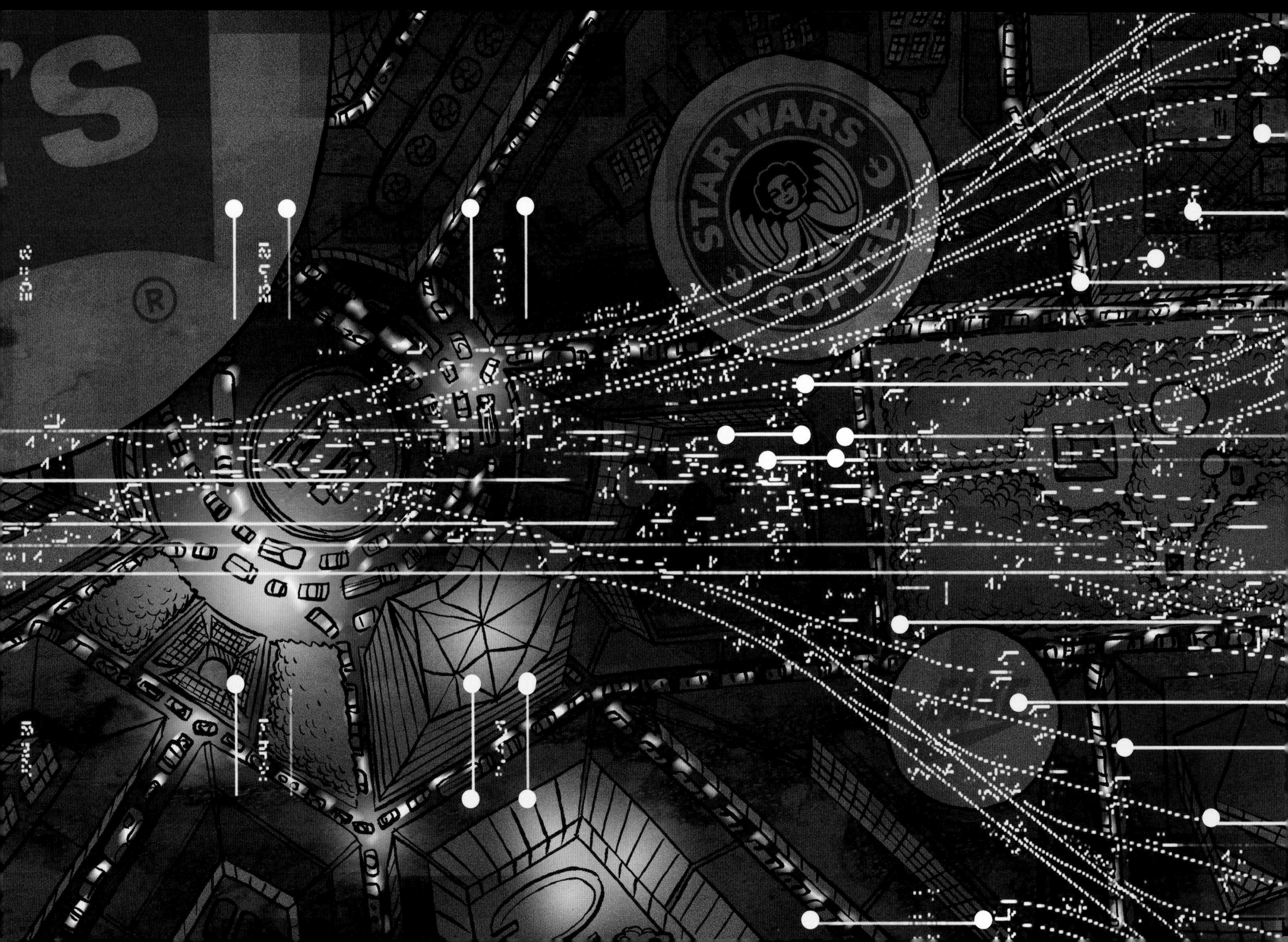
STAR WARS
COFFEE

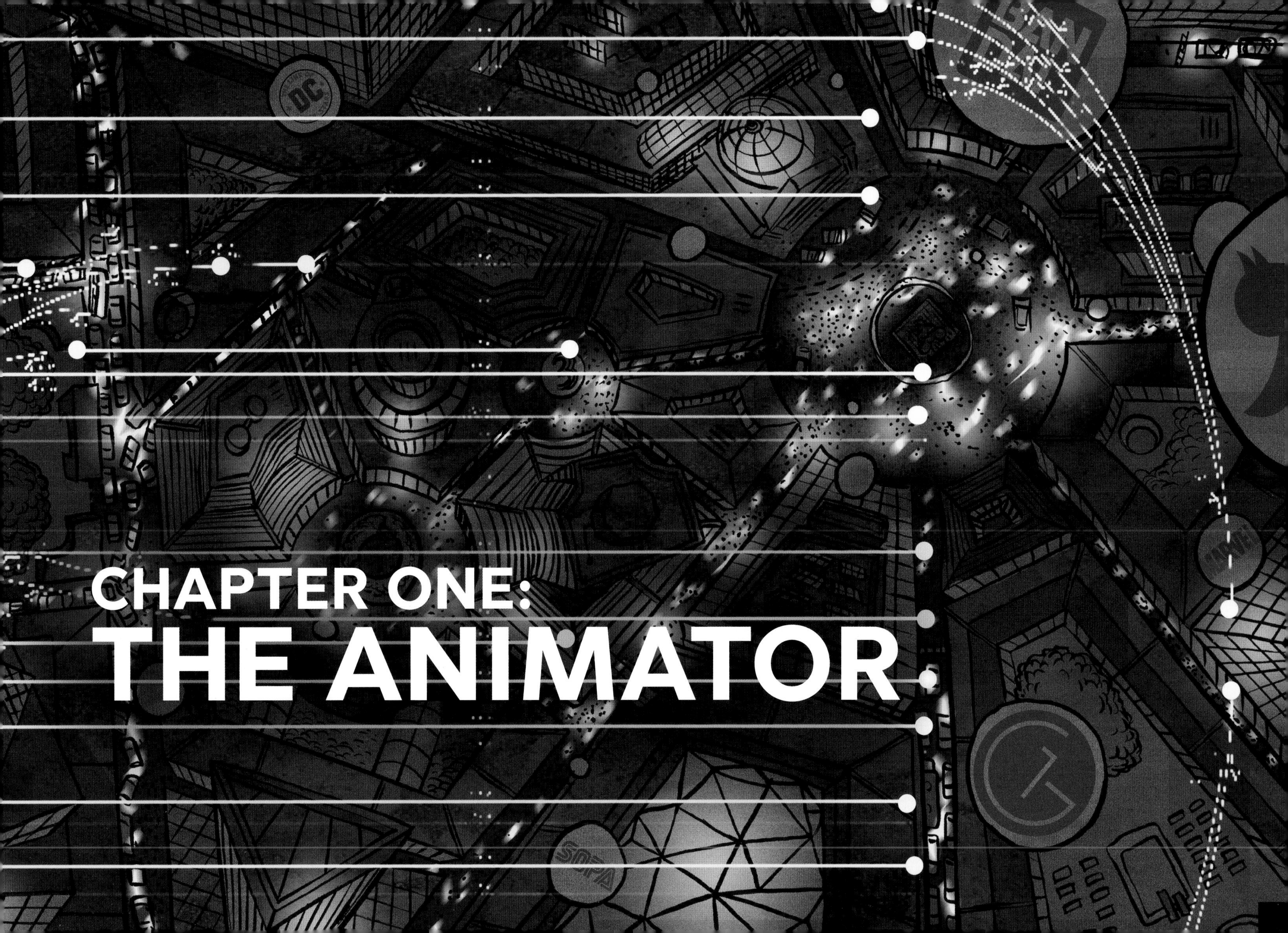

CHAPTER ONE: THE ANIMATOR

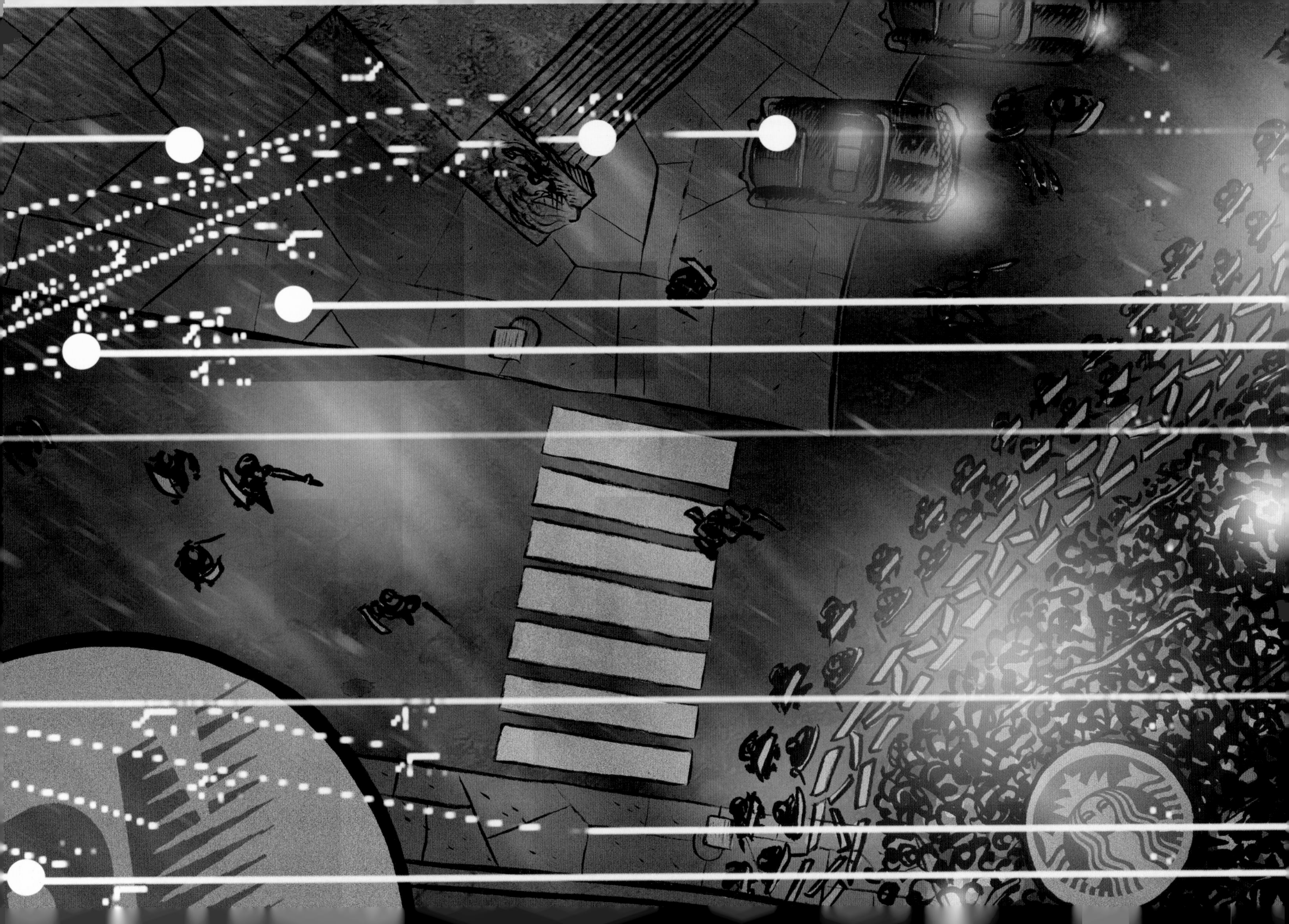

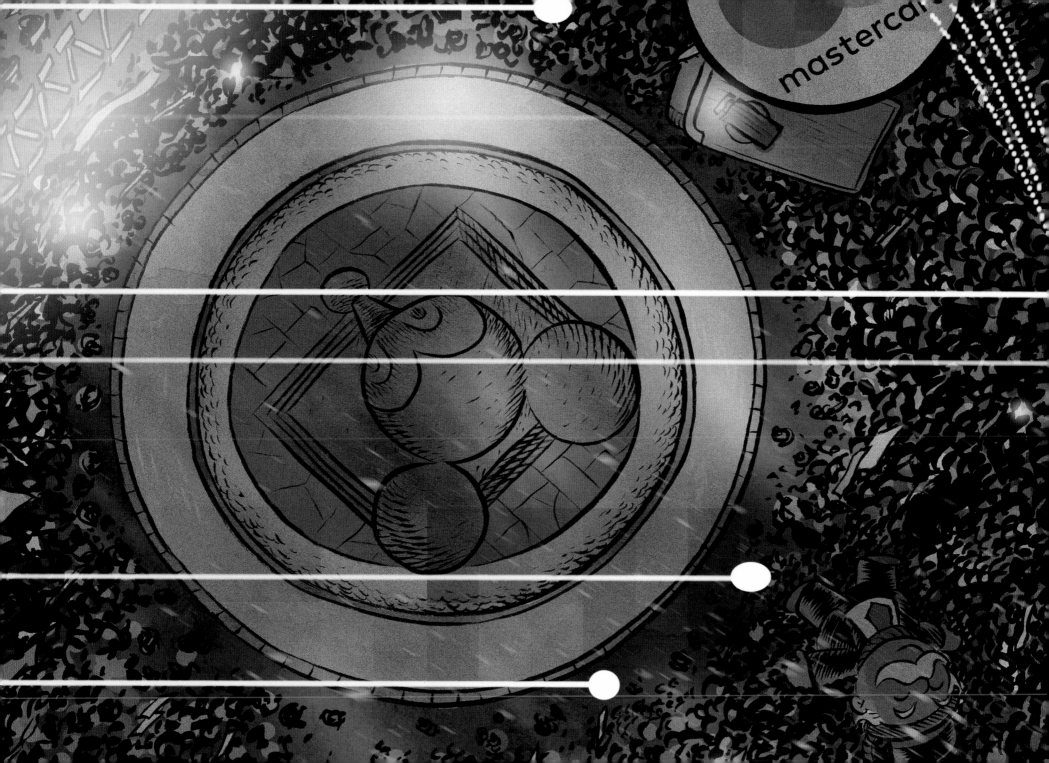

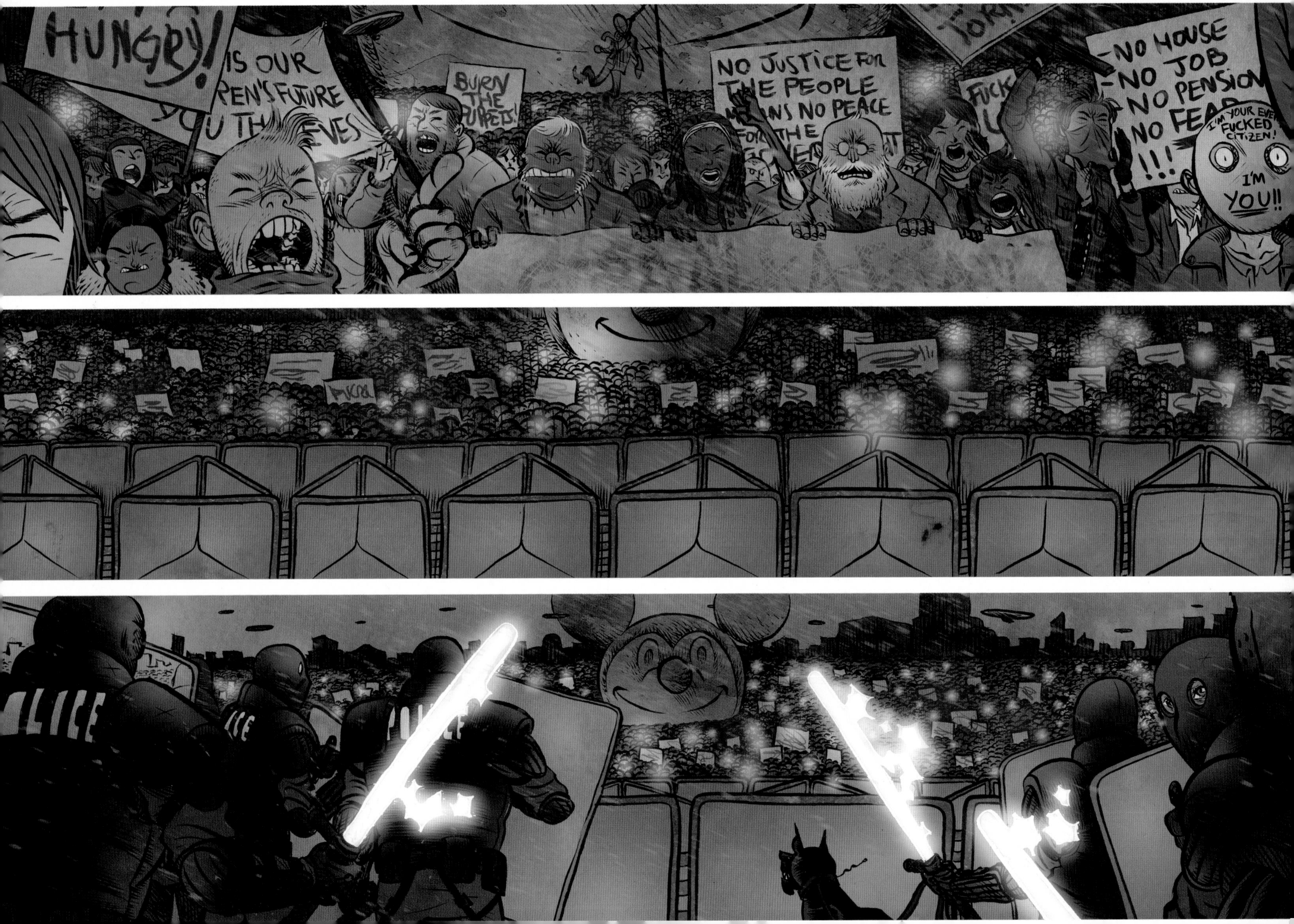
HUNGRY!
IS OUR
REN'S FUTURE
YOU TH EVES
BURN THE PUPPETS!
NO JUSTICE FOR
THE PEOPLE
NO PEACE
-NO HOUSE
-NO JOB
-NO PENSION
NO FEA
!!!
I'M YOUR EVE
FUCKED
CITIZEN!
I'M
YOU!!
POLICE

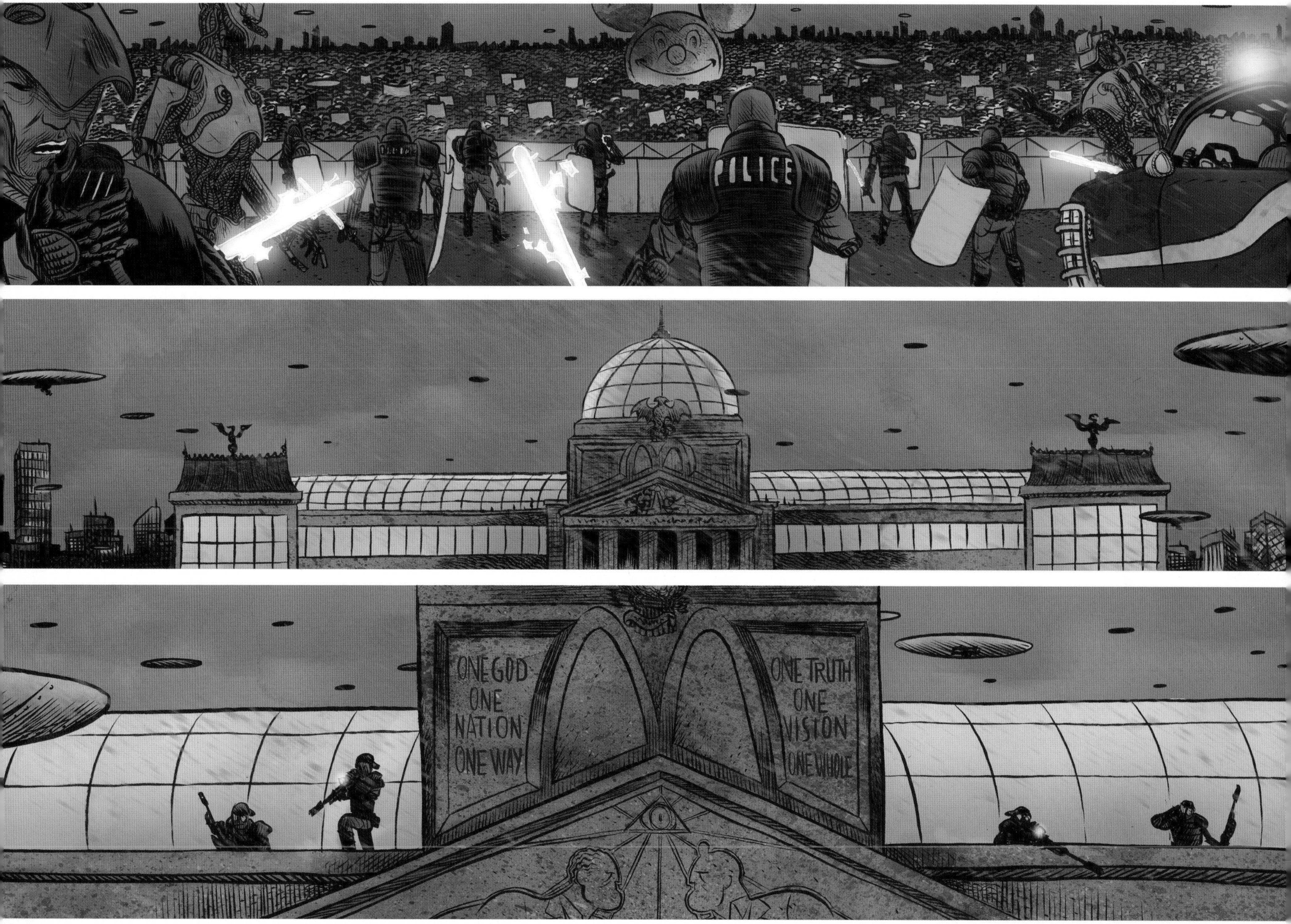
ONE GOD
ONE
NATION
ONE WAY
ONE TRUTH
ONE
VISION
ONE WHOLE

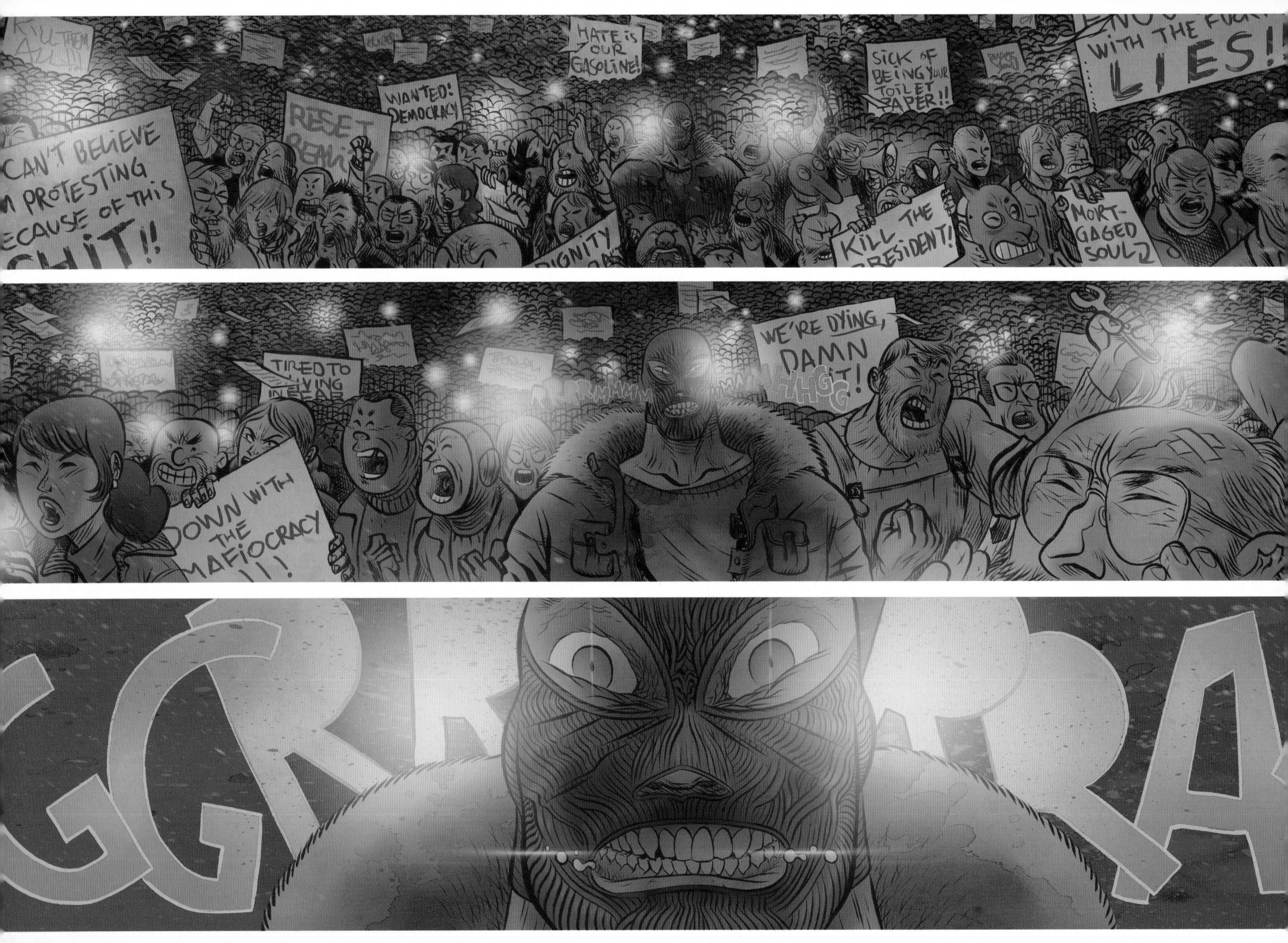
HATE IS OUR GASOLINE!
WANTED: DEMOCRACY
SICK OF BEING YOUR TOILET PAPER!!
WITH THE FUCK
LIES!!
CAN'T BELIEVE
M PROTESTING
ECAUSE OF THIS
SHIT!!
RESET
DIGNITY
KILL THE
RESIDENT!
MORT-GAGED SOUL2
WE'RE DYING, DAMN
RRRMMMMM
MMMNHHGG
DOWN WITH THE MAFIOCRACY !!!
GGR RA

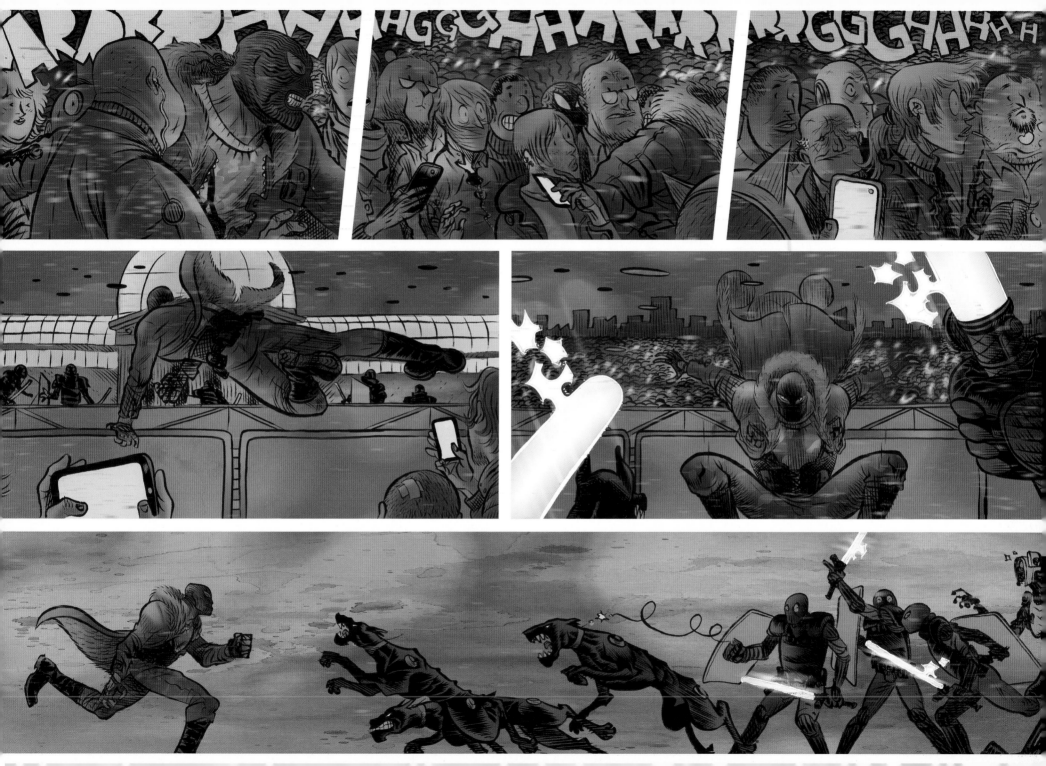

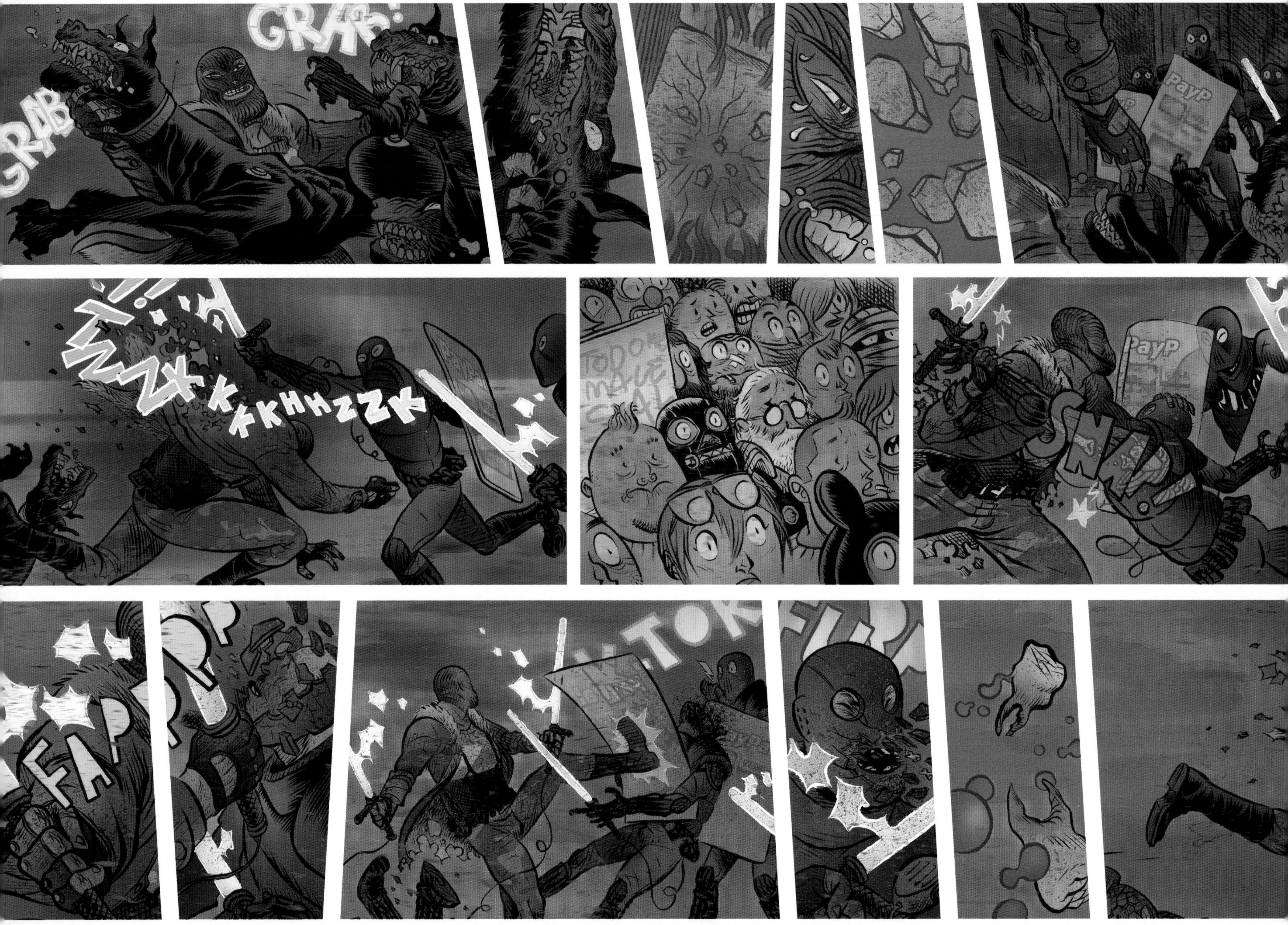
GRAB
GRAB!
PayP
TZZZKKKKHHZZZK
PayP
SNAP!
FAP

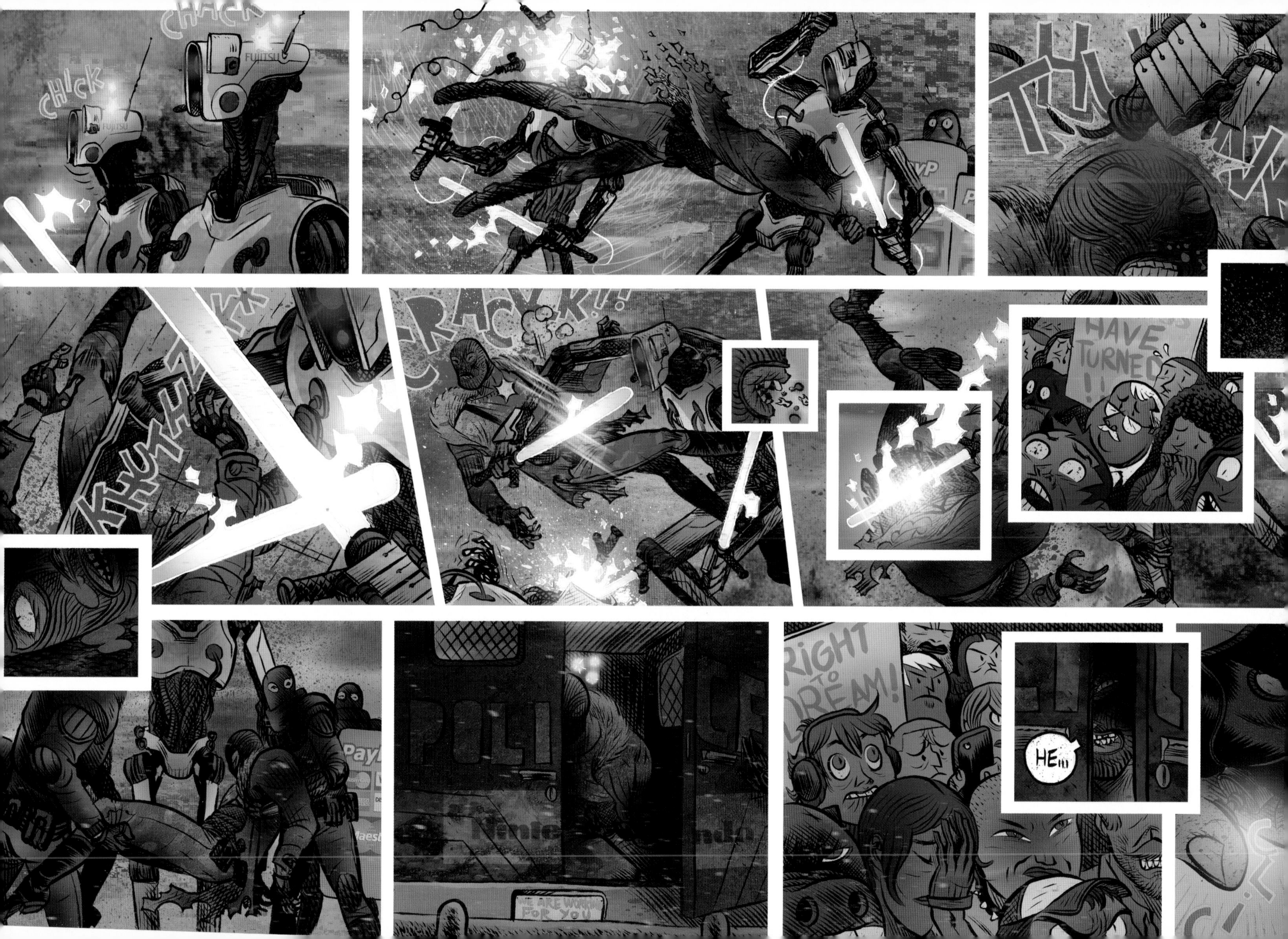
CHICK
CHACK
FUJITSU
FUJITSU
HAVE TURNED !!
RIGHT TO DREAM!
HE...

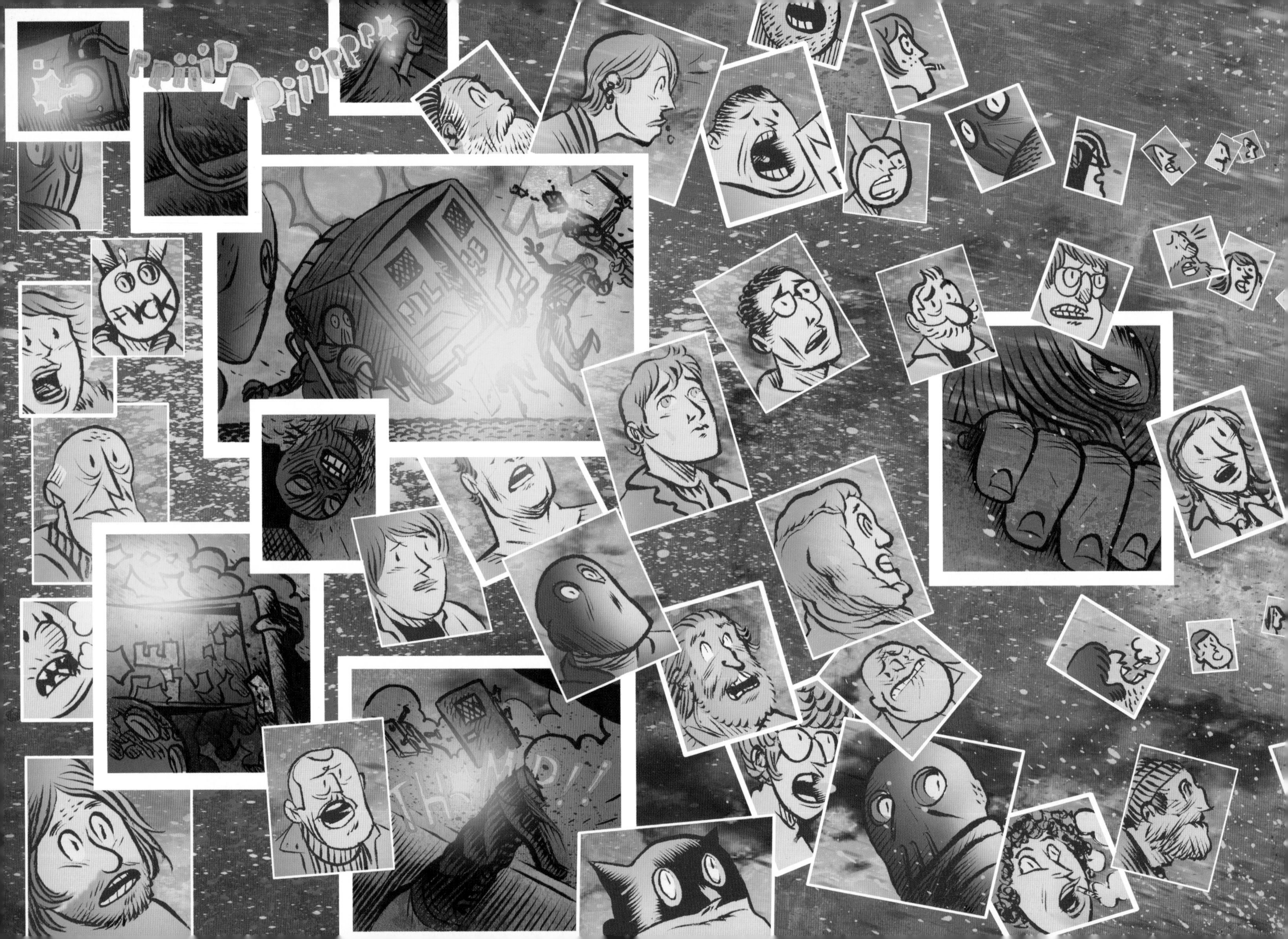
PPIIIP PPIIIIRPPP
FVCK

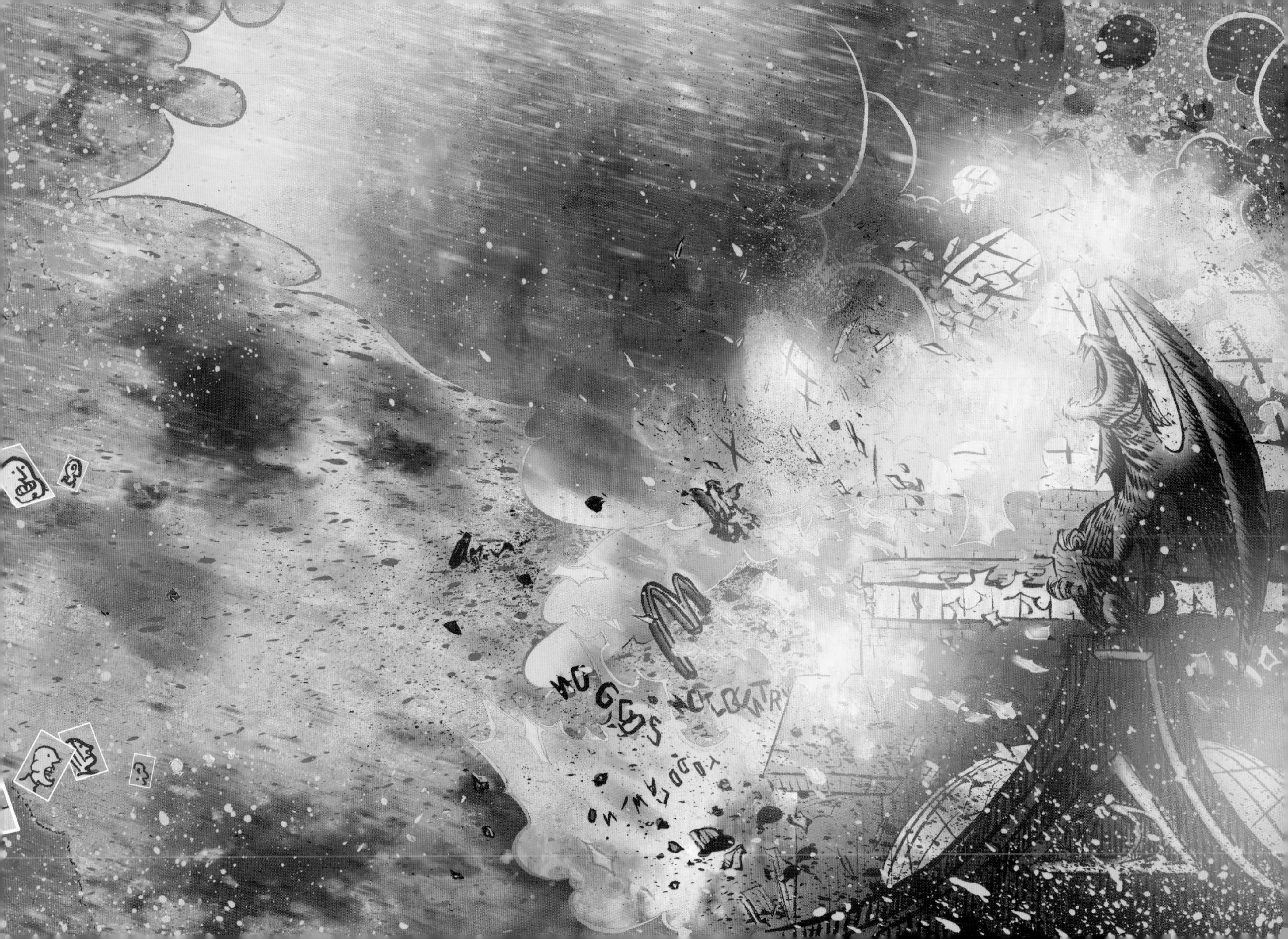
NO GODS NO COUNTRY

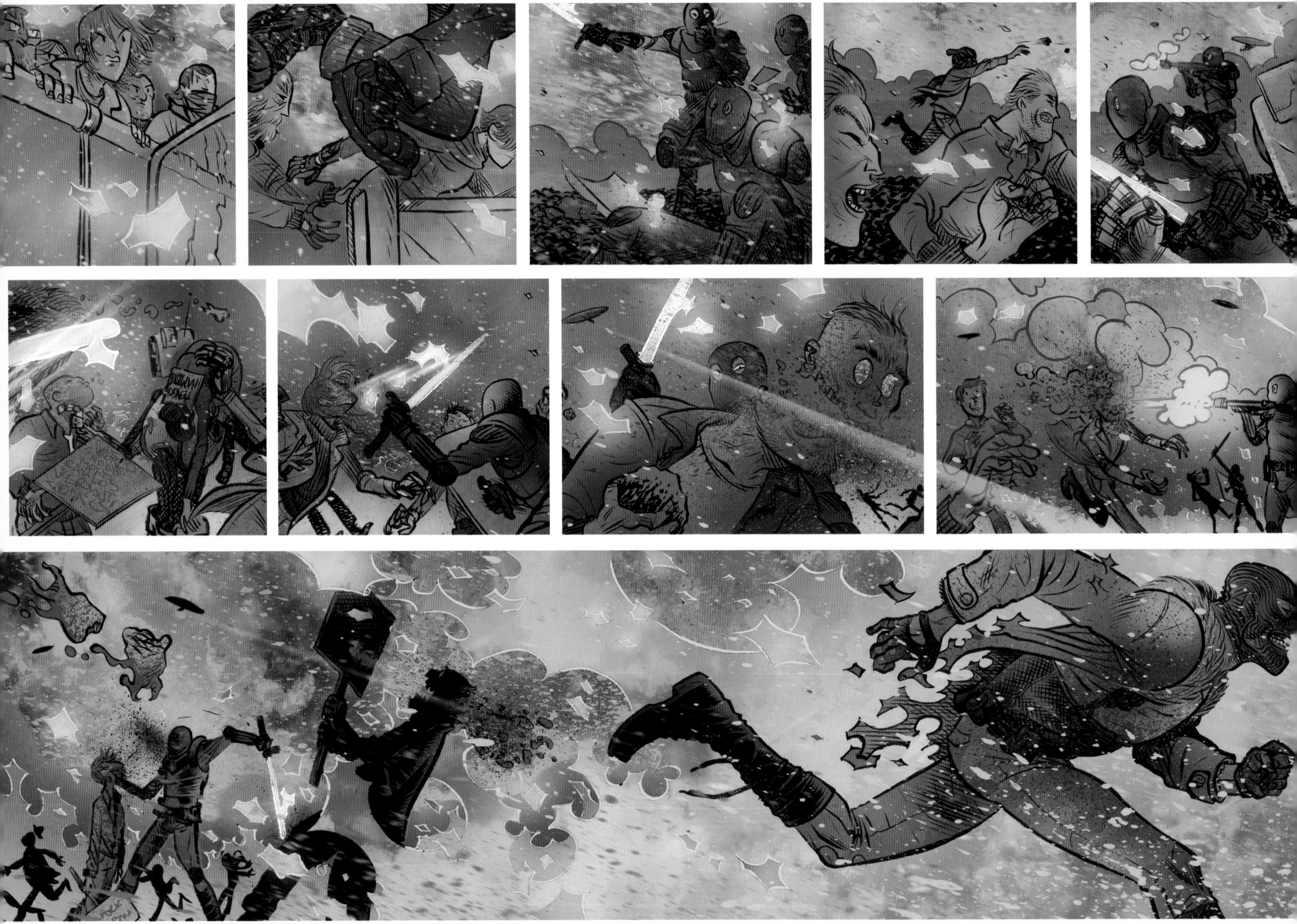

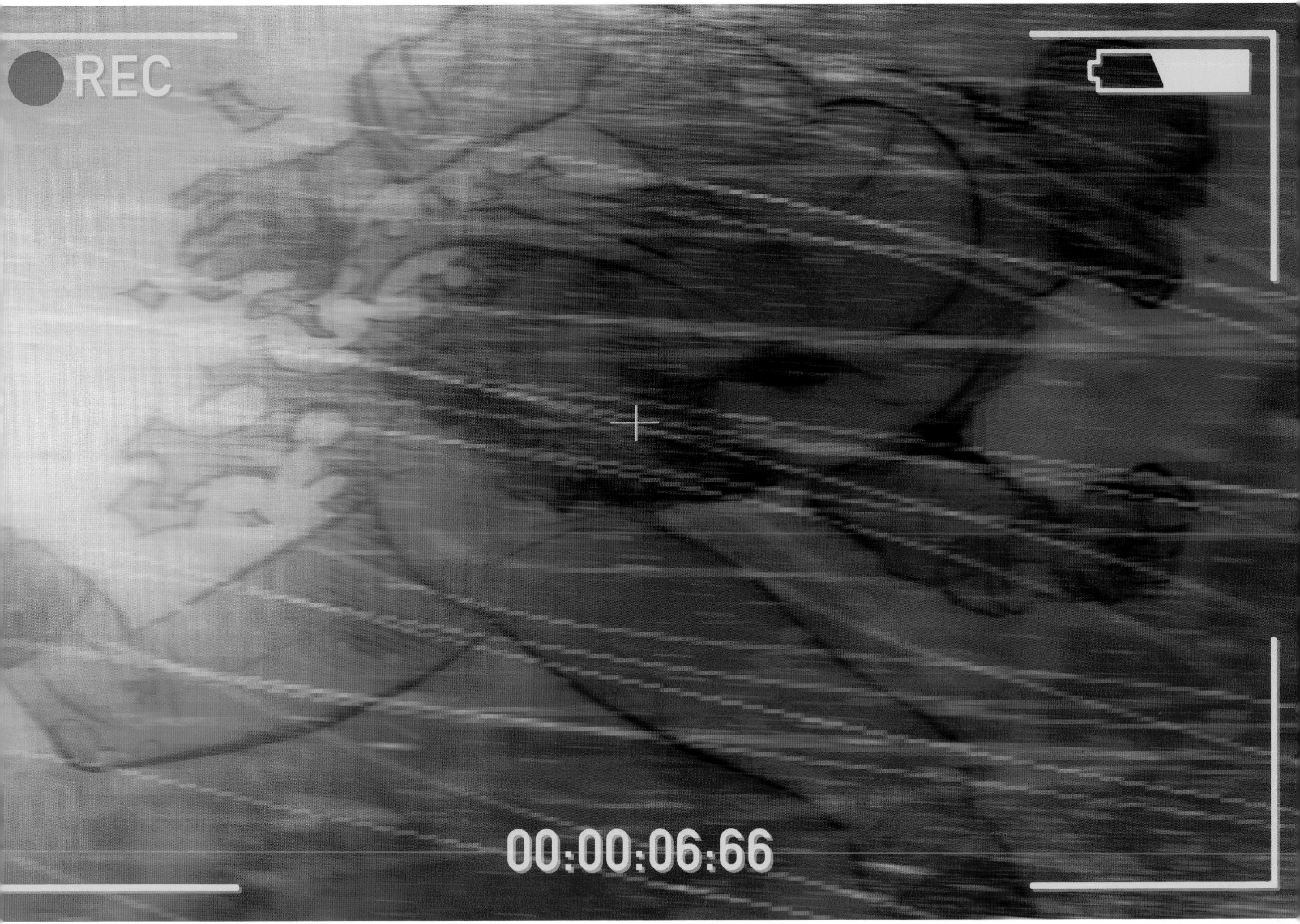
REC
00:00:06:66

Marsupalia @leviathan_strikes! --Just now

A bunch of "pacifists" had amassed around parliament #20M3

Reply | Reposition | <3 Like | ⚡ Despise | ⊙⊙⊙+

Le Pin Ball @lepinball1995 --38s.

In case you haven't herd: that's the far left to a t, ready to bash a cops head in and set off a bomb in Parliament #20M

Reply | Reposition | <3 Like | ⚡ Despise | ⊙⊙⊙+

The State @TheState --1m.

Explosion at Parliament captured on surveillance video from the After Pop Museum #20M

Reply | Reposition | <3 Like | ⚡ Despise | ⊙⊙⊙+

Marina @marina162x97 --1m.

27 police officers treated for head injuries. #terrible #20m

Reply | Reposition | <3 Like | ⚡ Despise | ⊙⊙⊙+

Schwejk @bravesoldierschwejk --2m.

WHO benefits from this atttack? #20M

Reply | Reposition | <3 Like | ⚡ Despise | ⊙⊙⊙+

JKL @thebigone --2m.

Nobody's talking about indiscriminate #drone use? Oh, right—the Parliament fire is what matters #REICHSTAG #20M

Reply | Reposition | <3 Like | ⚡ Despise | ⊙⊙⊙+

Commissioner Flash Gordon @comicsionerflashgordon --3m.

#20M SUPER IMPRESSIVE. Amazing photo by @janloeuropez

Reply | Reposition | <3 Like | ⚡ Despise | ⊙⊙⊙+

Best price robes @bestpricerobes11 --4m.

Fantastic fireworks show. I'd like to know who's responsible so I can congratulate them personally #20M

I was at #20M and I completely condemn the attack on parliaments

Reply Reposition <3 Like Despise ⊙⊙⊙+

VON DOOOOOOM @viktoroviktoriavondoom --5m.

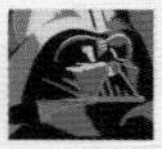

Congratulations to the creators/organizers of #20M.
yOu've earned an honorary doctorate in one of the most contemptible -isms

Reply Reposition <3 Like Despise ⊙⊙⊙+

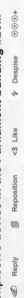

The State @The_State --5m.

URGENT: Government sources confirm the detonation of an explosive device in the Parliament building #20M

Reply Reposition <3 Like Despise ⊙⊙⊙+

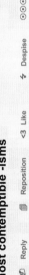

LAMOTHE @antoinedelamothe-cadillac --5m.

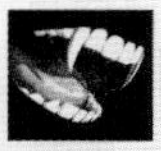

Introducing the new LAMOTHE ESCALADE MONSTER TRUCK, capable of surmounting any obstacle and securing the safety of you and yours #20M

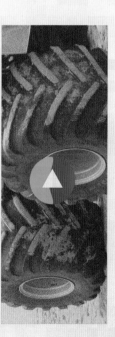

Reply Reposition <3 Like Despise ⊙⊙⊙+

Comeclavos @naileater --5m.

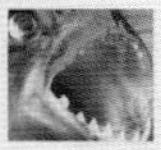

The parliament was already destroyed before #20M

Reply Reposition <3 Like Despise ⊙⊙⊙+

LILY MARLENE @mariemagdalenevonlosch --6m.

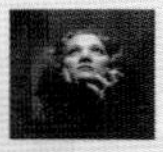

Looks like they're putting on a hell of a fireworks show around the parliament building ;) #20M

Reply Reposition <3 Like Despise ⊙⊙⊙+

Spin Top Halley's Comet @madeinsaturn --6m.

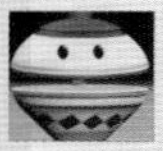

If the bomb claim is true, that crosses a red line.
#20M is hit and sunk. #RIP

Reply Reposition <3 Like Despise ⊙⊙⊙+

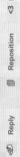

Thomas & Chips @thomasandchips --6m.

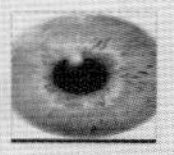

THIS ISNT A JOKE: A bomb has gone off in Parliament.
We can see a column of smoke and fire #20M

Reply Reposition <3 Like Despise ⊙⊙⊙+

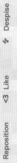

Christa V. @trollhunter --6m.

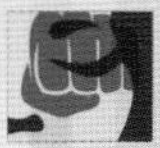

THE ROBOCOPS are disoriented #20M

Reply Reposition <3 Like Despise ⊙⊙⊙+

N'DEA @ndea --6m.

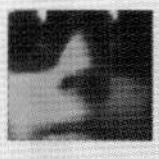

UNBELIEVABLE!!!!! We just heard a huge exokosion.
WE're far away, not sure whats going on #20M

Reply Reposition <3 Like Despise ⊙⊙⊙+

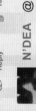

MASSAGES WITH BAMBOO STICKS @greatmassages --7m.

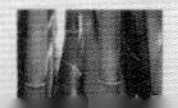

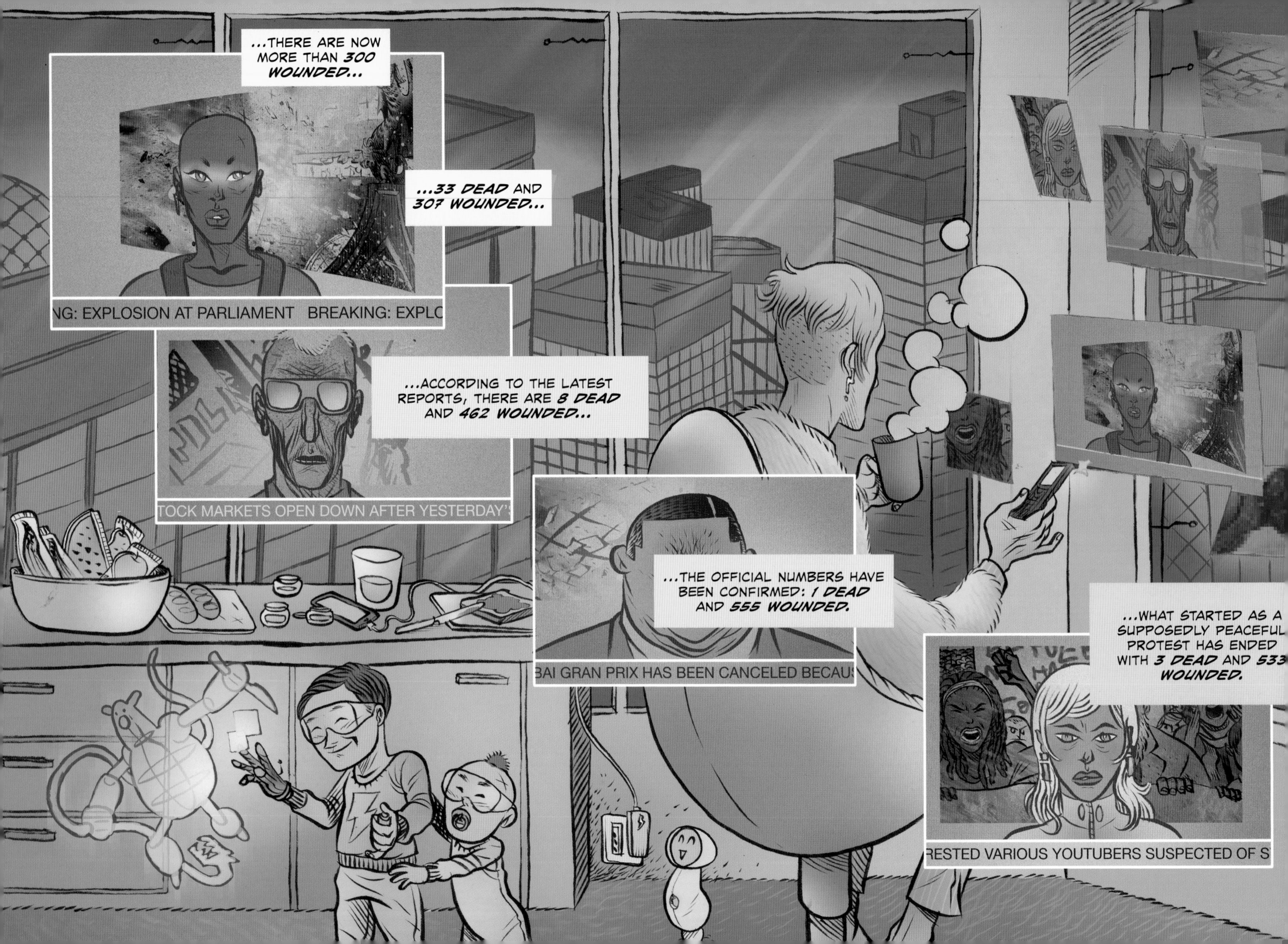
...THERE ARE NOW MORE THAN *300 WOUNDED...*
...33 DEAD AND *307 WOUNDED...*
NG: EXPLOSION AT PARLIAMENT BREAKING: EXPLO
...ACCORDING TO THE LATEST REPORTS, THERE ARE *8 DEAD* AND *462 WOUNDED...*
TOCK MARKETS OPEN DOWN AFTER YESTERDAY'S
...THE OFFICIAL NUMBERS HAVE BEEN CONFIRMED: *1 DEAD* AND *555 WOUNDED.*
BAI GRAN PRIX HAS BEEN CANCELED BECAUS
...WHAT STARTED AS A SUPPOSEDLY PEACEFUL PROTEST HAS ENDED WITH *3 DEAD* AND *533 WOUNDED.*
RESTED VARIOUS YOUTUBERS SUSPECTED OF S

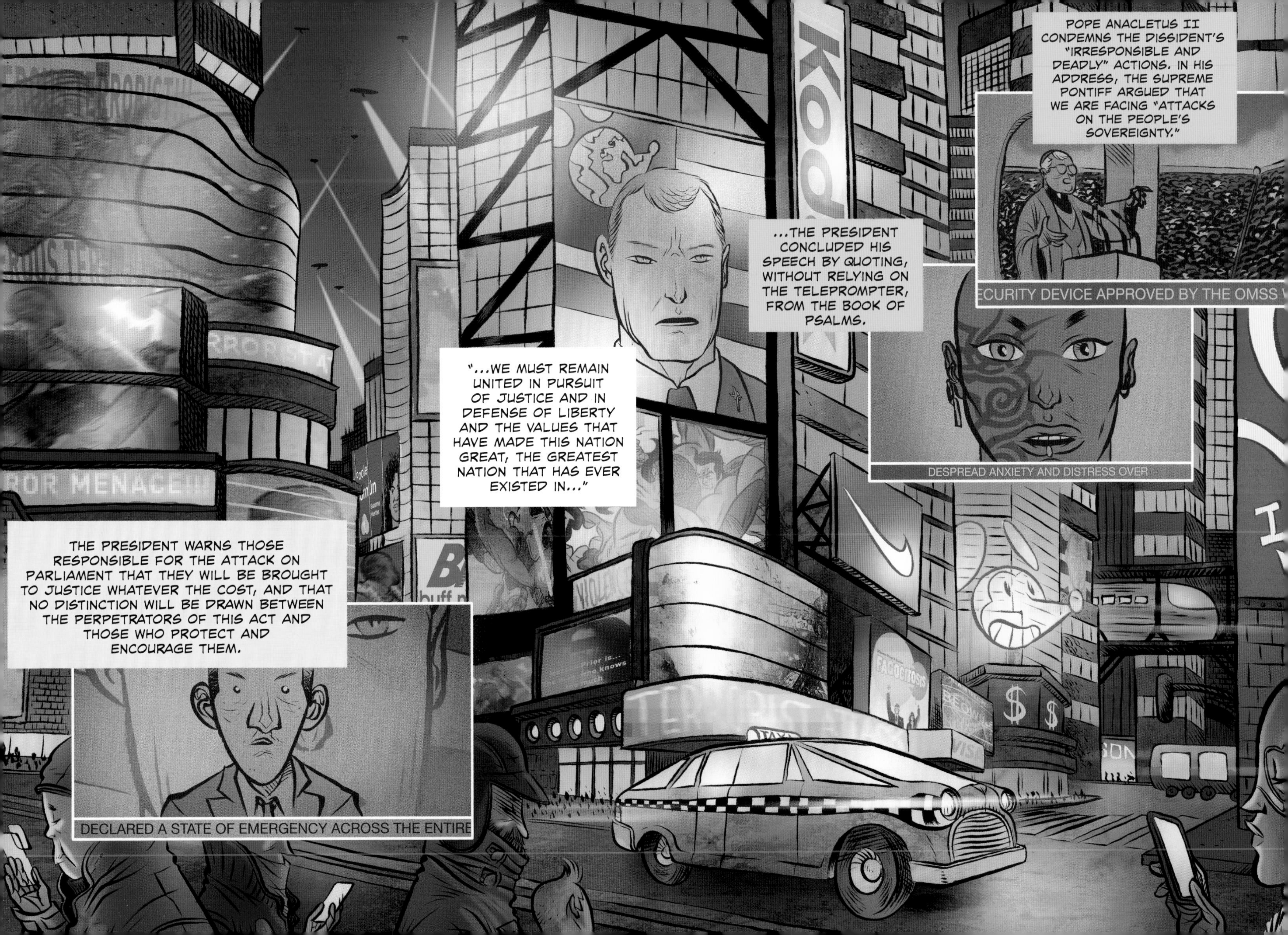
THE PRESIDENT WARNS THOSE RESPONSIBLE FOR THE ATTACK ON PARLIAMENT THAT THEY WILL BE BROUGHT TO JUSTICE WHATEVER THE COST, AND THAT NO DISTINCTION WILL BE DRAWN BETWEEN THE PERPETRATORS OF THIS ACT AND THOSE WHO PROTECT AND ENCOURAGE THEM.
DECLARED A STATE OF EMERGENCY ACROSS THE ENTIRE
"...WE MUST REMAIN UNITED IN PURSUIT OF JUSTICE AND IN DEFENSE OF LIBERTY AND THE VALUES THAT HAVE MADE THIS NATION GREAT, THE GREATEST NATION THAT HAS EVER EXISTED IN..."
...THE PRESIDENT CONCLUDED HIS SPEECH BY QUOTING, WITHOUT RELYING ON THE TELEPROMPTER, FROM THE BOOK OF PSALMS.
DESPREAD ANXIETY AND DISTRESS OVER
POPE ANACLETUS II CONDEMNS THE DISSIDENT'S "IRRESPONSIBLE AND DEADLY" ACTIONS. IN HIS ADDRESS, THE SUPREME PONTIFF ARGUED THAT WE ARE FACING "ATTACKS ON THE PEOPLE'S SOVEREIGNTY."
ECURITY DEVICE APPROVED BY THE OMSS W
ROR MENACE!!!

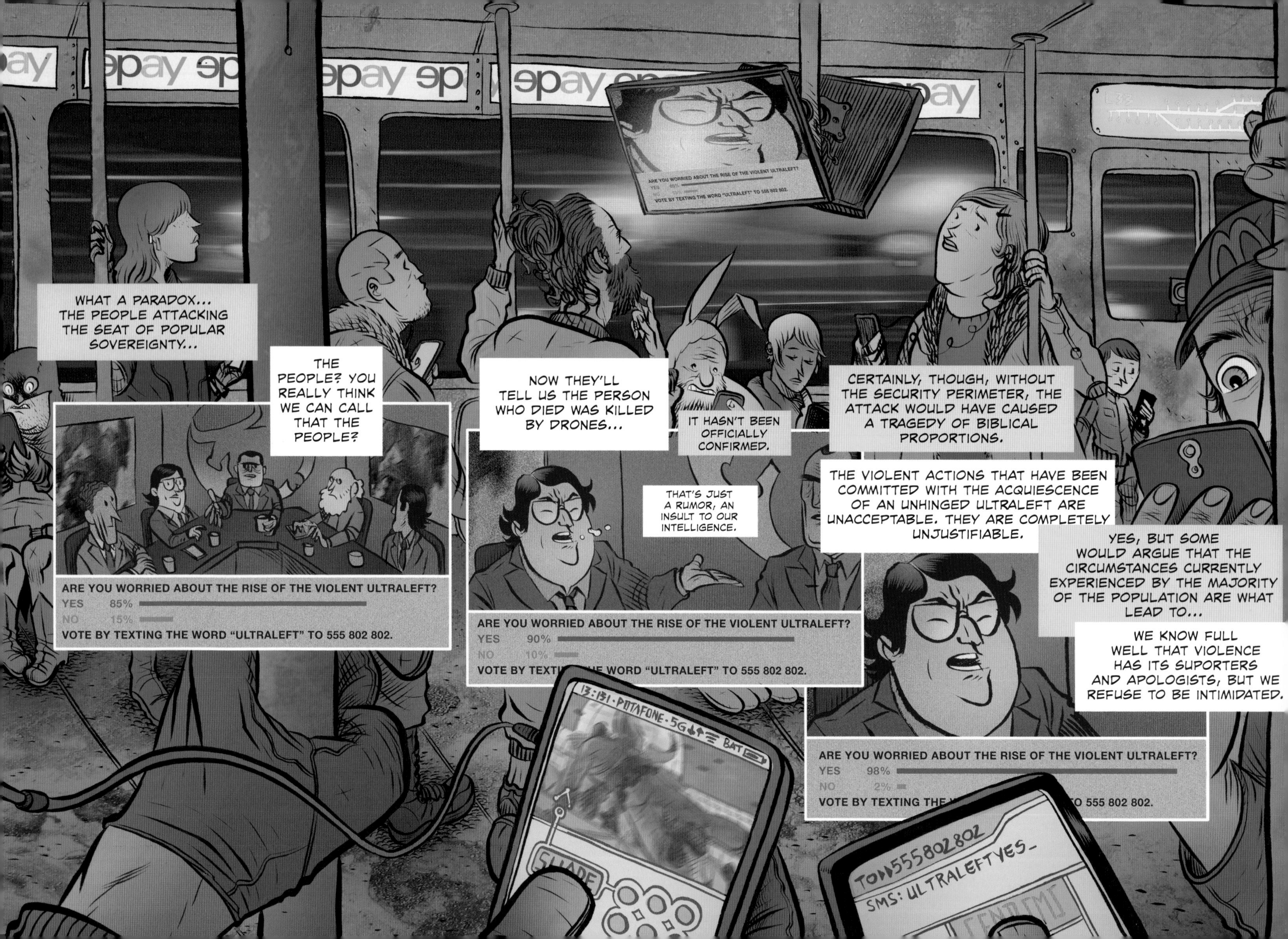
epay
ARE YOU WORRIED ABOUT THE RISE OF THE VIOLENT ULTRALEFT?
VOTE BY TEXTING THE WORD "ULTRALEFT" TO 555 802 802.
WHAT A PARADOX... THE PEOPLE ATTACKING THE SEAT OF POPULAR SOVEREIGNTY...
THE PEOPLE? YOU REALLY THINK WE CAN CALL THAT THE PEOPLE?
ARE YOU WORRIED ABOUT THE RISE OF THE VIOLENT ULTRALEFT?
YES 85%
NO 15%
VOTE BY TEXTING THE WORD "ULTRALEFT" TO 555 802 802.
NOW THEY'LL TELL US THE PERSON WHO DIED WAS KILLED BY DRONES...
IT HASN'T BEEN OFFICIALLY CONFIRMED.
THAT'S JUST A RUMOR, AN INSULT TO OUR INTELLIGENCE.
ARE YOU WORRIED ABOUT THE RISE OF THE VIOLENT ULTRALEFT?
YES 90%
NO 10%
VOTE BY TEXTI WORD "ULTRALEFT" TO 555 802 802.
CERTAINLY, THOUGH, WITHOUT THE SECURITY PERIMETER, THE ATTACK WOULD HAVE CAUSED A TRAGEDY OF BIBLICAL PROPORTIONS.
THE VIOLENT ACTIONS THAT HAVE BEEN COMMITTED WITH THE ACQUIESCENCE OF AN UNHINGED ULTRALEFT ARE UNACCEPTABLE. THEY ARE COMPLETELY UNJUSTIFIABLE.
YES, BUT SOME WOULD ARGUE THAT THE CIRCUMSTANCES CURRENTLY EXPERIENCED BY THE MAJORITY OF THE POPULATION ARE WHAT LEAD TO...
WE KNOW FULL WELL THAT VIOLENCE HAS ITS SUPORTERS AND APOLOGISTS, BUT WE REFUSE TO BE INTIMIDATED.
ARE YOU WORRIED ABOUT THE RISE OF THE VIOLENT ULTRALEFT?
YES 98%
NO 2%
VOTE BY TEXTING THE O 555 802 802.
13:131 · POTAFONE · 5G BAT
SLIDE
TO 555802802
SMS: ULTRALEFTYES_

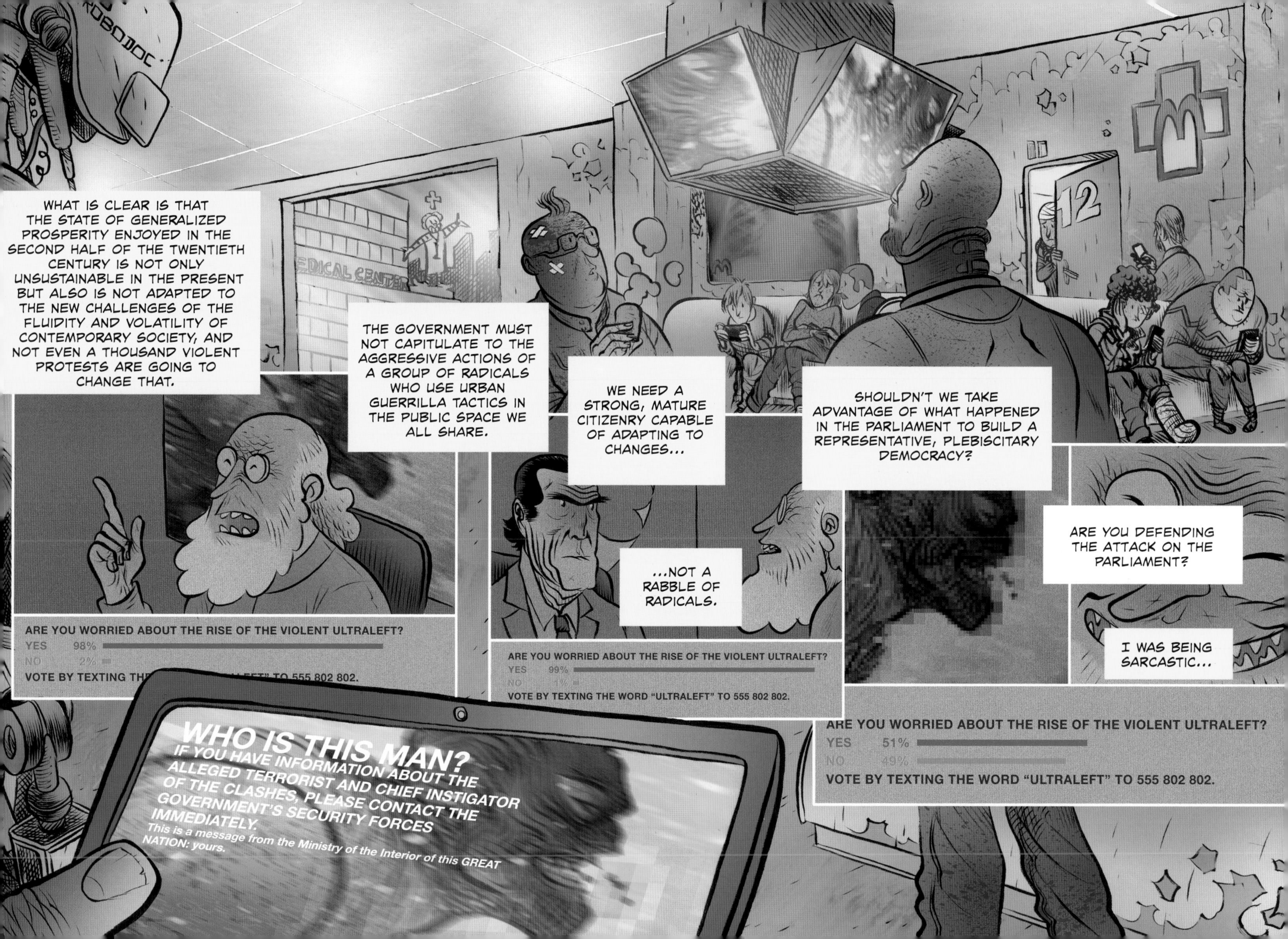

ROBODOC
EDICAL CENTER
12
WHAT IS CLEAR IS THAT THE STATE OF GENERALIZED PROSPERITY ENJOYED IN THE SECOND HALF OF THE TWENTIETH CENTURY IS NOT ONLY UNSUSTAINABLE IN THE PRESENT BUT ALSO IS NOT ADAPTED TO THE NEW CHALLENGES OF THE FLUIDITY AND VOLATILITY OF CONTEMPORARY SOCIETY; AND NOT EVEN A THOUSAND VIOLENT PROTESTS ARE GOING TO CHANGE THAT.
ARE YOU WORRIED ABOUT THE RISE OF THE VIOLENT ULTRALEFT?
YES 98%
NO 2%
VOTE BY TEXTING TH "LEFT" TO 555 802 802.
THE GOVERNMENT MUST NOT CAPITULATE TO THE AGGRESSIVE ACTIONS OF A GROUP OF RADICALS WHO USE URBAN GUERRILLA TACTICS IN THE PUBLIC SPACE WE ALL SHARE.
WE NEED A STRONG, MATURE CITIZENRY CAPABLE OF ADAPTING TO CHANGES...
...NOT A RABBLE OF RADICALS.
ARE YOU WORRIED ABOUT THE RISE OF THE VIOLENT ULTRALEFT?
YES 99%
NO 1%
VOTE BY TEXTING THE WORD "ULTRALEFT" TO 555 802 802.
SHOULDN'T WE TAKE ADVANTAGE OF WHAT HAPPENED IN THE PARLIAMENT TO BUILD A REPRESENTATIVE, PLEBISCITARY DEMOCRACY?
ARE YOU DEFENDING THE ATTACK ON THE PARLIAMENT?
I WAS BEING SARCASTIC...
ARE YOU WORRIED ABOUT THE RISE OF THE VIOLENT ULTRALEFT?
YES 51%
NO 49%
VOTE BY TEXTING THE WORD "ULTRALEFT" TO 555 802 802.
WHO IS THIS MAN?
IF YOU HAVE INFORMATION ABOUT THE ALLEGED TERRORIST AND CHIEF INSTIGATOR OF THE CLASHES, PLEASE CONTACT THE GOVERNMENT'S SECURITY FORCES IMMEDIATELY.
This is a message from the Ministry of the Interior of this GREAT NATION: yours.

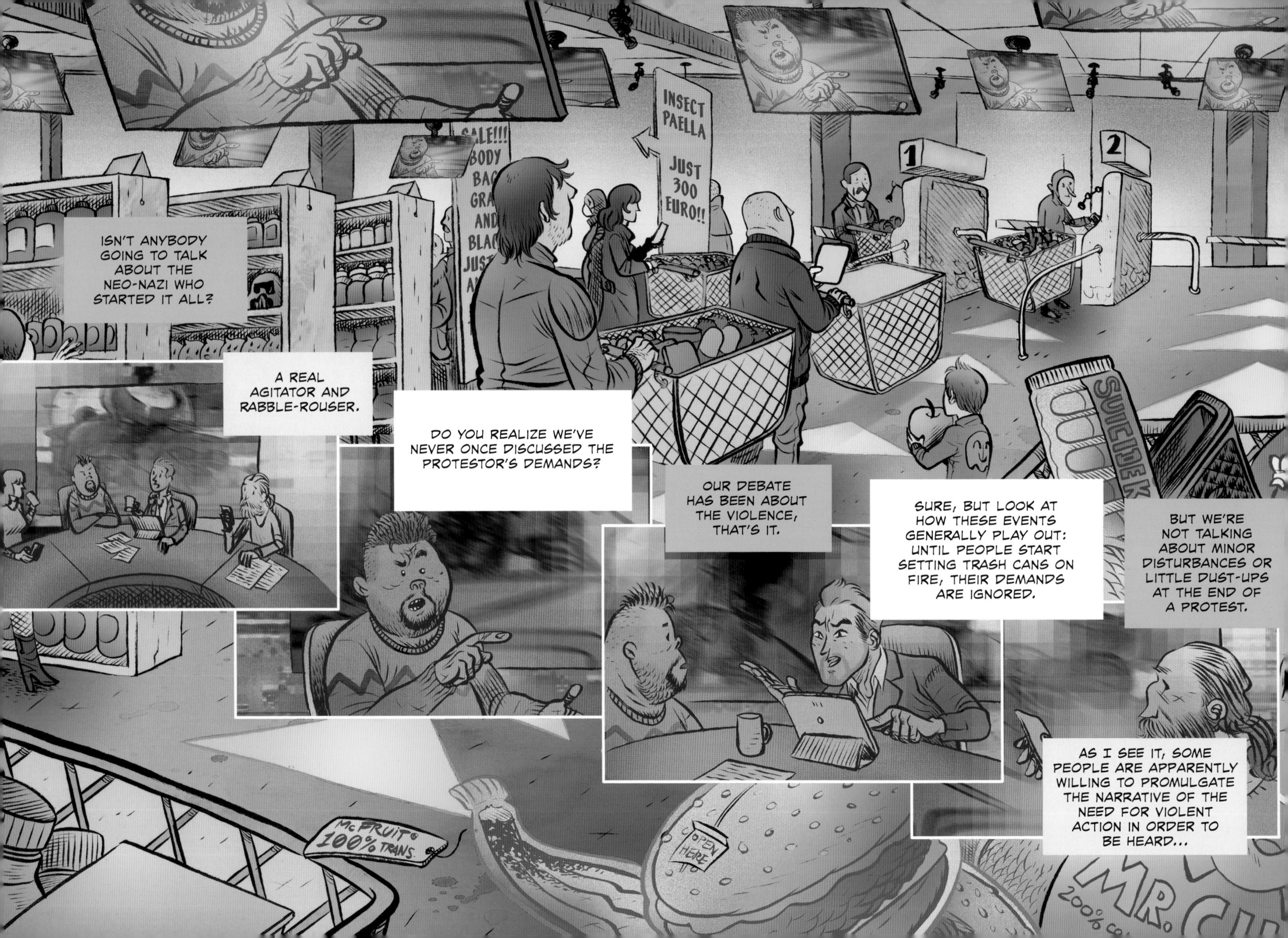
INSECT PAELLA
JUST 300 EURO!!
1
2
ISN'T ANYBODY GOING TO TALK ABOUT THE NEO-NAZI WHO STARTED IT ALL?
A REAL AGITATOR AND RABBLE-ROUSER.
DO YOU REALIZE WE'VE NEVER ONCE DISCUSSED THE PROTESTOR'S DEMANDS?
OUR DEBATE HAS BEEN ABOUT THE VIOLENCE, THAT'S IT.
SURE, BUT LOOK AT HOW THESE EVENTS GENERALLY PLAY OUT: UNTIL PEOPLE START SETTING TRASH CANS ON FIRE, THEIR DEMANDS ARE IGNORED.
BUT WE'RE NOT TALKING ABOUT MINOR DISTURBANCES OR LITTLE DUST-UPS AT THE END OF A PROTEST.
AS I SEE IT, SOME PEOPLE ARE APPARENTLY WILLING TO PROMULGATE THE NARRATIVE OF THE NEED FOR VIOLENT ACTION IN ORDER TO BE HEARD...
McFRUIT 100% TRANS.
OPEN HERE

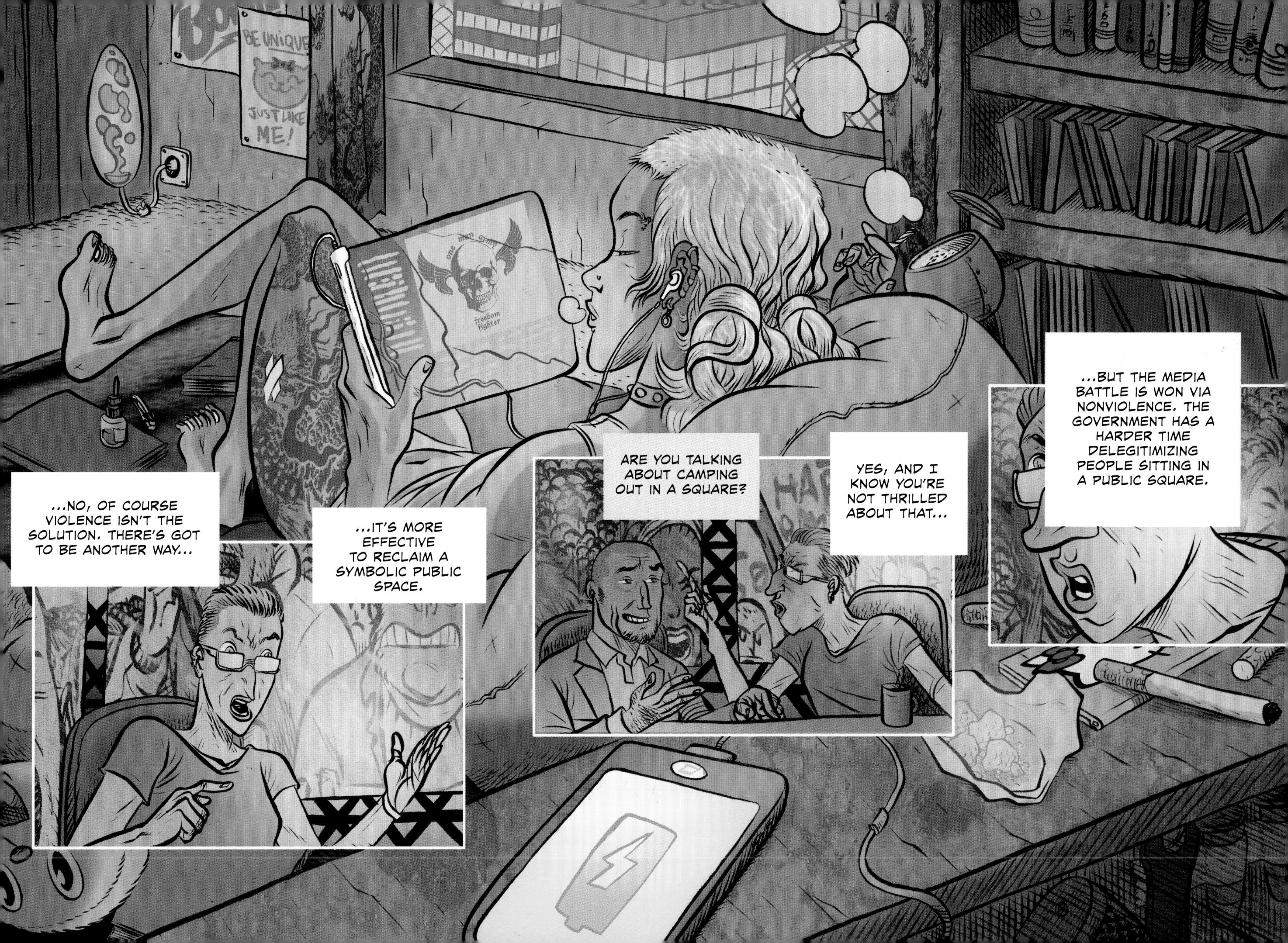
BE UNIQUE JUST LIKE ME!
one man army
freedom fighter
...NO, OF COURSE VIOLENCE ISN'T THE SOLUTION. THERE'S GOT TO BE ANOTHER WAY...
...IT'S MORE EFFECTIVE TO RECLAIM A SYMBOLIC PUBLIC SPACE.
ARE YOU TALKING ABOUT CAMPING OUT IN A SQUARE?
YES, AND I KNOW YOU'RE NOT THRILLED ABOUT THAT...
...BUT THE MEDIA BATTLE IS WON VIA NONVIOLENCE. THE GOVERNMENT HAS A HARDER TIME DELEGITIMIZING PEOPLE SITTING IN A PUBLIC SQUARE.

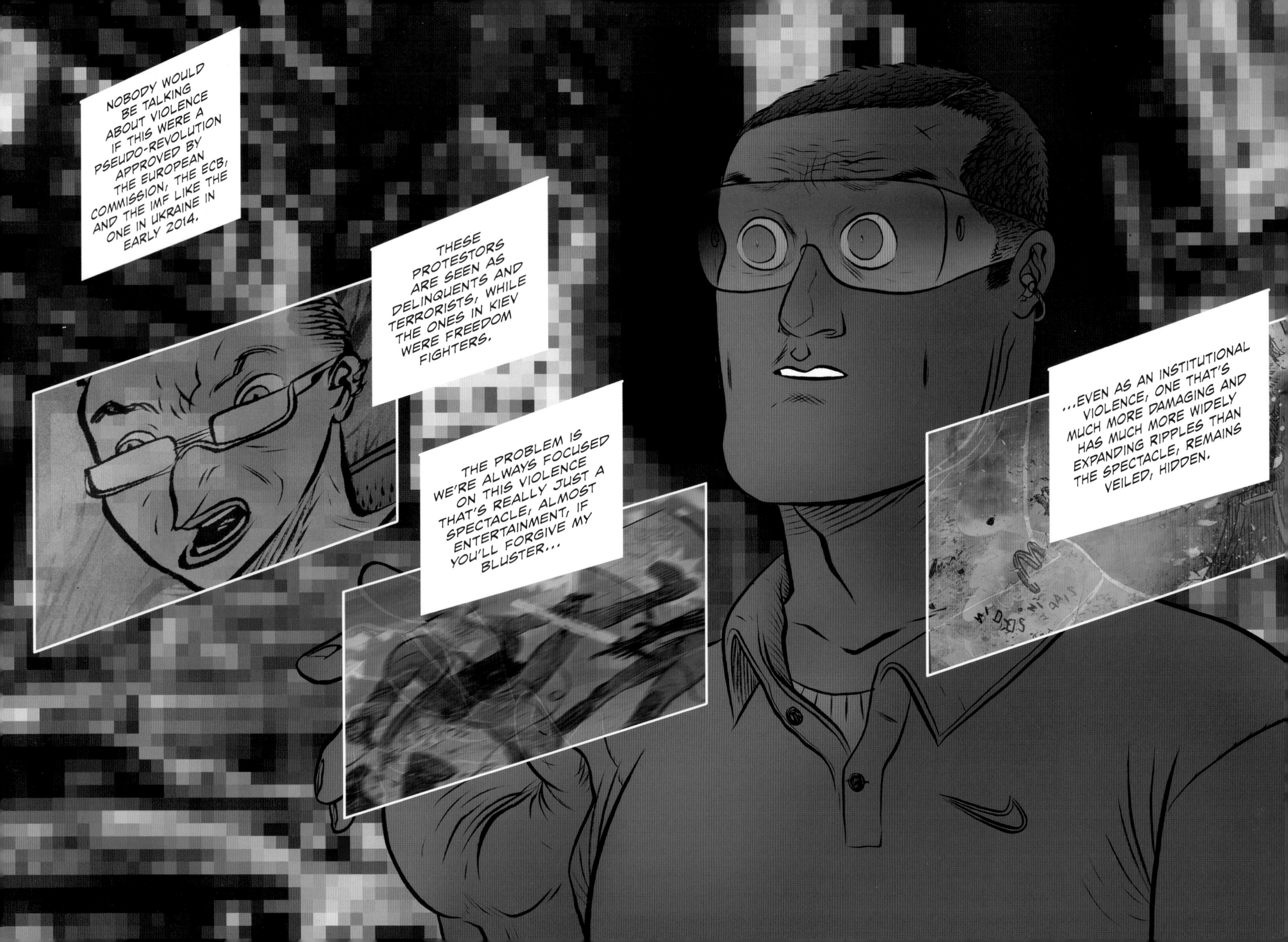
NOBODY WOULD BE TALKING ABOUT VIOLENCE IF THIS WERE A PSEUDO-REVOLUTION APPROVED BY THE EUROPEAN COMMISSION, THE ECB, AND THE IMF LIKE THE ONE IN UKRAINE IN EARLY 2014.
THESE PROTESTORS ARE SEEN AS DELINQUENTS AND TERRORISTS, WHILE THE ONES IN KIEV WERE FREEDOM FIGHTERS.
THE PROBLEM IS WE'RE ALWAYS FOCUSED ON THIS VIOLENCE THAT'S REALLY JUST A SPECTACLE, ALMOST ENTERTAINMENT, IF YOU'LL FORGIVE MY BLUSTER...
...EVEN AS AN INSTITUTIONAL VIOLENCE, ONE THAT'S MUCH MORE DAMAGING AND HAS MUCH MORE WIDELY EXPANDING RIPPLES THAN THE SPECTACLE, REMAINS VEILED, HIDDEN.

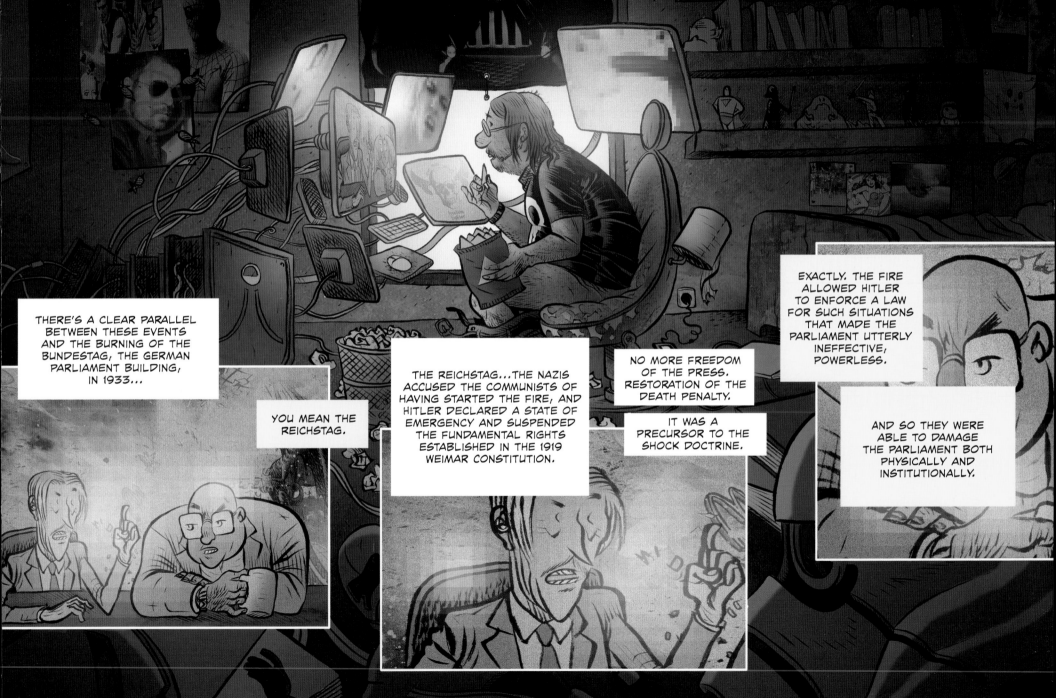

THERE'S A CLEAR PARALLEL BETWEEN THESE EVENTS AND THE BURNING OF THE BUNDESTAG, THE GERMAN PARLIAMENT BUILDING, IN 1933...

YOU MEAN THE REICHSTAG.

THE REICHSTAG...THE NAZIS ACCUSED THE COMMUNISTS OF HAVING STARTED THE FIRE, AND HITLER DECLARED A STATE OF EMERGENCY AND SUSPENDED THE FUNDAMENTAL RIGHTS ESTABLISHED IN THE 1919 WEIMAR CONSTITUTION.

NO MORE FREEDOM OF THE PRESS. RESTORATION OF THE DEATH PENALTY.

IT WAS A PRECURSOR TO THE SHOCK DOCTRINE.

EXACTLY. THE FIRE ALLOWED HITLER TO ENFORCE A LAW FOR SUCH SITUATIONS THAT MADE THE PARLIAMENT UTTERLY INEFFECTIVE, POWERLESS.

AND SO THEY WERE ABLE TO DAMAGE THE PARLIAMENT BOTH PHYSICALLY AND INSTITUTIONALLY.

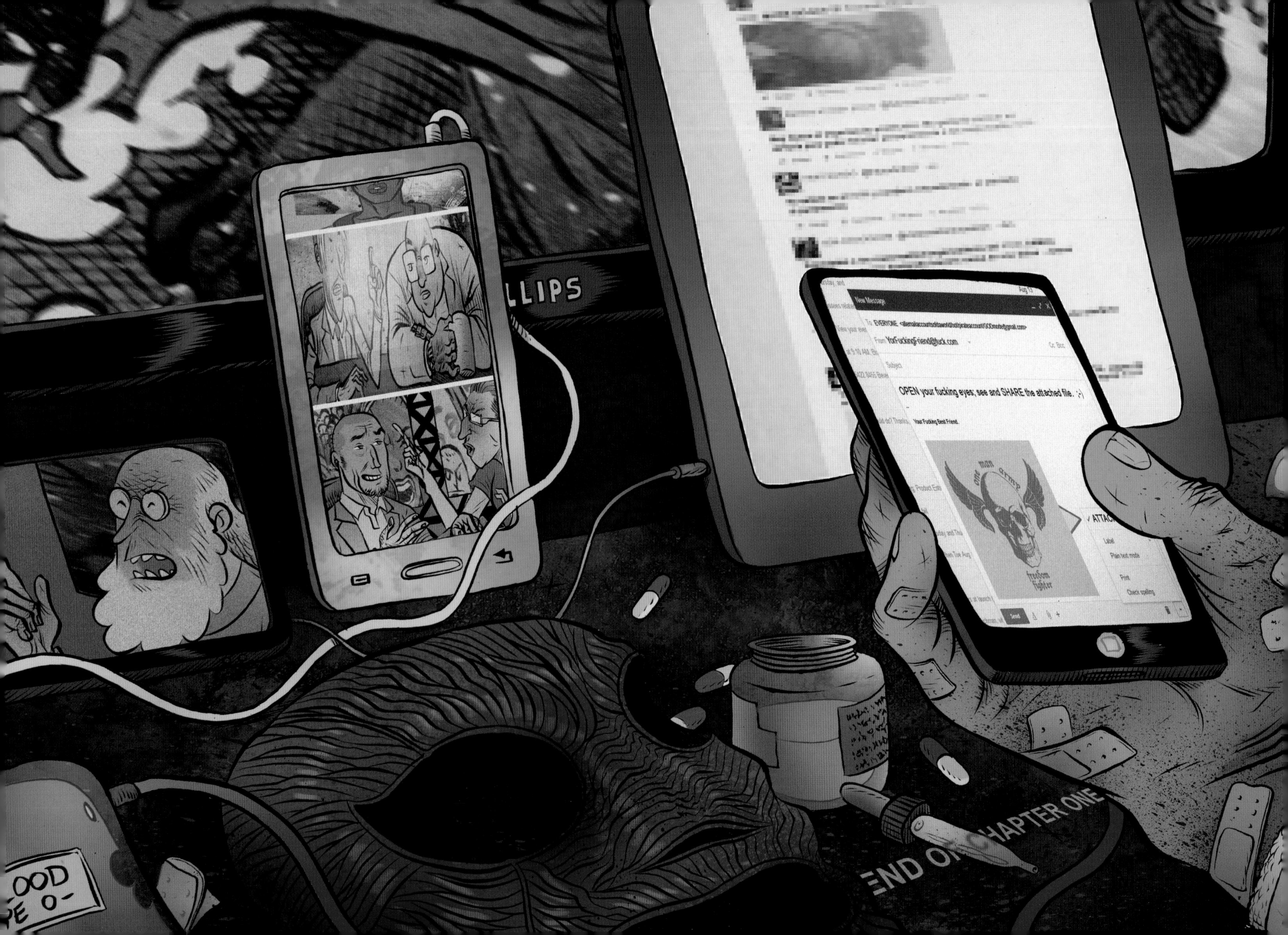

LLIPS
New Message
To EVERYONE
From YorFuckingFriend@fuck.com
Cc Bcc
Subject
OPEN your fucking eyes; see and SHARE the attached file. ;-)
Your Fucking Best Friend.
one man army
freedom fighter
Label
Plain text mode
Print
Check spelling
Send
END OF CHAPTER ONE

CHAPTER TWO:
SUITE

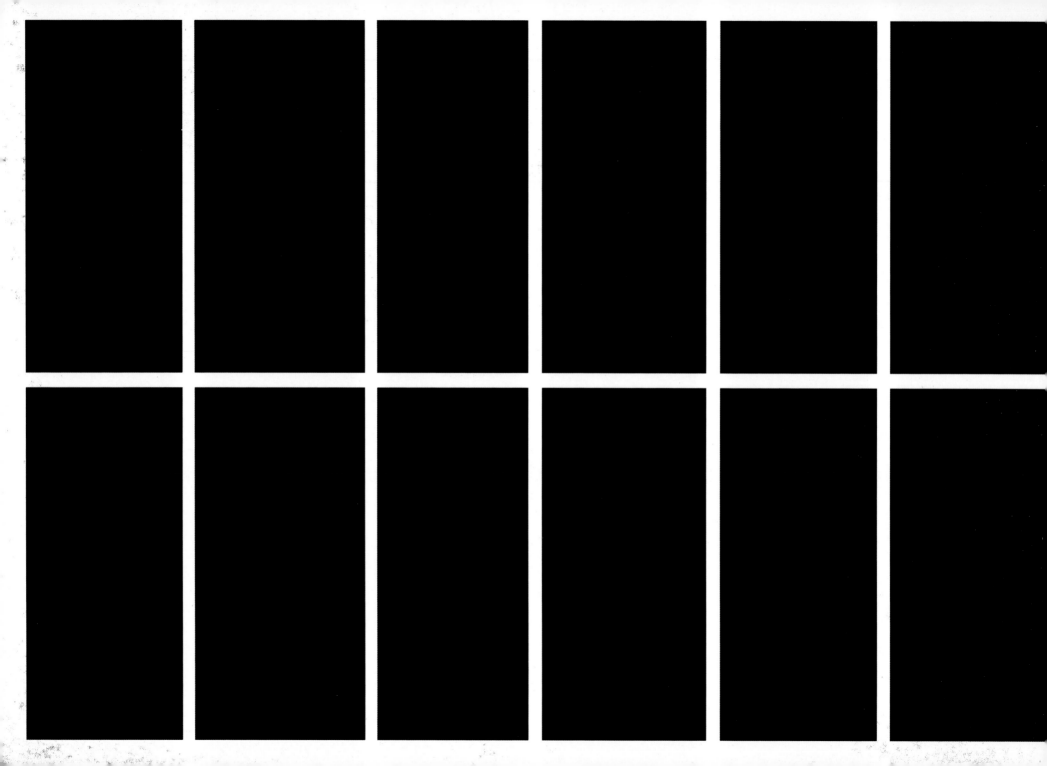

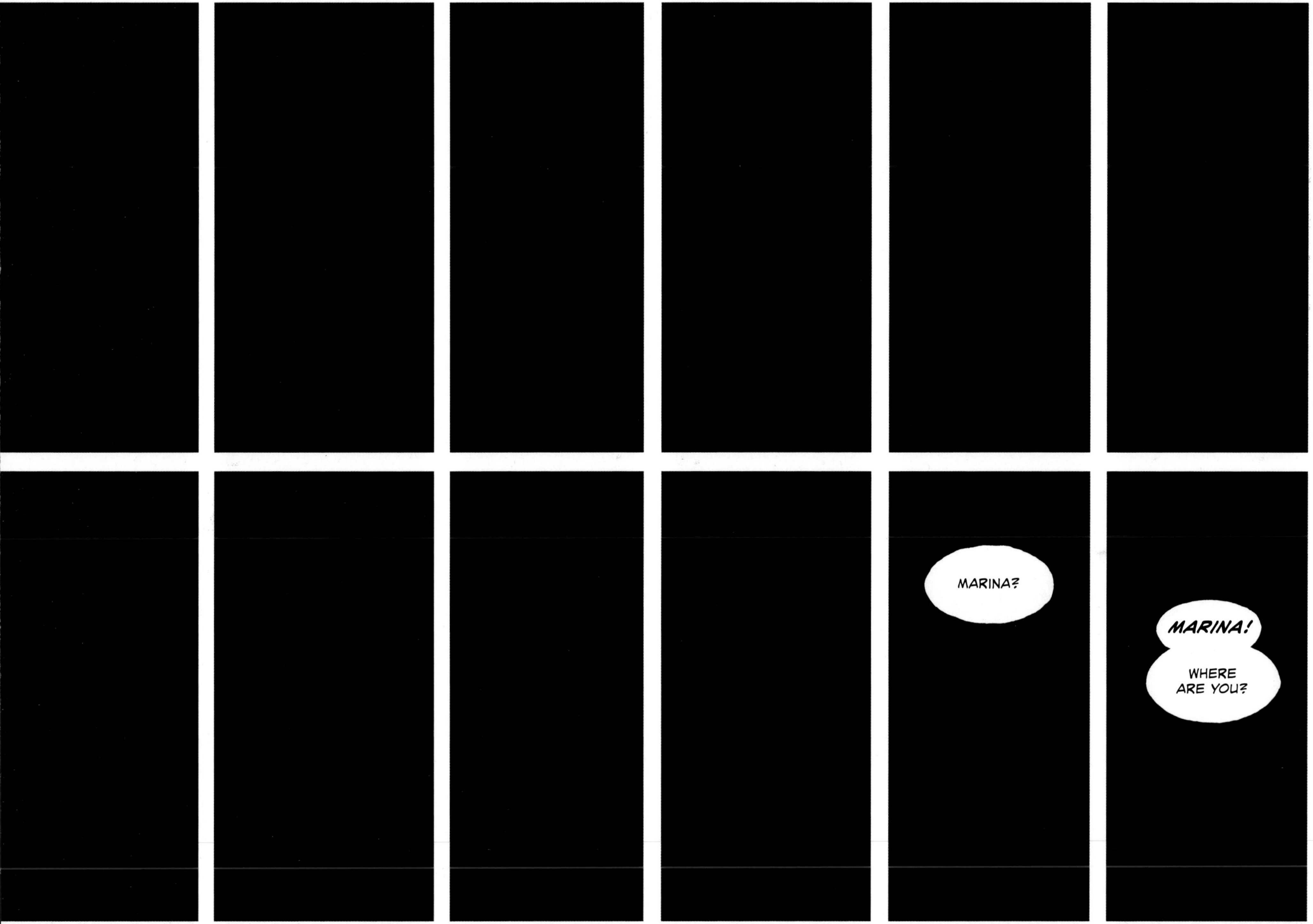
MARINA?
MARINA!
WHERE ARE YOU?

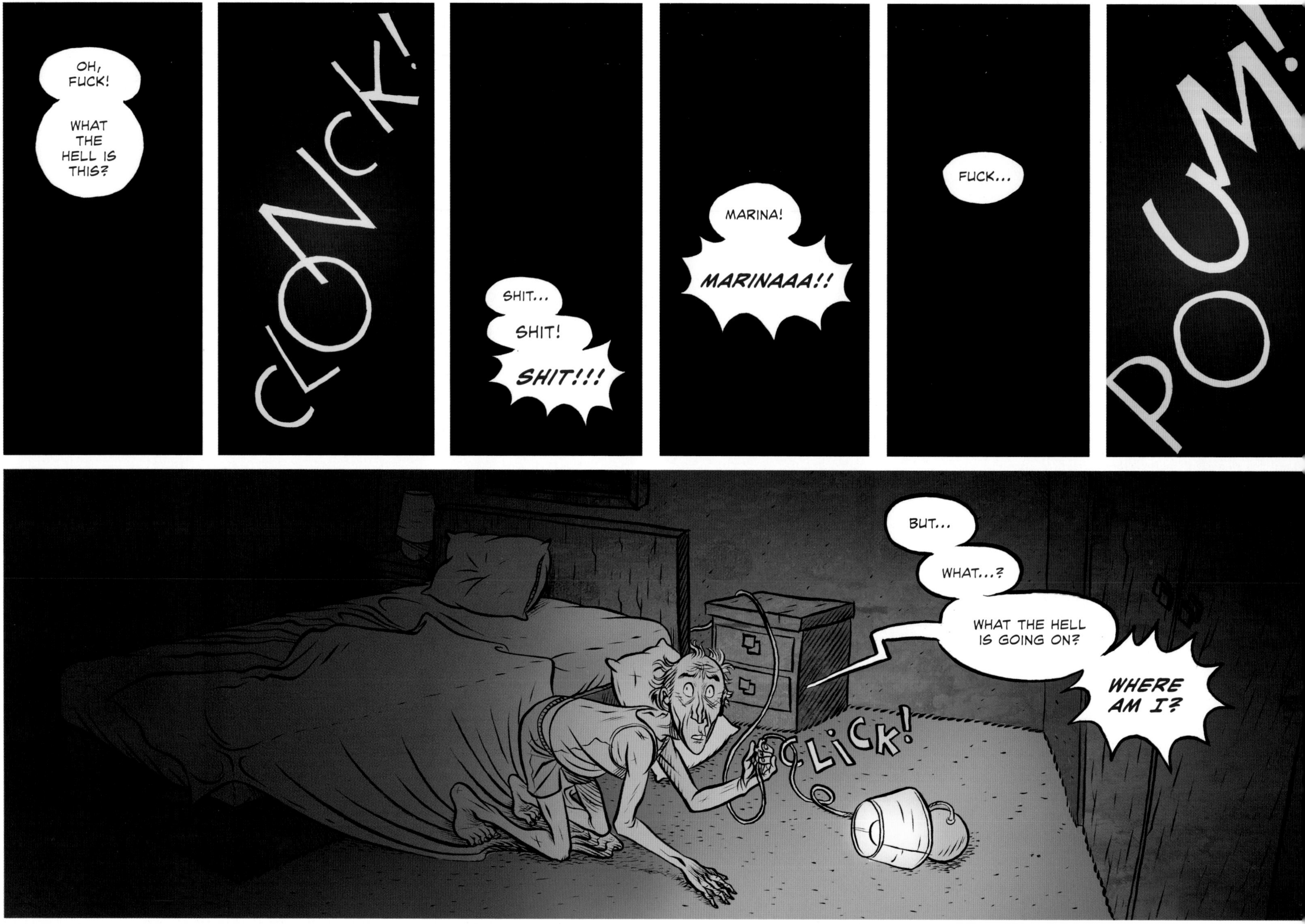

OH, FUCK!
WHAT THE HELL IS THIS?
CLONCK!
SHIT...
SHIT!
SHIT!!!
MARINA!
MARINAAA!!
FUCK...
POUM!
BUT...
WHAT...?
WHAT THE HELL IS GOING ON?
WHERE AM I?
CLICK!

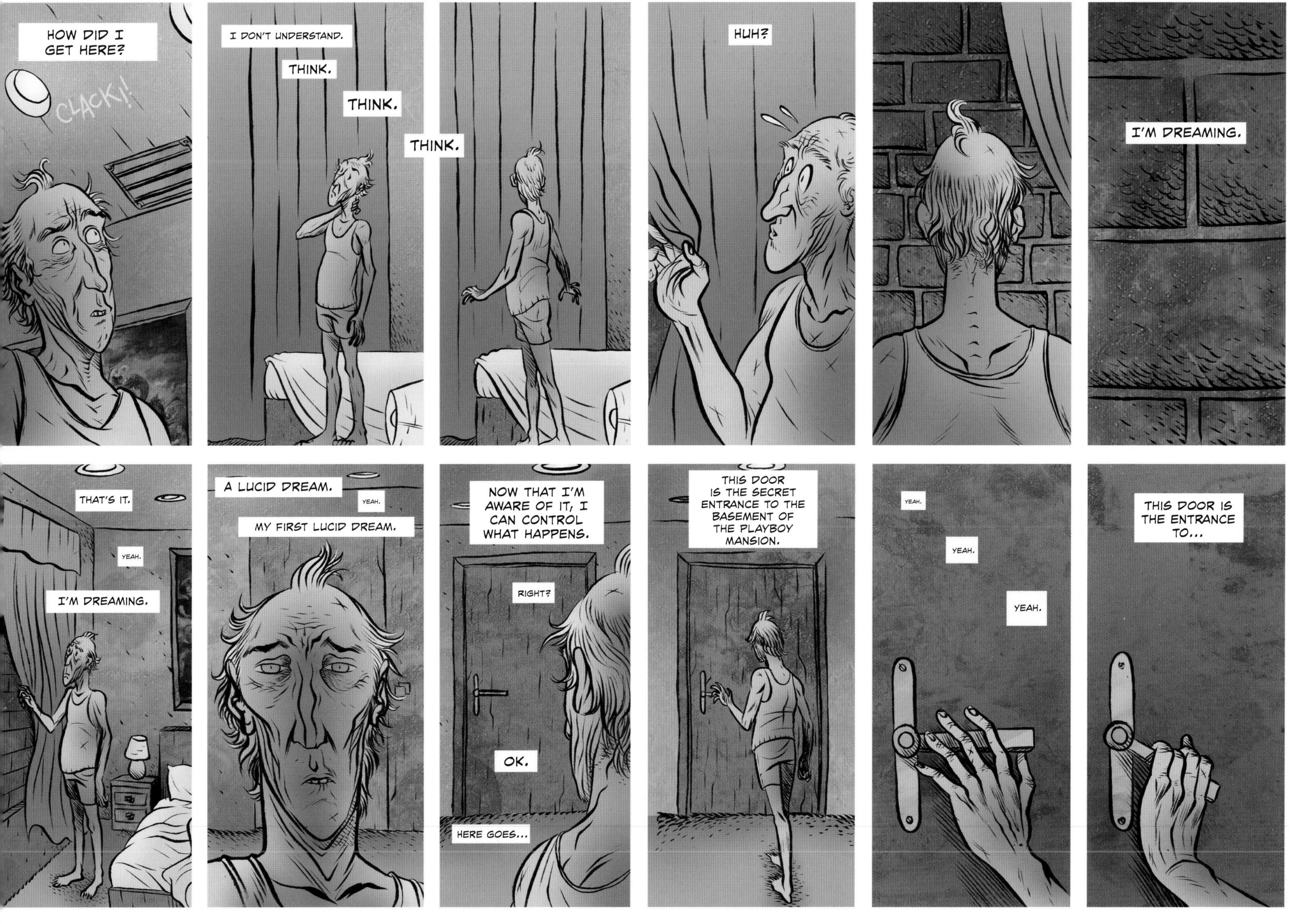

HOW DID I GET HERE?
CLACK!
I DON'T UNDERSTAND.
THINK.
THINK.
THINK.
HUH?
I'M DREAMING.
THAT'S IT.
YEAH.
I'M DREAMING.
A LUCID DREAM.
YEAH.
MY FIRST LUCID DREAM.
NOW THAT I'M AWARE OF IT, I CAN CONTROL WHAT HAPPENS.
RIGHT?
OK.
HERE GOES...
THIS DOOR IS THE SECRET ENTRANCE TO THE BASEMENT OF THE PLAYBOY MANSION.
YEAH.
YEAH.
YEAH.
THIS DOOR IS THE ENTRANCE TO...

NO.

NO.

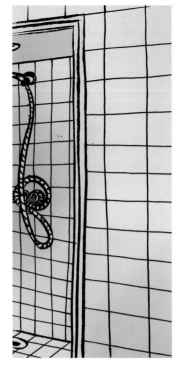

GOOD MORNING!

GOOD MORNING, MR. MANCINI!

WELCOME TO YOUR NEW HOME!

WE HOPE YOU'LL FIND THE TIME YOU SPEND HERE PLEASANT AND FULFILLING.

WHAT KIND OF JOKE IS THIS?

IT'S NOT A JOKE, IT'S A--LET'S CALL IT AN EXPERIMENT.

WHAT DO YOU MEAN, AN EXPERIMENT?

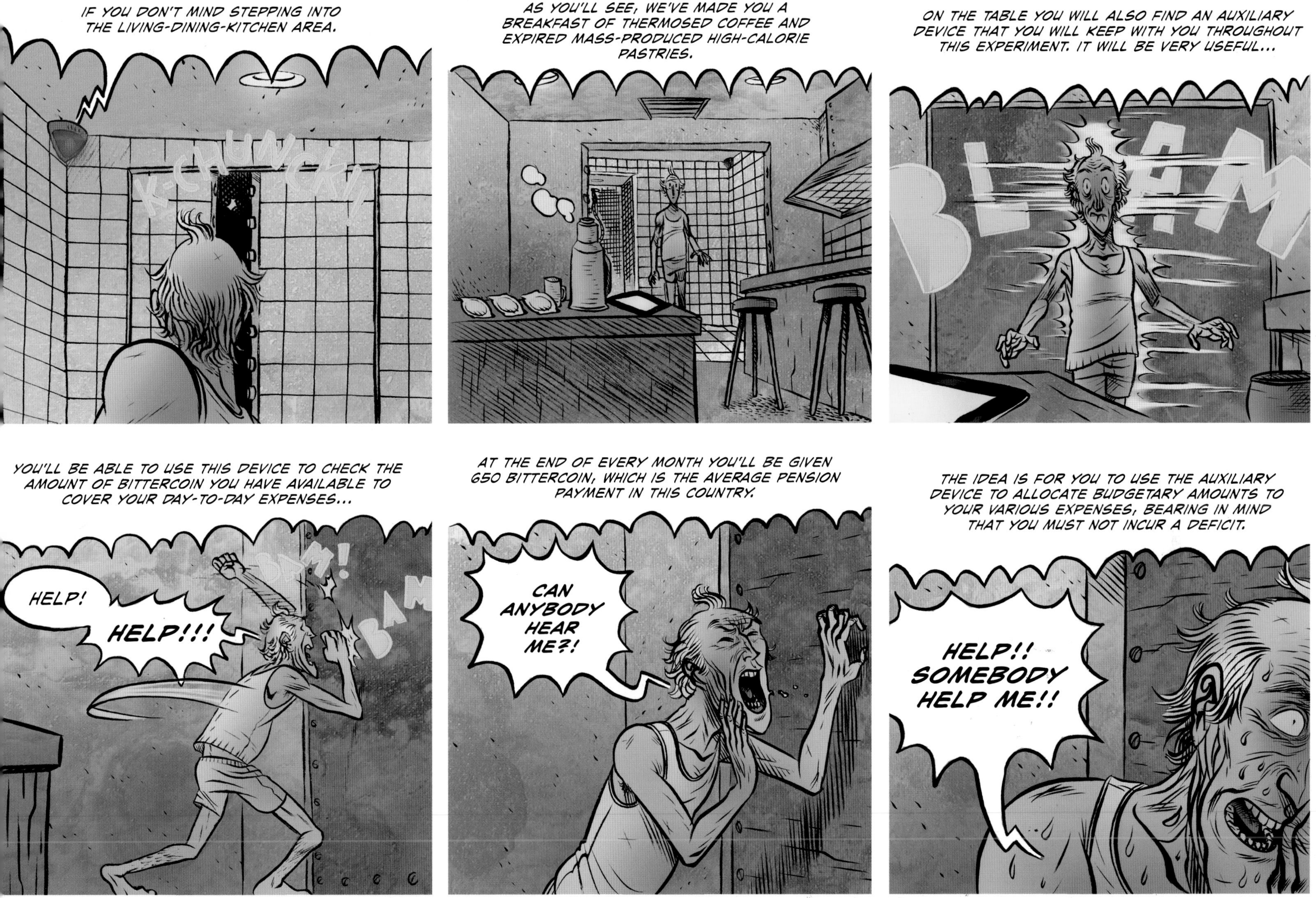
IF YOU DON'T MIND STEPPING INTO THE LIVING-DINING-KITCHEN AREA.
K-CHUNCK!!
AS YOU'LL SEE, WE'VE MADE YOU A BREAKFAST OF THERMOSED COFFEE AND EXPIRED MASS-PRODUCED HIGH-CALORIE PASTRIES.
ON THE TABLE YOU WILL ALSO FIND AN AUXILIARY DEVICE THAT YOU WILL KEEP WITH YOU THROUGHOUT THIS EXPERIMENT. IT WILL BE VERY USEFUL...
BLAM
YOU'LL BE ABLE TO USE THIS DEVICE TO CHECK THE AMOUNT OF BITTERCOIN YOU HAVE AVAILABLE TO COVER YOUR DAY-TO-DAY EXPENSES...
HELP!
HELP!!!
BAM!
BAM
AT THE END OF EVERY MONTH YOU'LL BE GIVEN 650 BITTERCOIN, WHICH IS THE AVERAGE PENSION PAYMENT IN THIS COUNTRY.
CAN ANYBODY HEAR ME?!
THE IDEA IS FOR YOU TO USE THE AUXILIARY DEVICE TO ALLOCATE BUDGETARY AMOUNTS TO YOUR VARIOUS EXPENSES, BEARING IN MIND THAT YOU MUST NOT INCUR A DEFICIT.
HELP!! SOMEBODY HELP ME!!

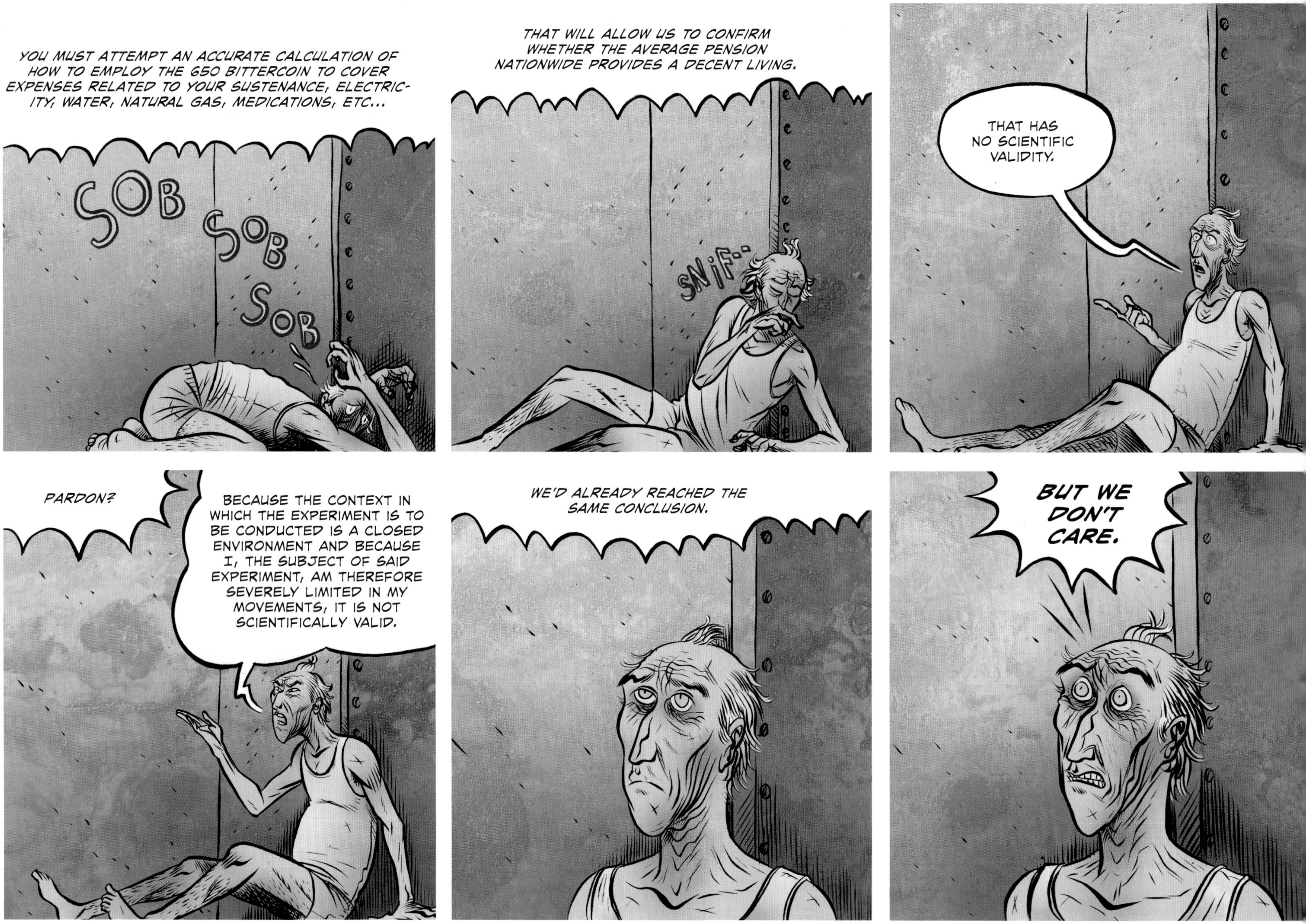
YOU MUST ATTEMPT AN ACCURATE CALCULATION OF HOW TO EMPLOY THE 650 BITTERCOIN TO COVER EXPENSES RELATED TO YOUR SUSTENANCE; ELECTRICITY; WATER; NATURAL GAS; MEDICATIONS; ETC...
SOB SOB SOB
THAT WILL ALLOW US TO CONFIRM WHETHER THE AVERAGE PENSION NATIONWIDE PROVIDES A DECENT LIVING.
SNIF..
THAT HAS NO SCIENTIFIC VALIDITY.
PARDON?
BECAUSE THE CONTEXT IN WHICH THE EXPERIMENT IS TO BE CONDUCTED IS A CLOSED ENVIRONMENT AND BECAUSE I, THE SUBJECT OF SAID EXPERIMENT, AM THEREFORE SEVERELY LIMITED IN MY MOVEMENTS, IT IS NOT SCIENTIFICALLY VALID.
WE'D ALREADY REACHED THE SAME CONCLUSION.
BUT WE DON'T CARE.

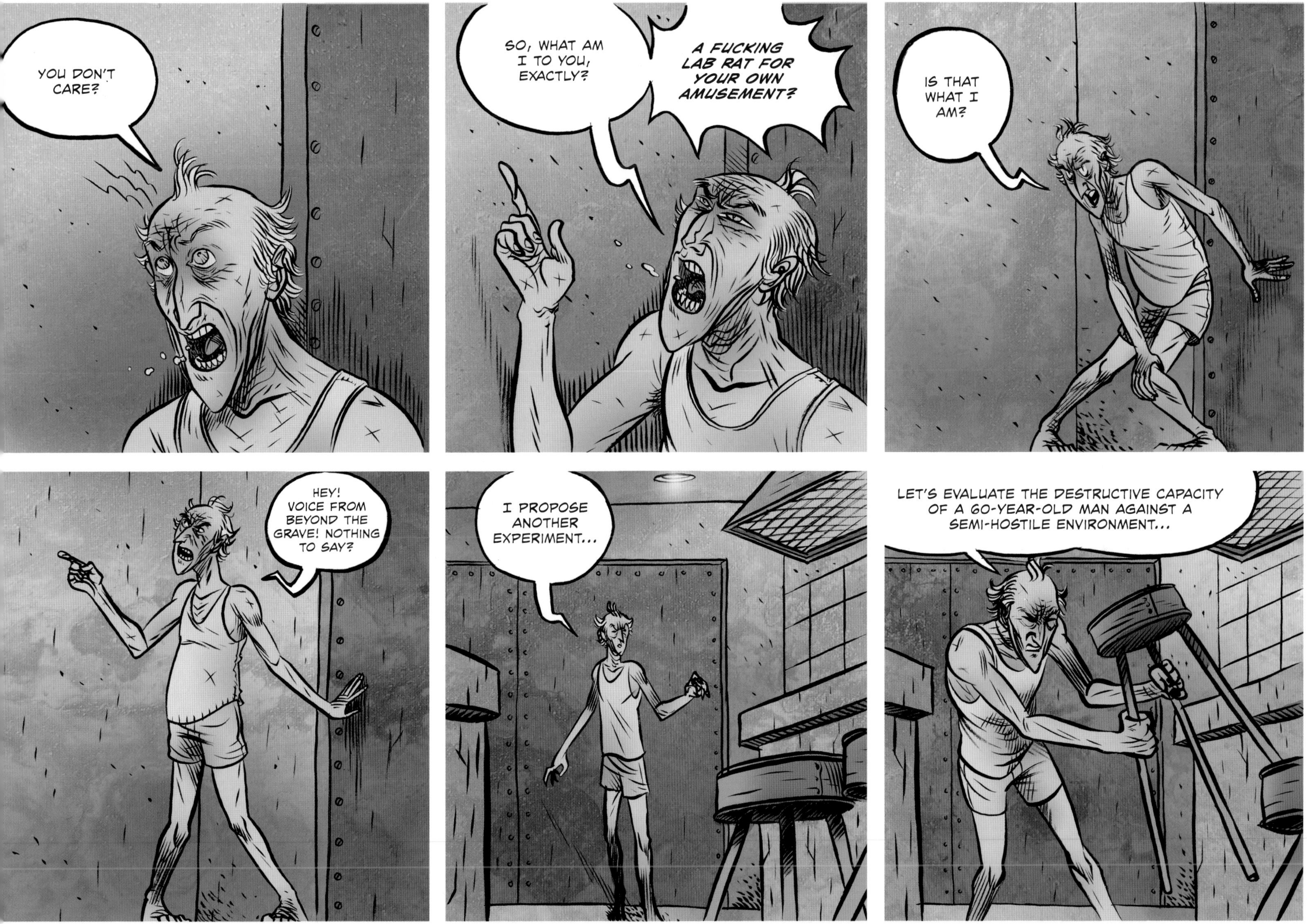
YOU DON'T CARE?
SO, WHAT AM I TO YOU, EXACTLY?
A FUCKING LAB RAT FOR YOUR OWN AMUSEMENT?
IS THAT WHAT I AM?
HEY! VOICE FROM BEYOND THE GRAVE! NOTHING TO SAY?
I PROPOSE ANOTHER EXPERIMENT...
LET'S EVALUATE THE DESTRUCTIVE CAPACITY OF A 60-YEAR-OLD MAN AGAINST A SEMI-HOSTILE ENVIRONMENT...

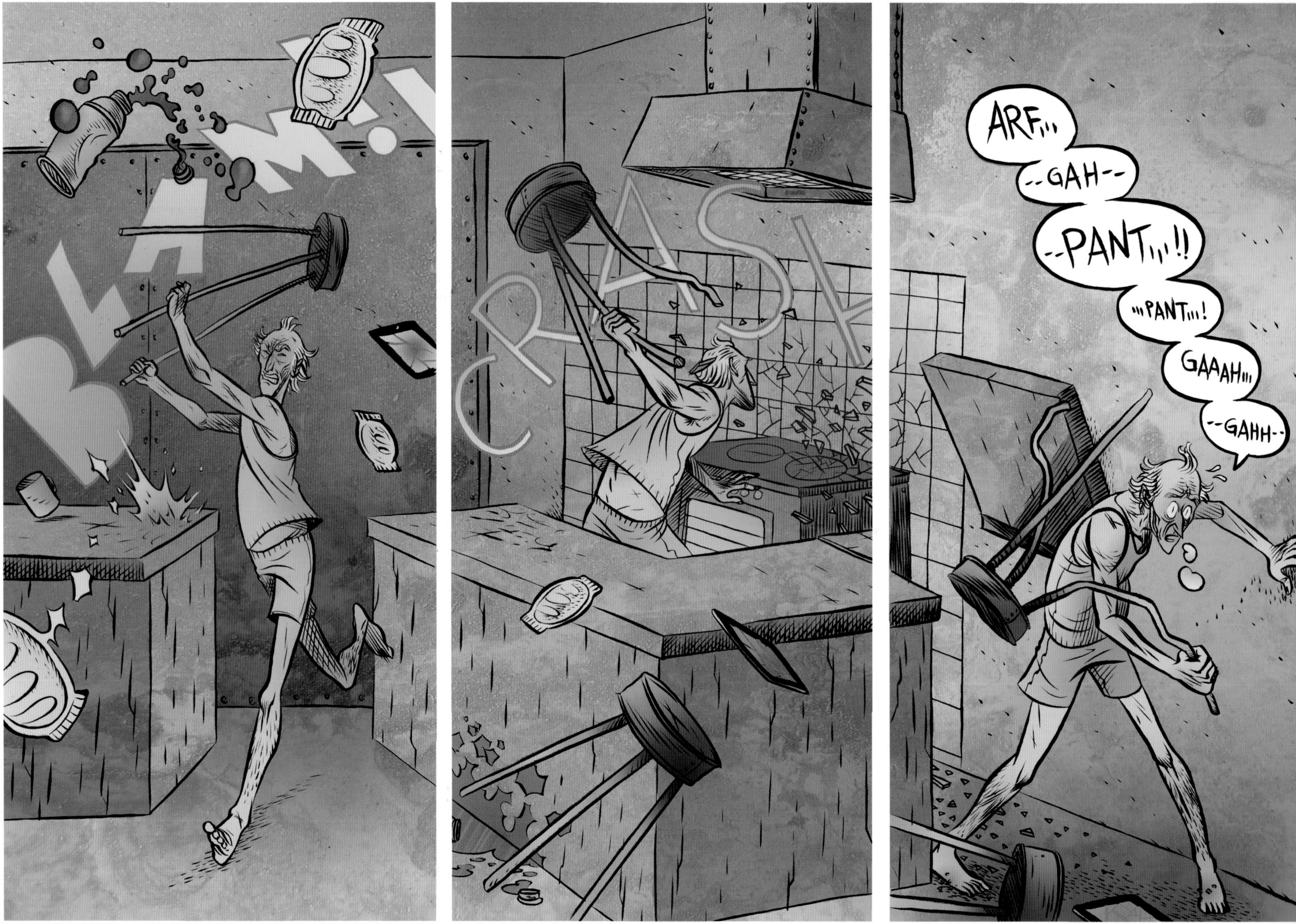
BLAM!
CRAS
ARF...
--GAH--
--PANT...!!
...PANT...!
GAAAH...
--GAHH--

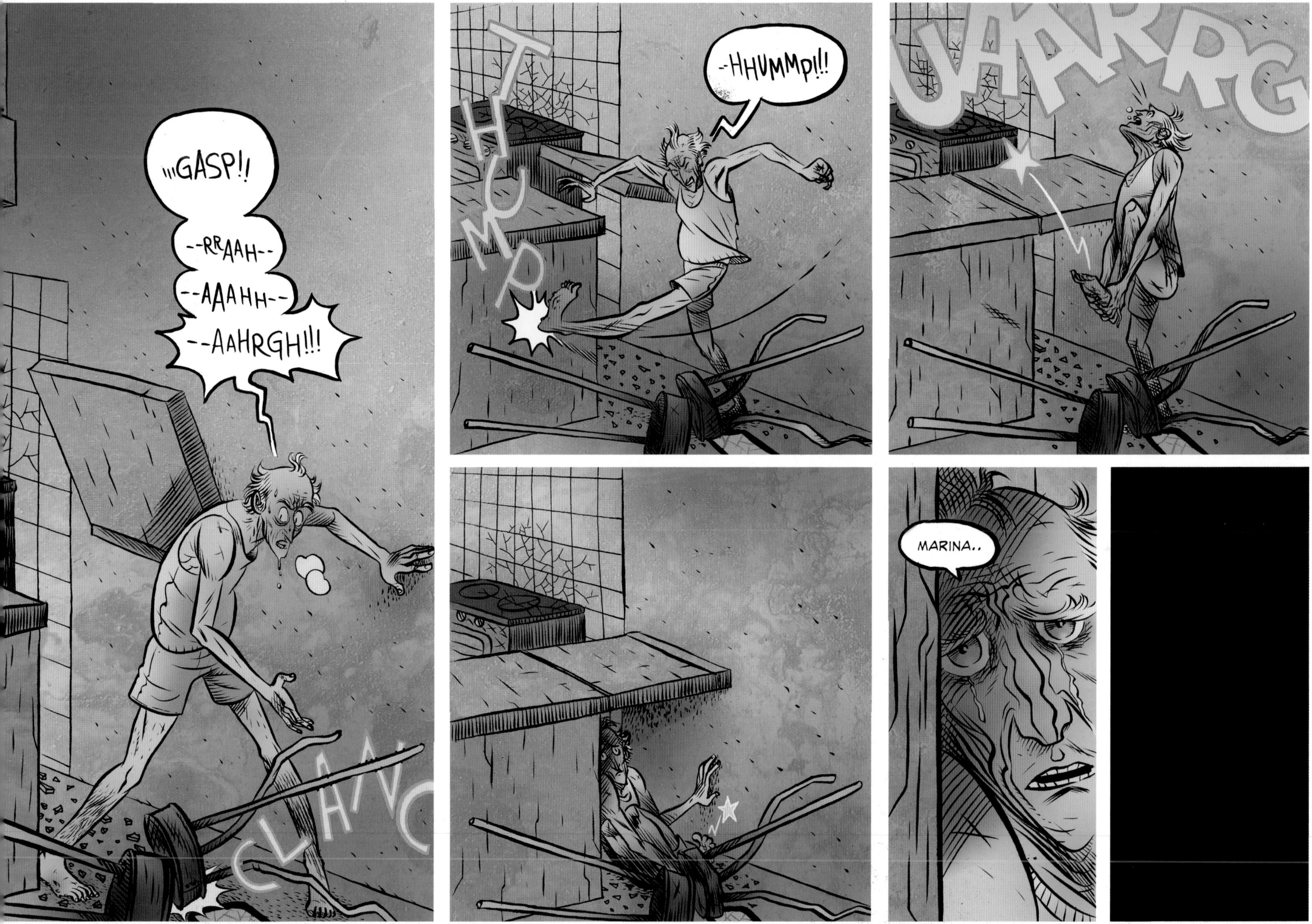
¡¡¡GASP!!
--RRAAH--
--AAAHH--
--AAHRGH!!!
CLANC
THUMP
-HHUMMP!!!
UARRG
MARINA..

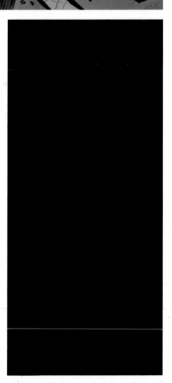

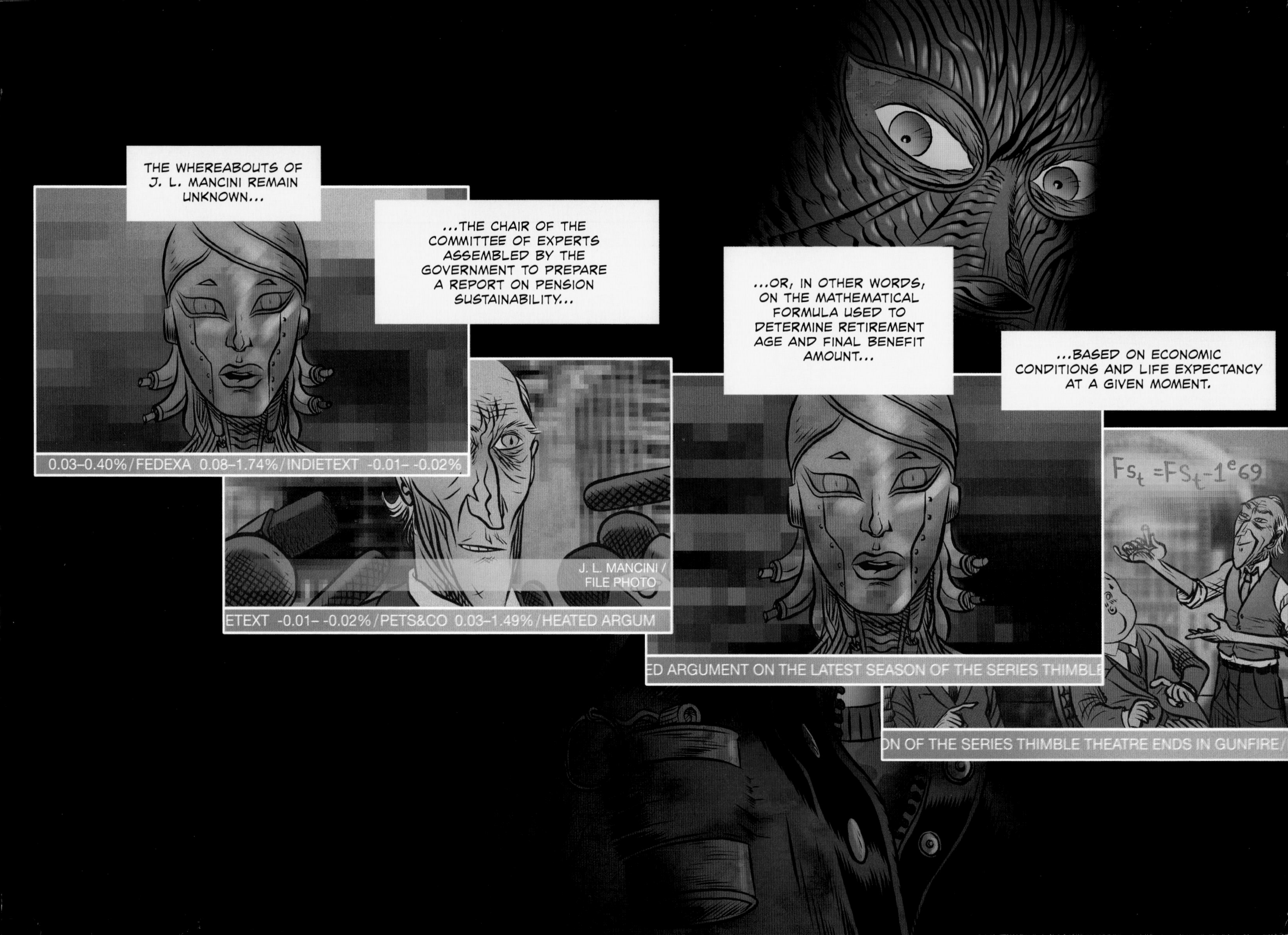
THE WHEREABOUTS OF J. L. MANCINI REMAIN UNKNOWN...
0.03–0.40% / FEDEXA 0.08–1.74% / INDIETEXT -0.01– -0.02%
...THE CHAIR OF THE COMMITTEE OF EXPERTS ASSEMBLED BY THE GOVERNMENT TO PREPARE A REPORT ON PENSION SUSTAINABILITY...
J. L. MANCINI / FILE PHOTO
ETEXT -0.01– -0.02% / PETS&CO 0.03–1.49% / HEATED ARGUM
...OR, IN OTHER WORDS, ON THE MATHEMATICAL FORMULA USED TO DETERMINE RETIREMENT AGE AND FINAL BENEFIT AMOUNT...
ED ARGUMENT ON THE LATEST SEASON OF THE SERIES THIMBLE
...BASED ON ECONOMIC CONDITIONS AND LIFE EXPECTANCY AT A GIVEN MOMENT.
Fst =FSt-1e69
N OF THE SERIES THIMBLE THEATRE ENDS IN GUNFIRE /

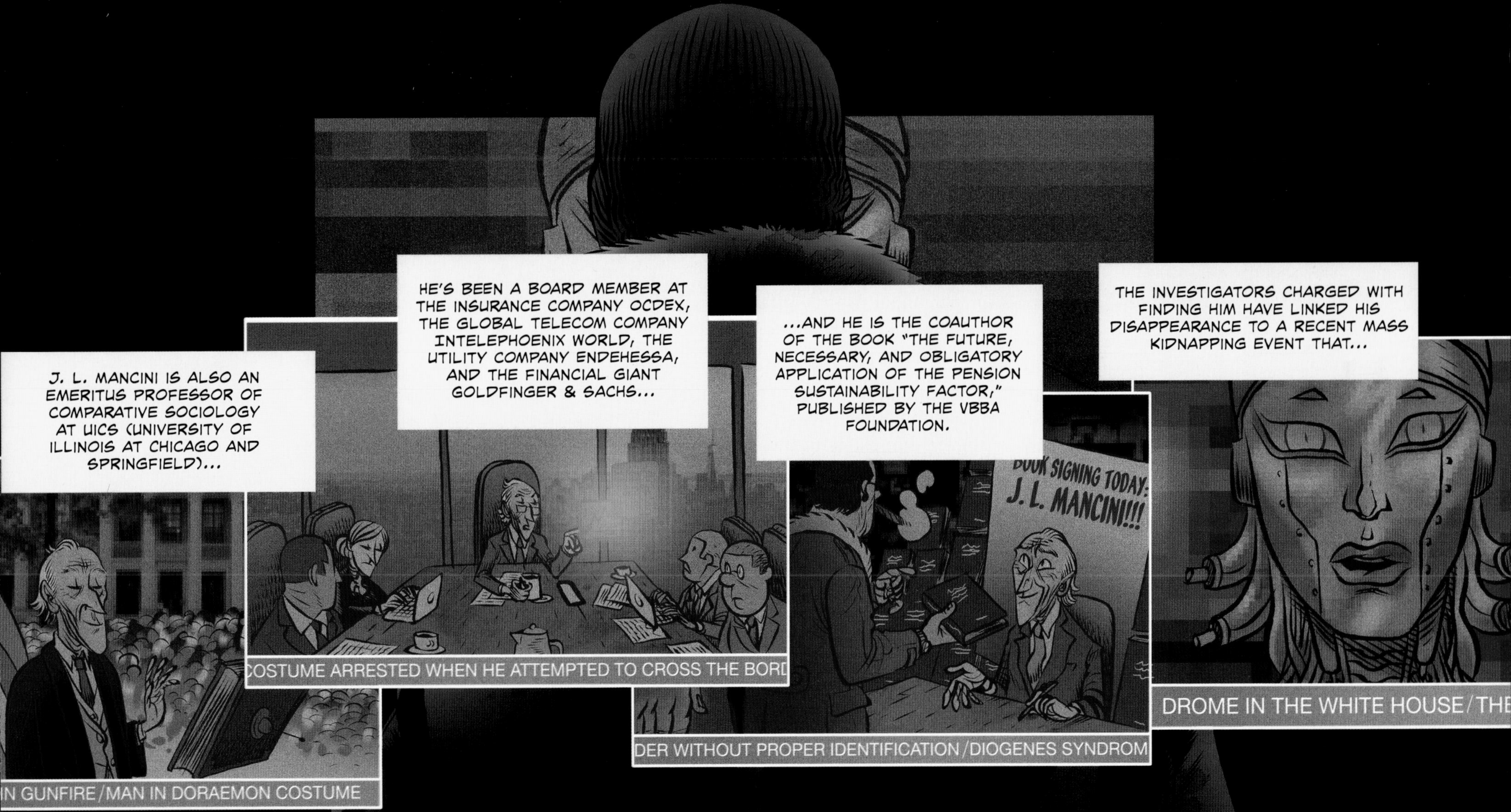
J. L. MANCINI IS ALSO AN EMERITUS PROFESSOR OF COMPARATIVE SOCIOLOGY AT UICS (UNIVERSITY OF ILLINOIS AT CHICAGO AND SPRINGFIELD)...
HE'S BEEN A BOARD MEMBER AT THE INSURANCE COMPANY OCDEX, THE GLOBAL TELECOM COMPANY INTELEPHOENIX WORLD, THE UTILITY COMPANY ENDEHESSA, AND THE FINANCIAL GIANT GOLDFINGER & SACHS...
...AND HE IS THE COAUTHOR OF THE BOOK "THE FUTURE, NECESSARY, AND OBLIGATORY APPLICATION OF THE PENSION SUSTAINABILITY FACTOR," PUBLISHED BY THE VBBA FOUNDATION.
THE INVESTIGATORS CHARGED WITH FINDING HIM HAVE LINKED HIS DISAPPEARANCE TO A RECENT MASS KIDNAPPING EVENT THAT...
IN GUNFIRE/MAN IN DORAEMON COSTUME
COSTUME ARRESTED WHEN HE ATTEMPTED TO CROSS THE BORD
BOOK SIGNING TODAY: J. L. MANCINI!!!
DER WITHOUT PROPER IDENTIFICATION/DIOGENES SYNDROM
DROME IN THE WHITE HOUSE/THE

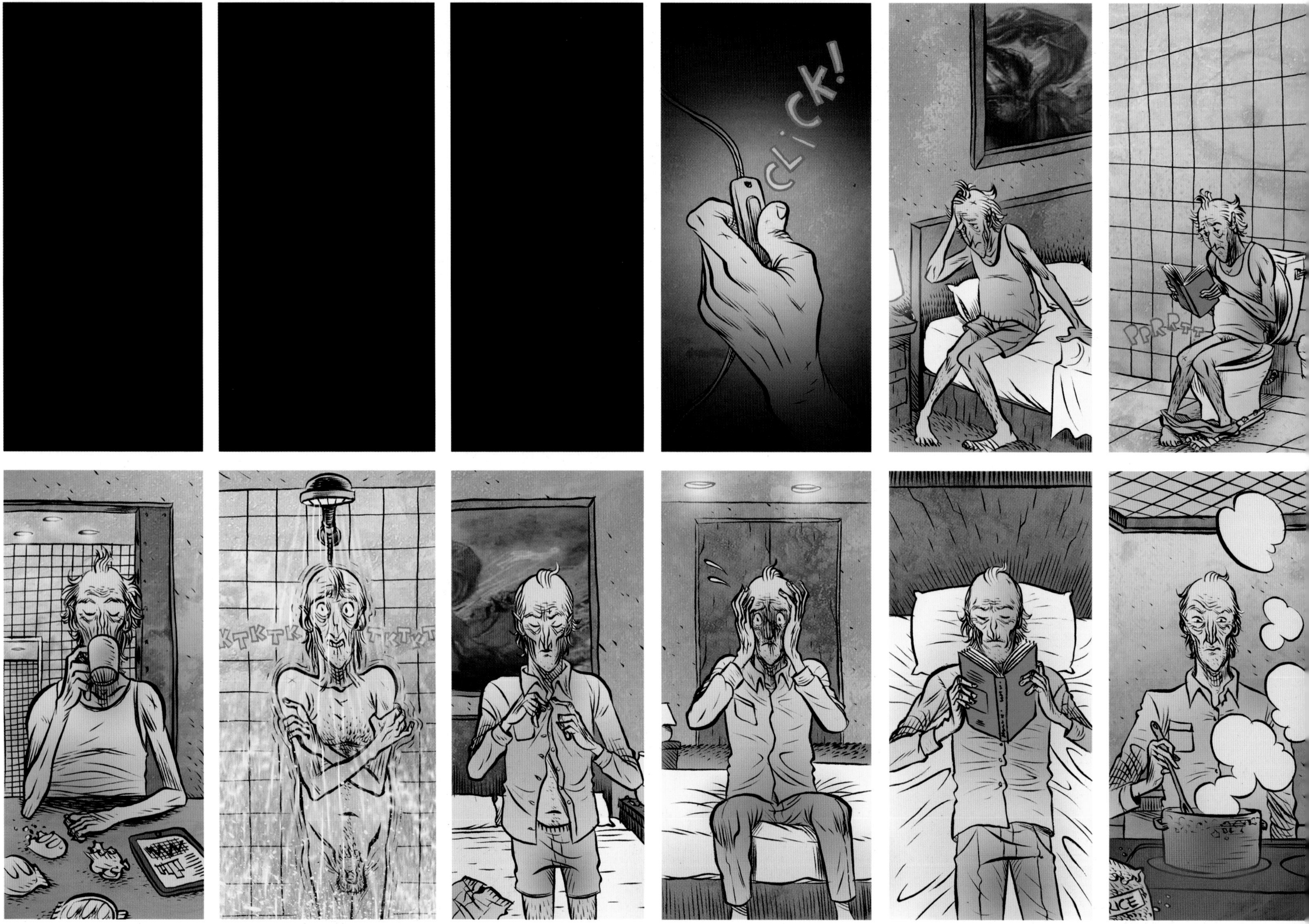
CLICK!
PPRRTTT
KTKTK
TKTKT

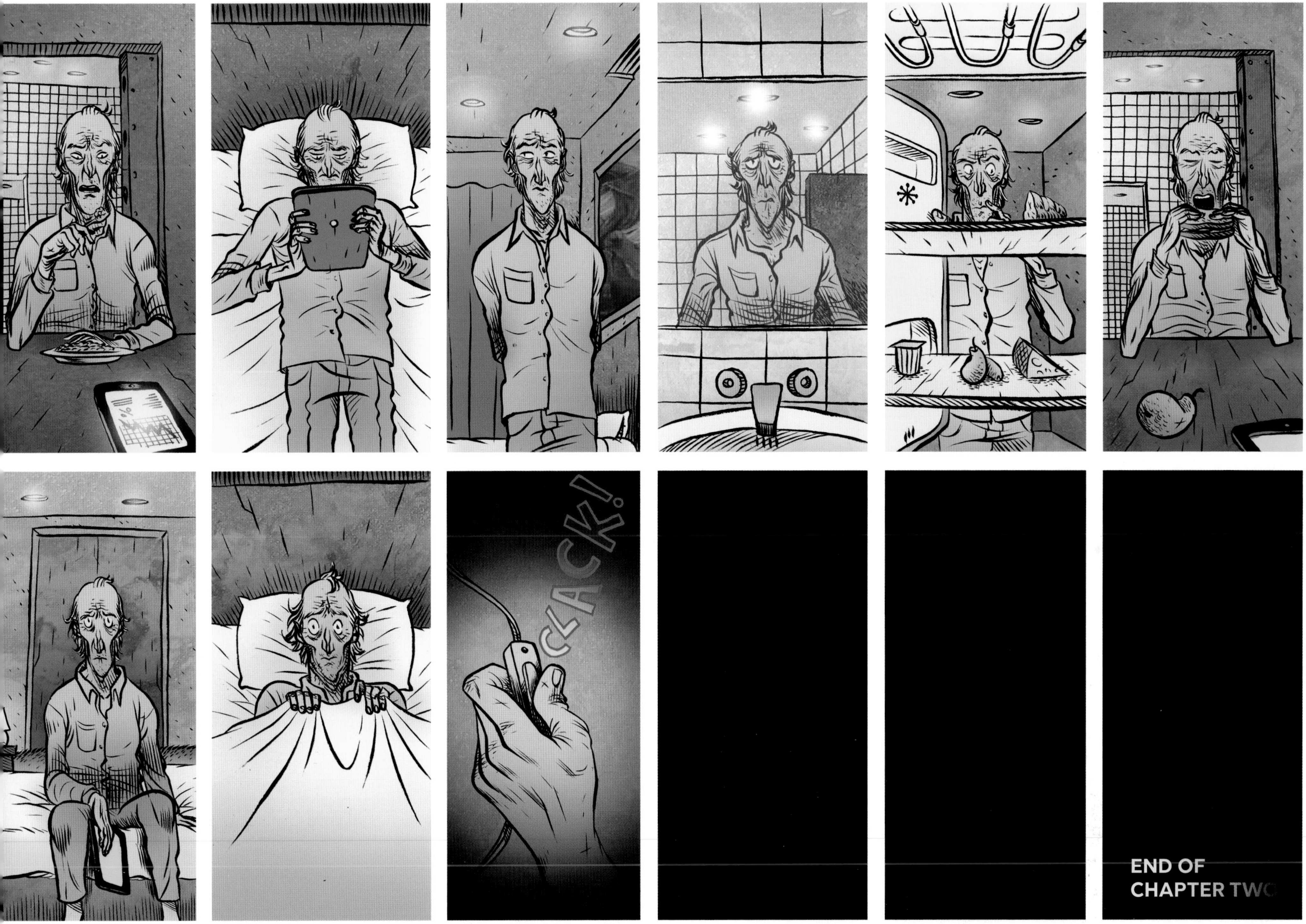
CLACK!
END OF
CHAPTER TWO

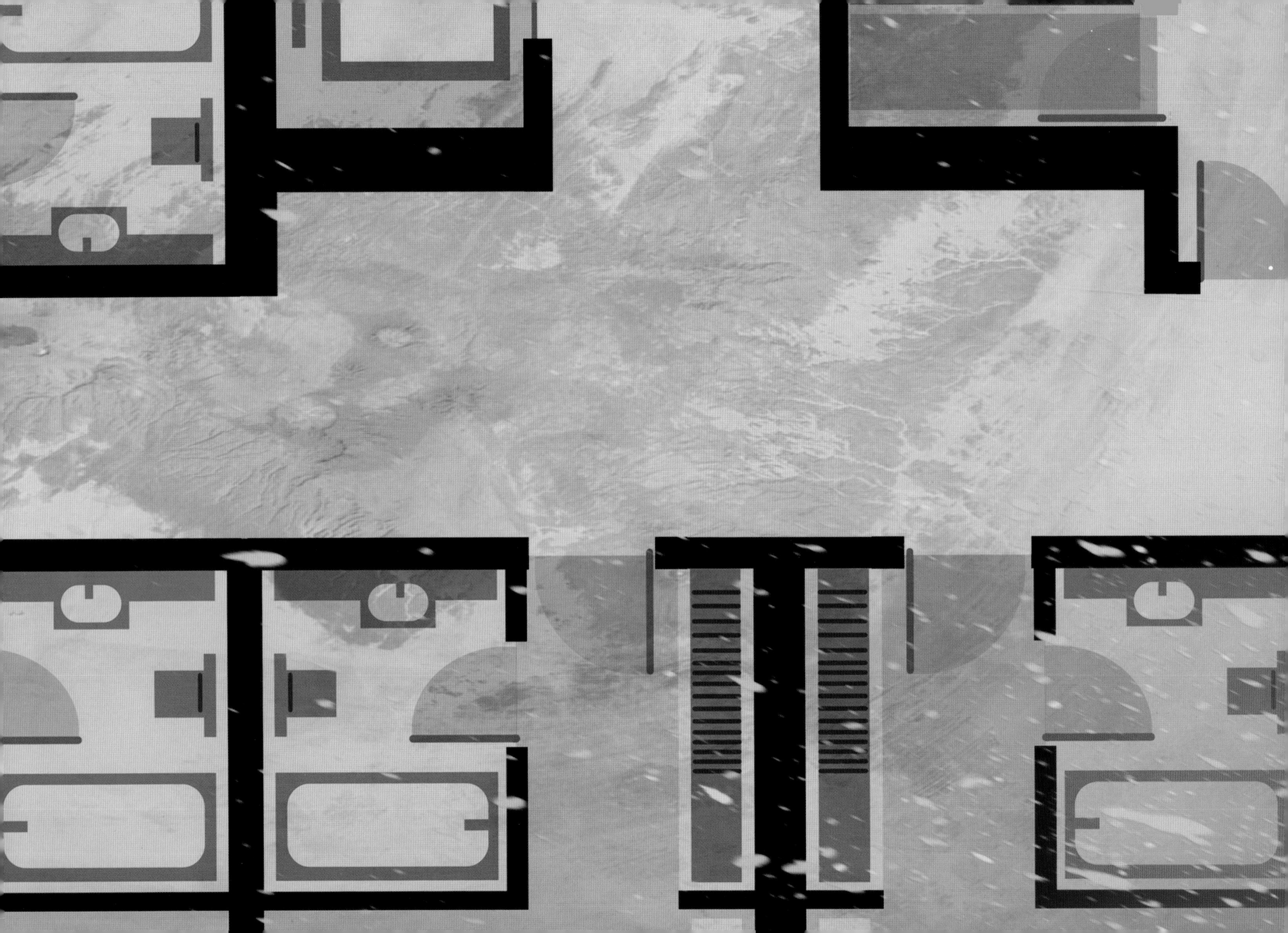

SERVICES

CHAPTER THREE:

YOU ARE HERE

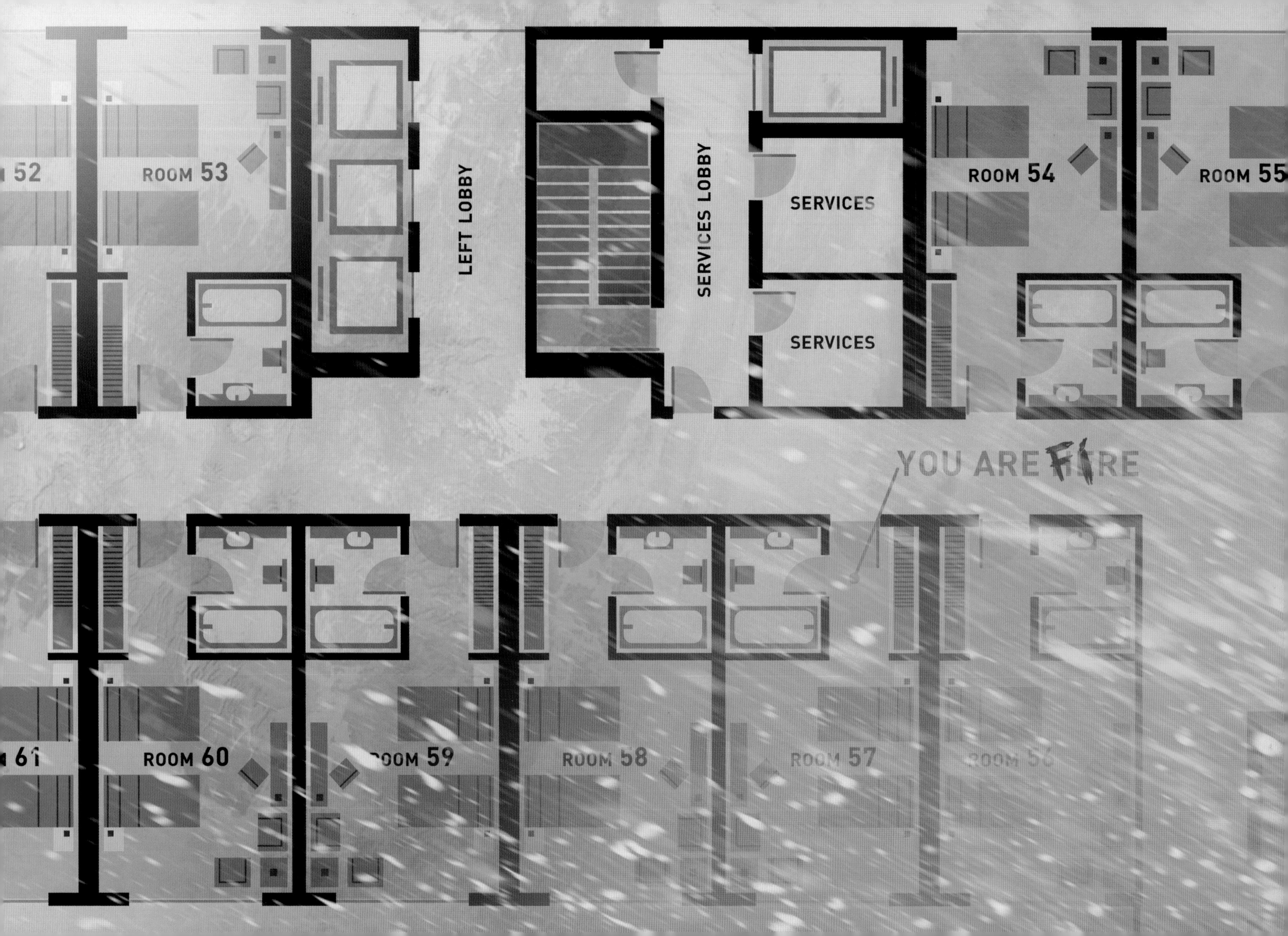
52
ROOM 53
LEFT LOBBY
SERVICES LOBBY
SERVICES
SERVICES
ROOM 54
ROOM 55
YOU ARE FIRE
61
ROOM 60
OOM 59
ROOM 58
ROOM 57

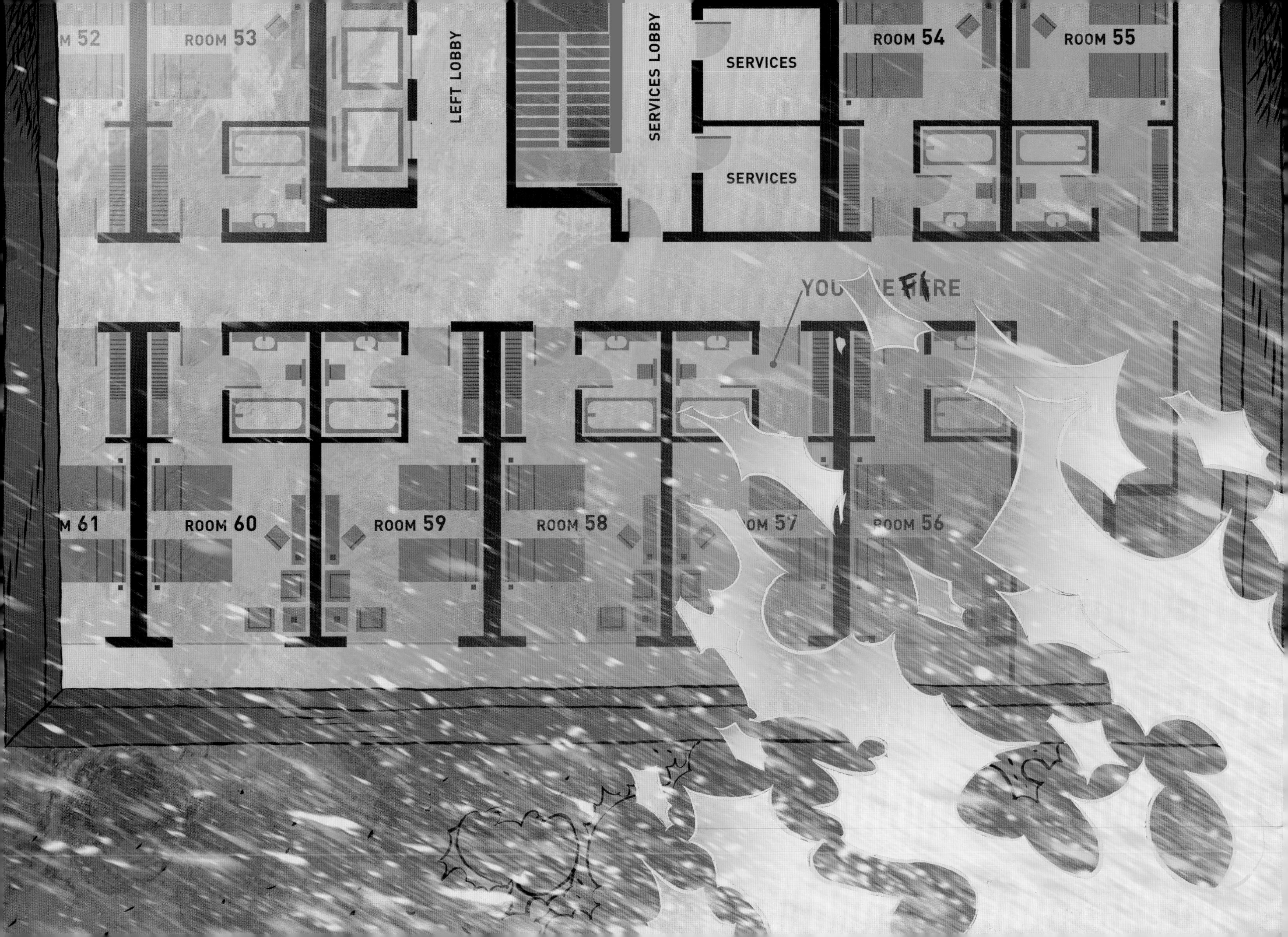

M 52
ROOM 53
LEFT LOBBY
SERVICES LOBBY
SERVICES
SERVICES
ROOM 54
ROOM 55
M 61
ROOM 60
ROOM 59
ROOM 58
OM 57
ROOM 56

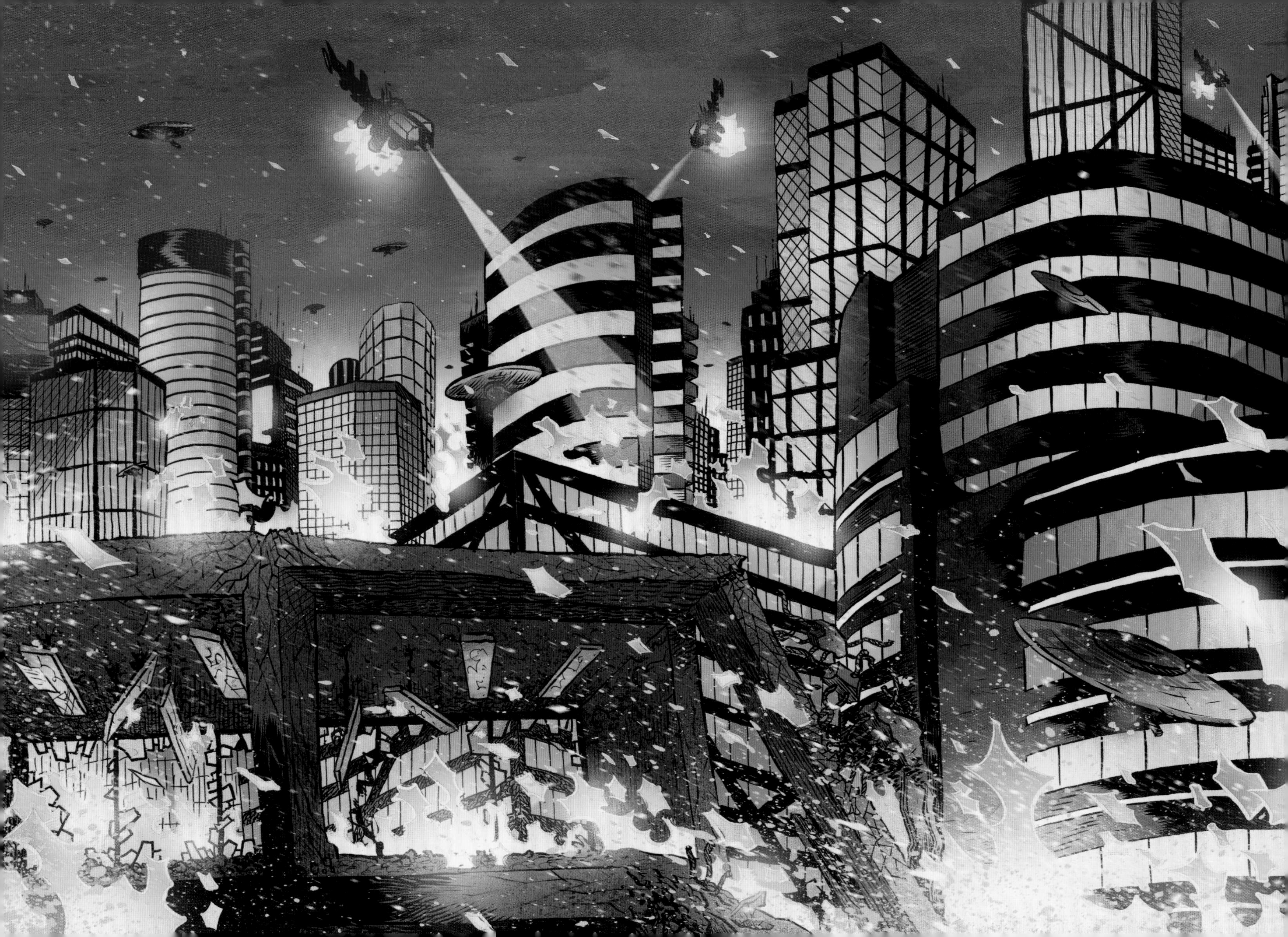

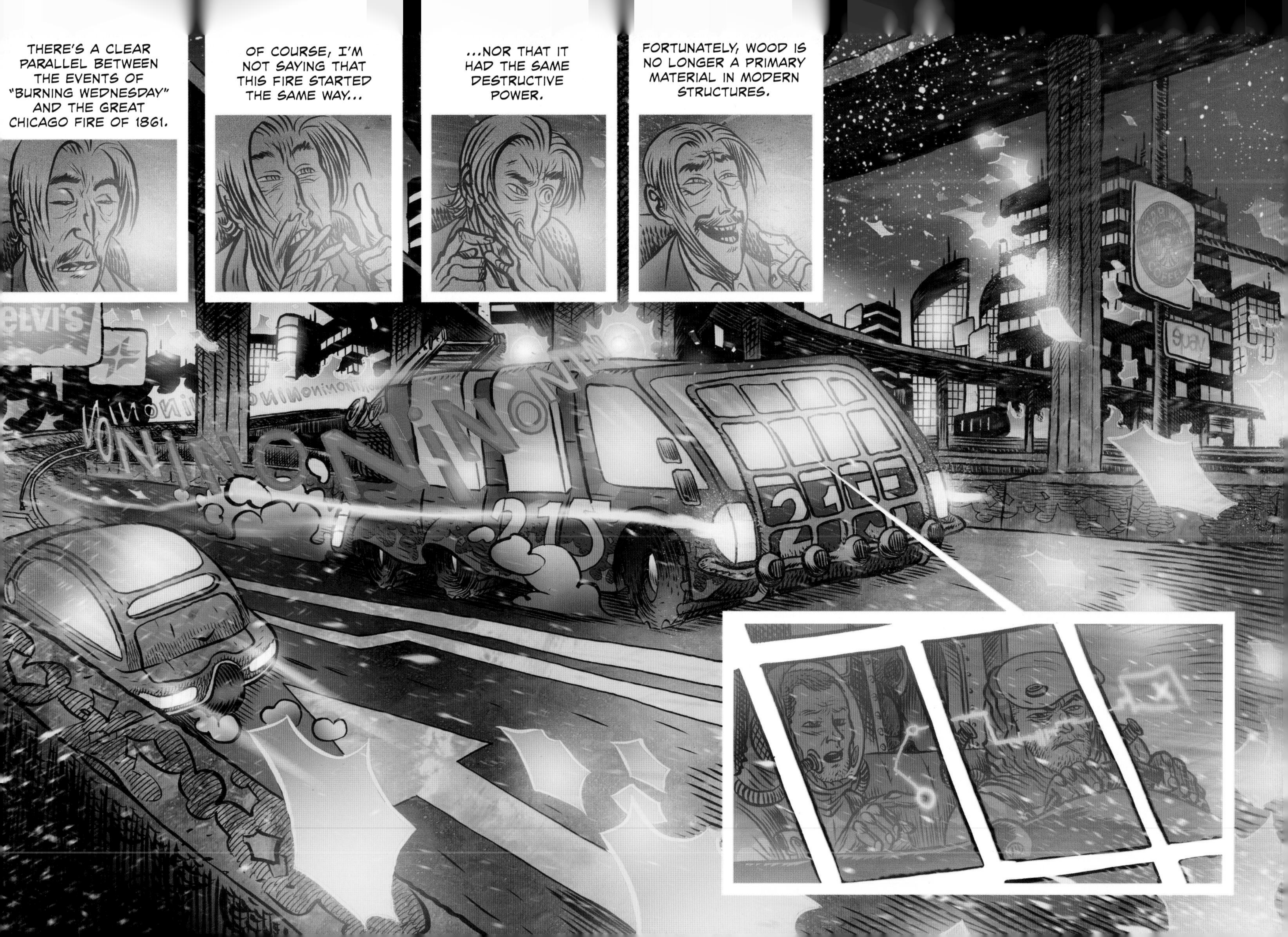
THERE'S A CLEAR PARALLEL BETWEEN THE EVENTS OF "BURNING WEDNESDAY" AND THE GREAT CHICAGO FIRE OF 1861.
OF COURSE, I'M NOT SAYING THAT THIS FIRE STARTED THE SAME WAY...
...NOR THAT IT HAD THE SAME DESTRUCTIVE POWER.
FORTUNATELY, WOOD IS NO LONGER A PRIMARY MATERIAL IN MODERN STRUCTURES.

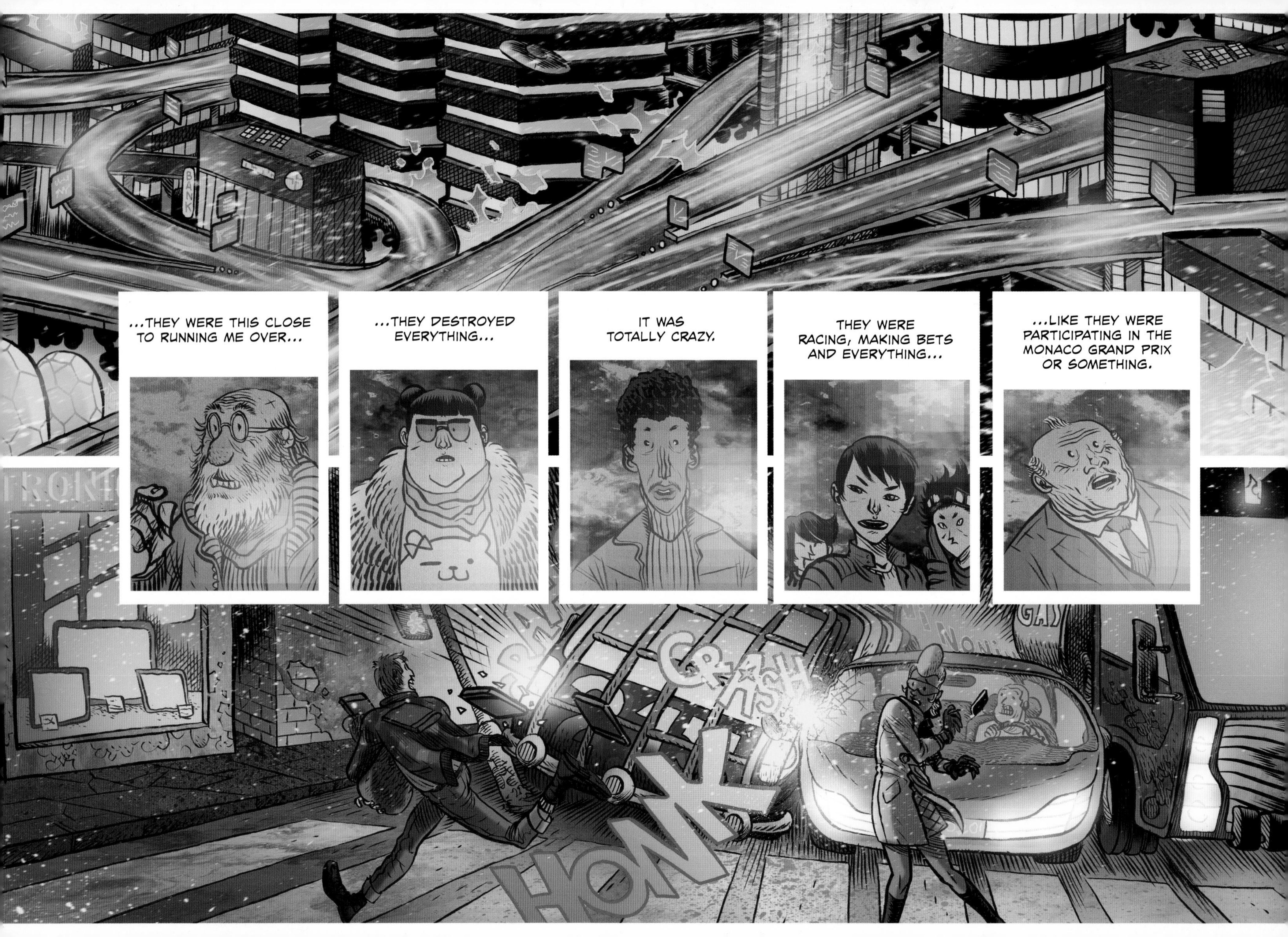

...THEY WERE THIS CLOSE TO RUNNING ME OVER...
...THEY DESTROYED EVERYTHING...
IT WAS TOTALLY CRAZY.
THEY WERE RACING, MAKING BETS AND EVERYTHING...
...LIKE THEY WERE PARTICIPATING IN THE MONACO GRAND PRIX OR SOMETHING.
BANK
CRASH
HONK

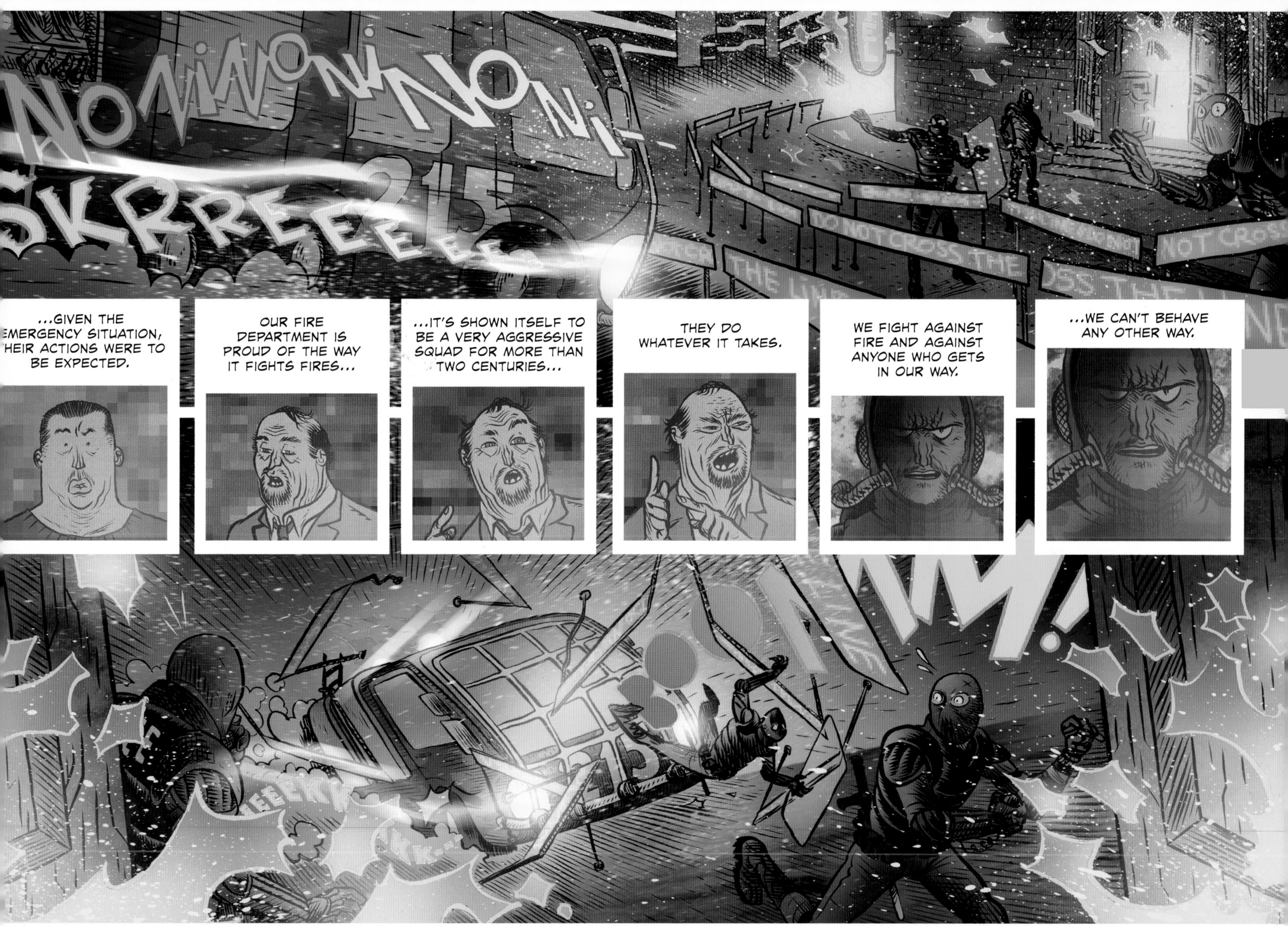
NONINONINONI-
SKREEEEEEE
...GIVEN THE EMERGENCY SITUATION, THEIR ACTIONS WERE TO BE EXPECTED.
OUR FIRE DEPARTMENT IS PROUD OF THE WAY IT FIGHTS FIRES...
...IT'S SHOWN ITSELF TO BE A VERY AGGRESSIVE SQUAD FOR MORE THAN TWO CENTURIES...
THEY DO WHATEVER IT TAKES.
WE FIGHT AGAINST FIRE AND AGAINST ANYONE WHO GETS IN OUR WAY.
...WE CAN'T BEHAVE ANY OTHER WAY.
DO NOT CROSS THE

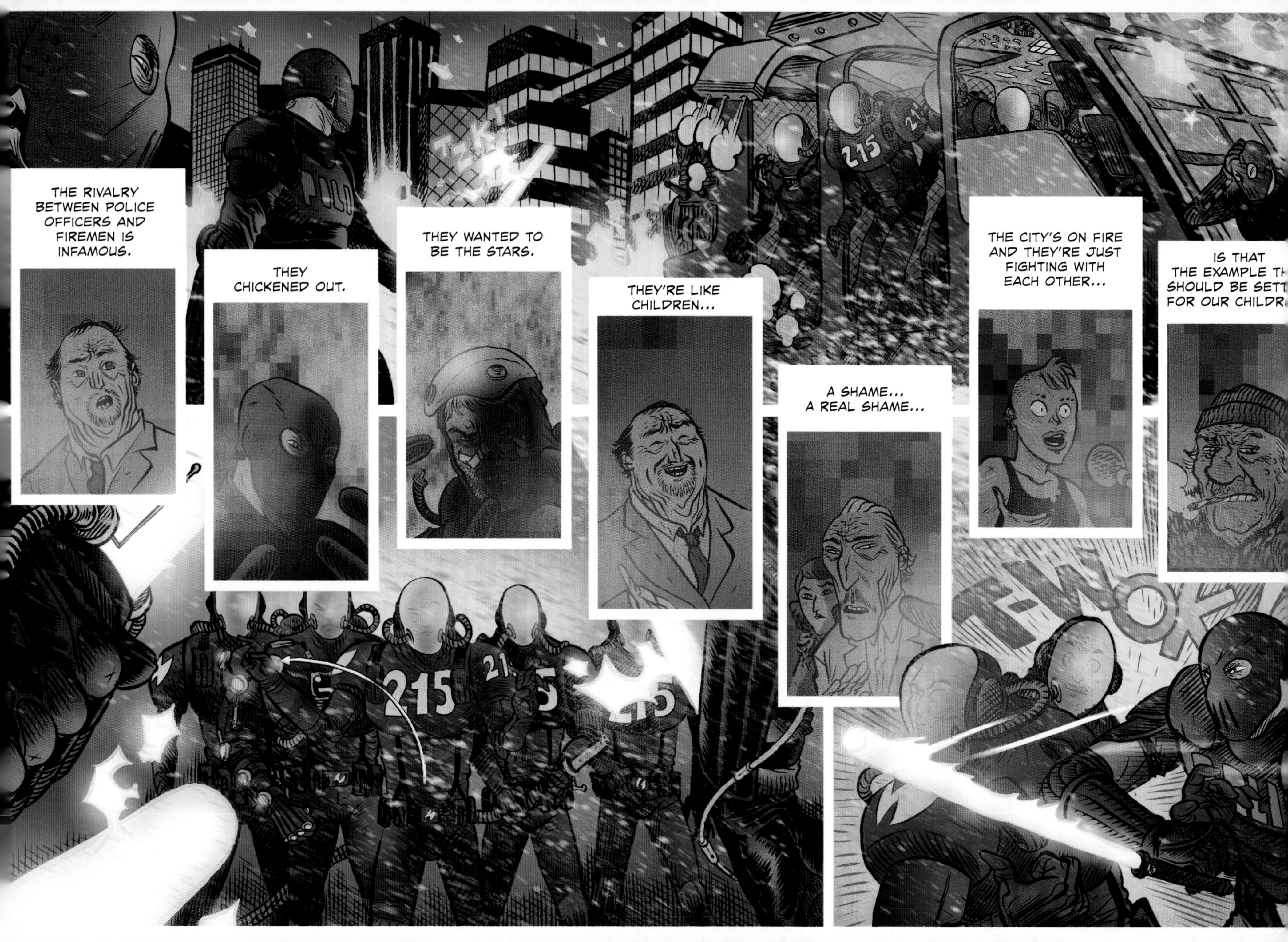
THE RIVALRY BETWEEN POLICE OFFICERS AND FIREMEN IS INFAMOUS.
THEY CHICKENED OUT.
THEY WANTED TO BE THE STARS.
THEY'RE LIKE CHILDREN...
A SHAME... A REAL SHAME...
THE CITY'S ON FIRE AND THEY'RE JUST FIGHTING WITH EACH OTHER...
IS THAT THE EXAMPLE TH SHOULD BE SETT FOR OUR CHILDR
215

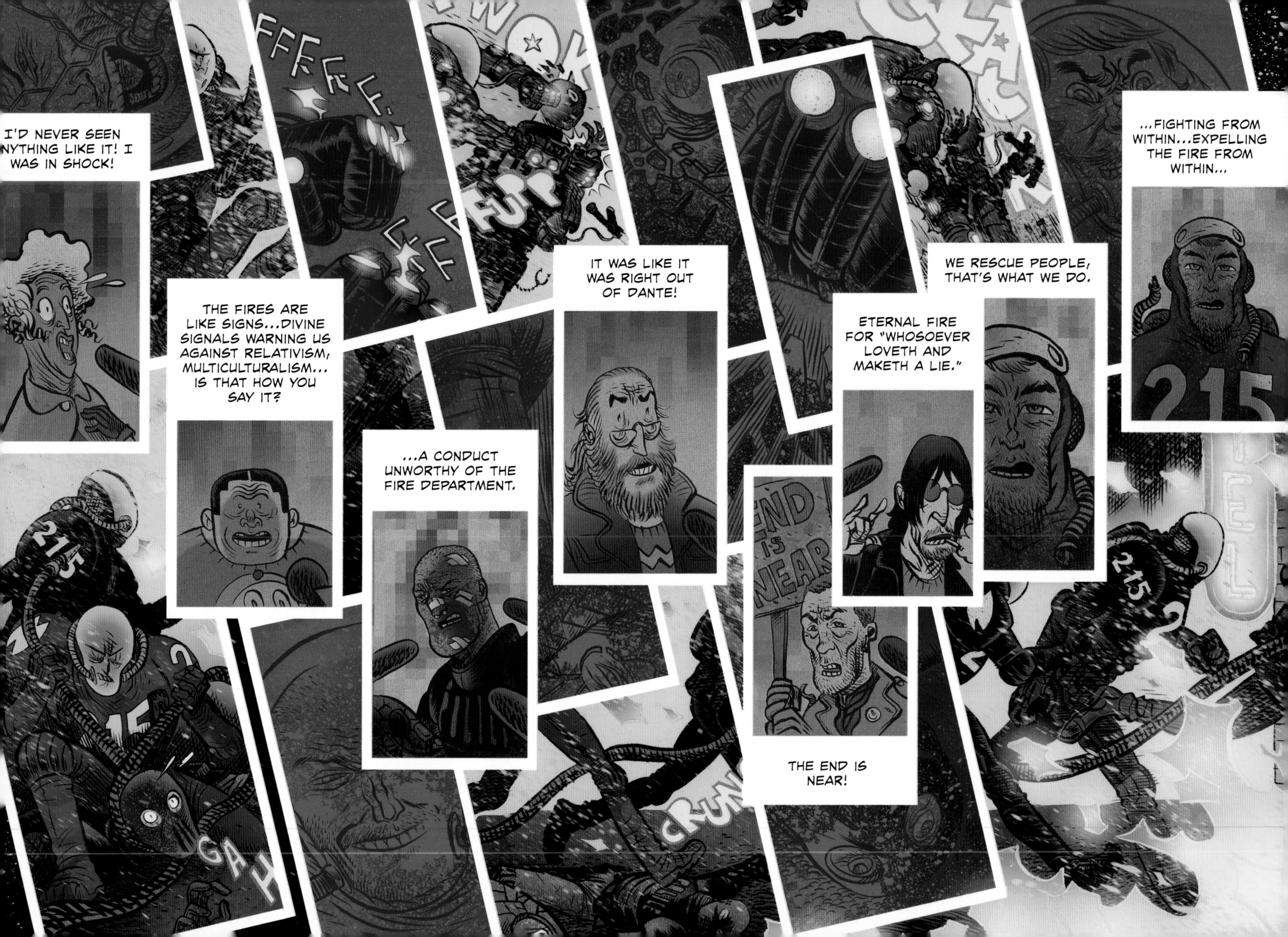

I'D NEVER SEEN NYTHING LIKE IT! I WAS IN SHOCK!
THE FIRES ARE LIKE SIGNS...DIVINE SIGNALS WARNING US AGAINST RELATIVISM, MULTICULTURALISM... IS THAT HOW YOU SAY IT?
...A CONDUCT UNWORTHY OF THE FIRE DEPARTMENT.
IT WAS LIKE IT WAS RIGHT OUT OF DANTE!
END IS NEAR
THE END IS NEAR!
ETERNAL FIRE FOR "WHOSOEVER LOVETH AND MAKETH A LIE."
WE RESCUE PEOPLE, THAT'S WHAT WE DO.
...FIGHTING FROM WITHIN...EXPELLING THE FIRE FROM WITHIN...
215
GAH

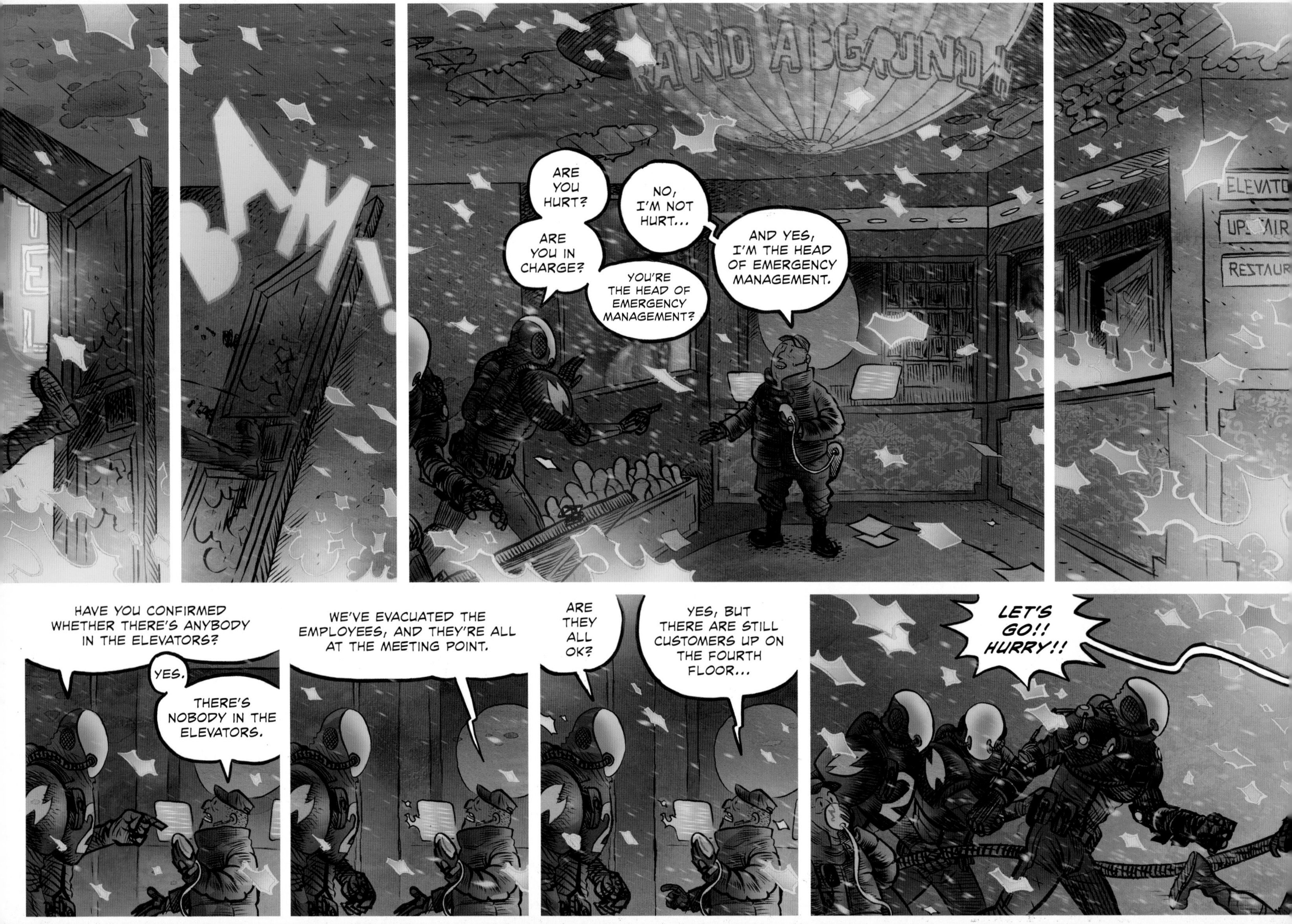
ARE YOU HURT?
ARE YOU IN CHARGE?
YOU'RE THE HEAD OF EMERGENCY MANAGEMENT?
NO, I'M NOT HURT...
AND YES, I'M THE HEAD OF EMERGENCY MANAGEMENT.
HAVE YOU CONFIRMED WHETHER THERE'S ANYBODY IN THE ELEVATORS?
YES.
THERE'S NOBODY IN THE ELEVATORS.
WE'VE EVACUATED THE EMPLOYEES, AND THEY'RE ALL AT THE MEETING POINT.
ARE THEY ALL OK?
YES, BUT THERE ARE STILL CUSTOMERS UP ON THE FOURTH FLOOR...
LET'S GO!! HURRY!!

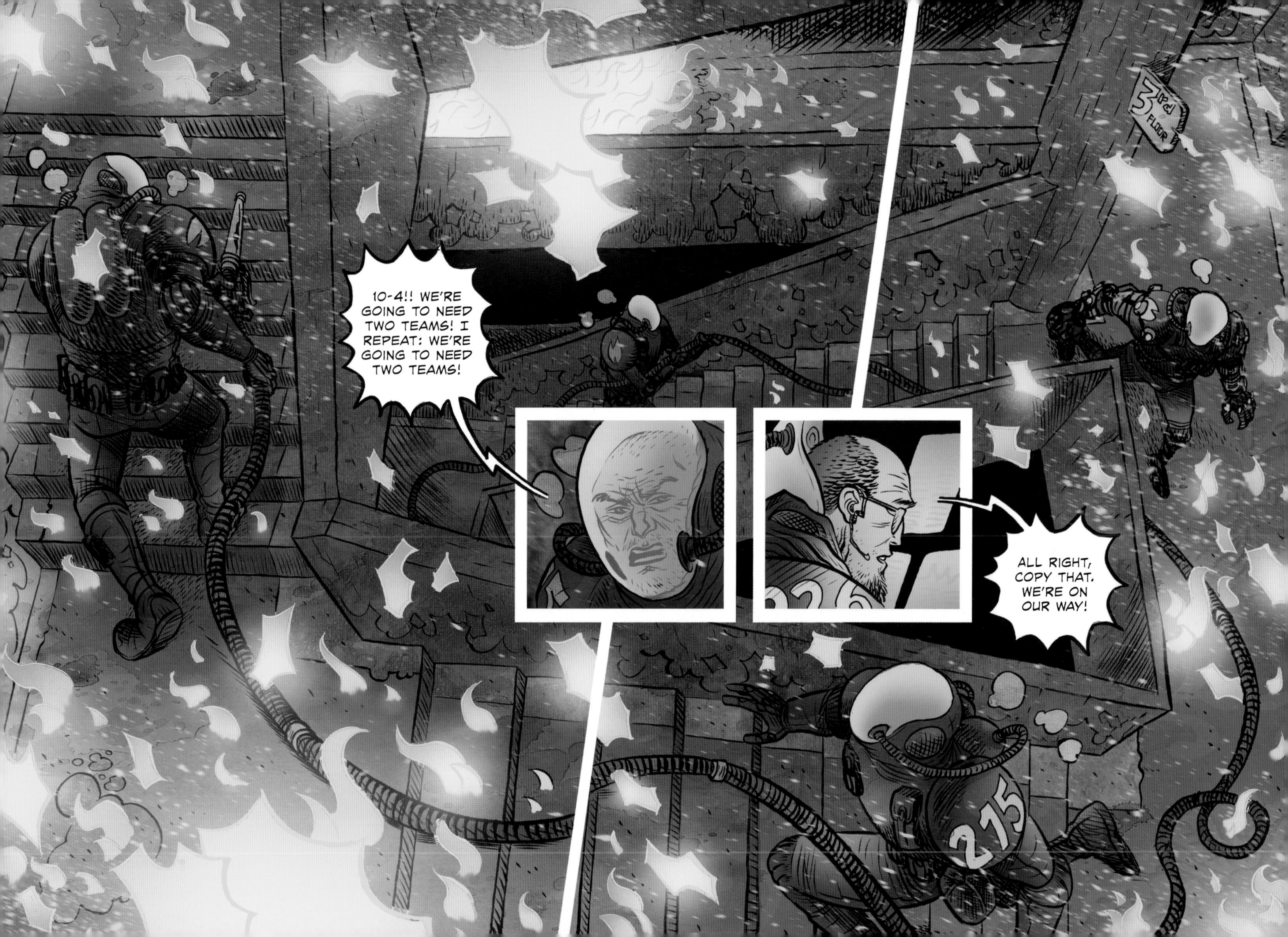

3rd FLOOR
10-4!! WE'RE GOING TO NEED TWO TEAMS! I REPEAT: WE'RE GOING TO NEED TWO TEAMS!
ALL RIGHT, COPY THAT. WE'RE ON OUR WAY!
215

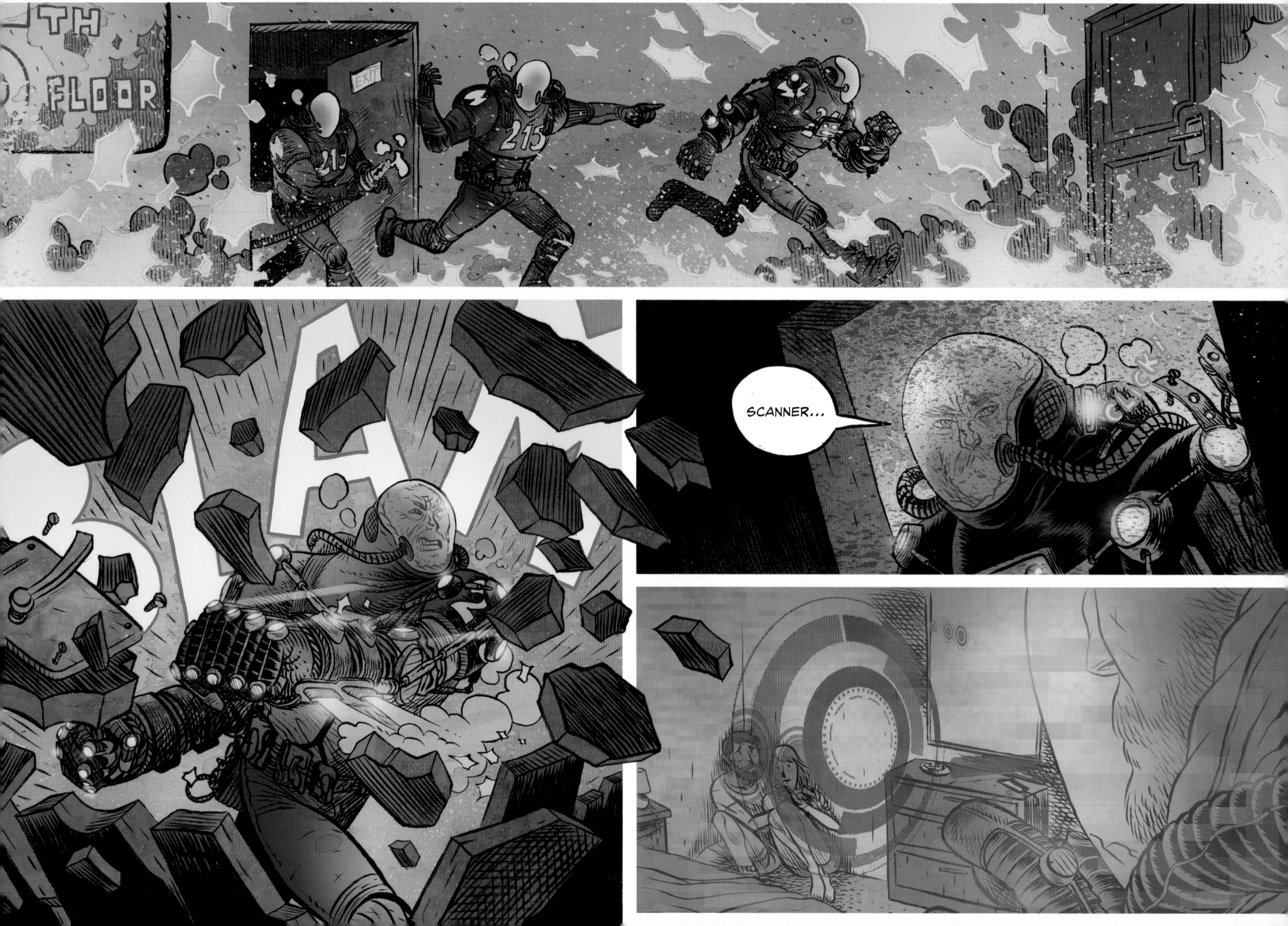
TH
FLOOR
EXIT
215
215
SCANNER...
CLICK!

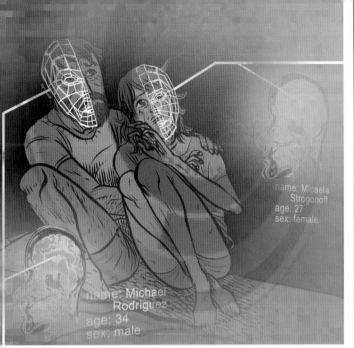

name: Micaela Strogonoff
age: 27
sex: female
name: Michael Rodriguez
age: 34
sex: male
Fakebox
Micaela Strogonoff Bolton
Online sommelier and off-hours ornithologist
0000458 followers
BIO
INFO
PHOTOS & MORE
D.A.R.K.E.T.
+ >
Involuntary guinea pig for the Fakebox study by the National Academy of Health Sciences and Martial Arts
http://www.zizekfans.blogspot.com
Micaela Strogonoff Bolton
May 17 at 10:16 a.m.
I read this in Zizek: "As Lacan...put it, truth has the structure of a fiction...[W]hen truth is too traumatic to be confronted directly, it can only be accepted in the guise of a fiction...When used in this way, the pleasure of aesthetic fiction is not a simple escape, but a mode of coping with traumatic memory: it is a survival mechanism . . .
akebox
Michael Rodriguez Jones
Community manager/Chief blogging officer
0000349 followers
BIO
INFO
PHOTOS & MORE
+ >
Michael Rodriguez Jones
Yesterday
I'm on here to share photos of cats being purrfectly adorable! ;) don't miss them!
at, bon vivant,
nity manager,
e love ambassador
ntire globe.
s in the existence
eyond this "solitary
the vast encircling
ss" that we call
Earth
CAN YOU HEAR ME?
CAN YOU BREATHE?
I NEED HELP! QUICK!

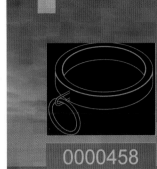

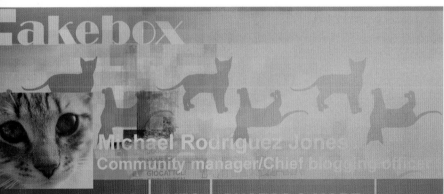

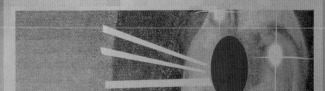

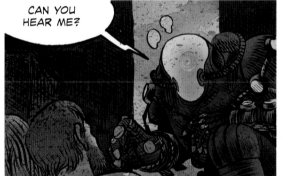

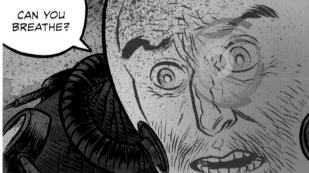

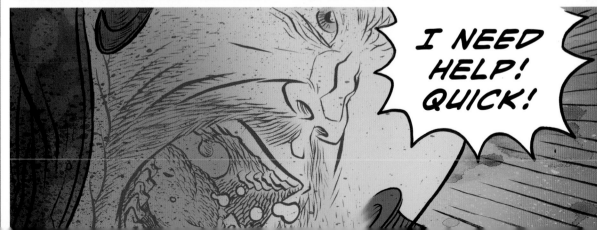

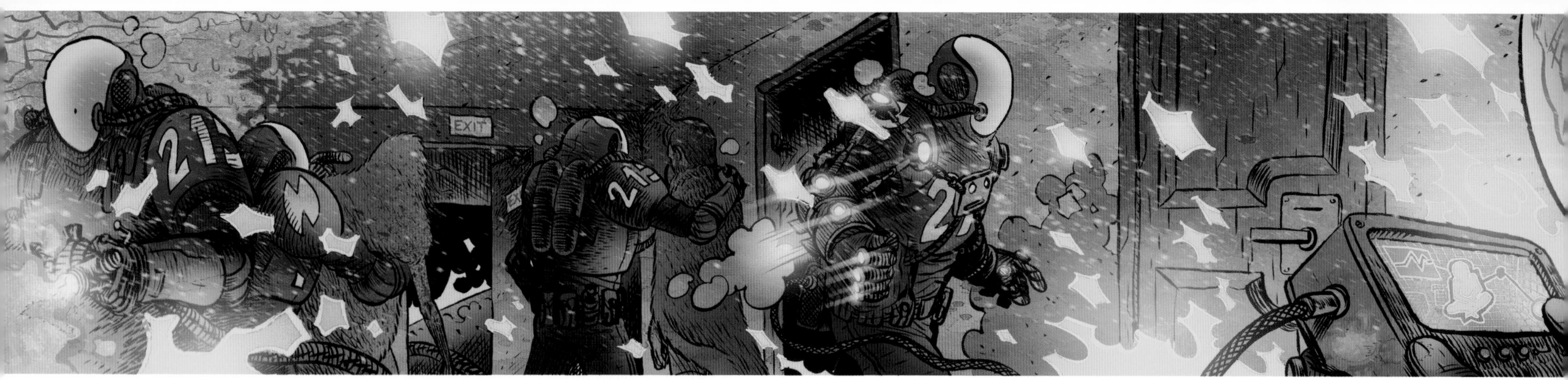
EXIT

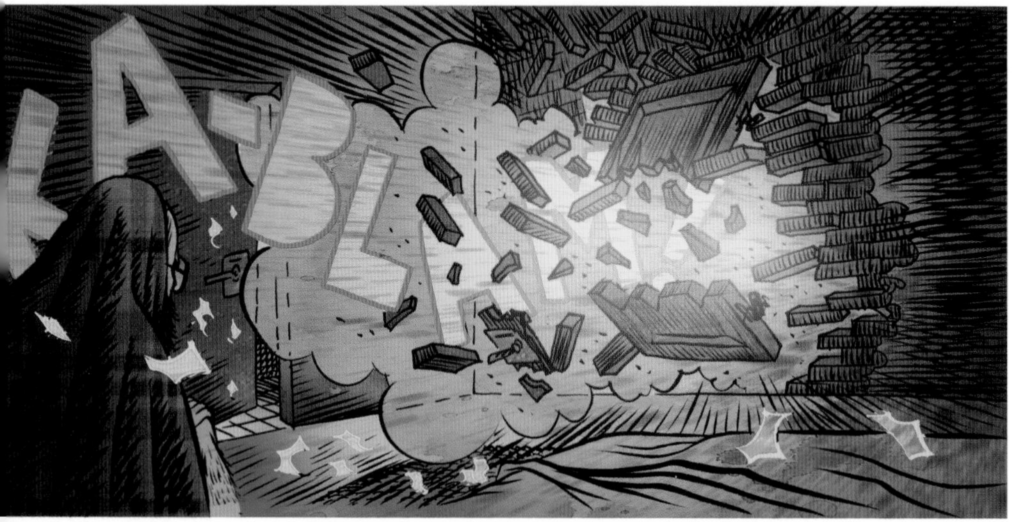

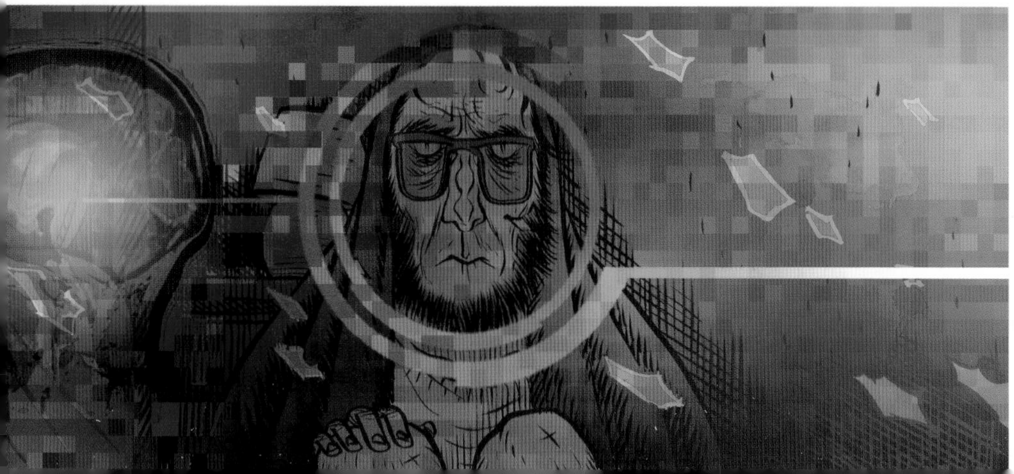

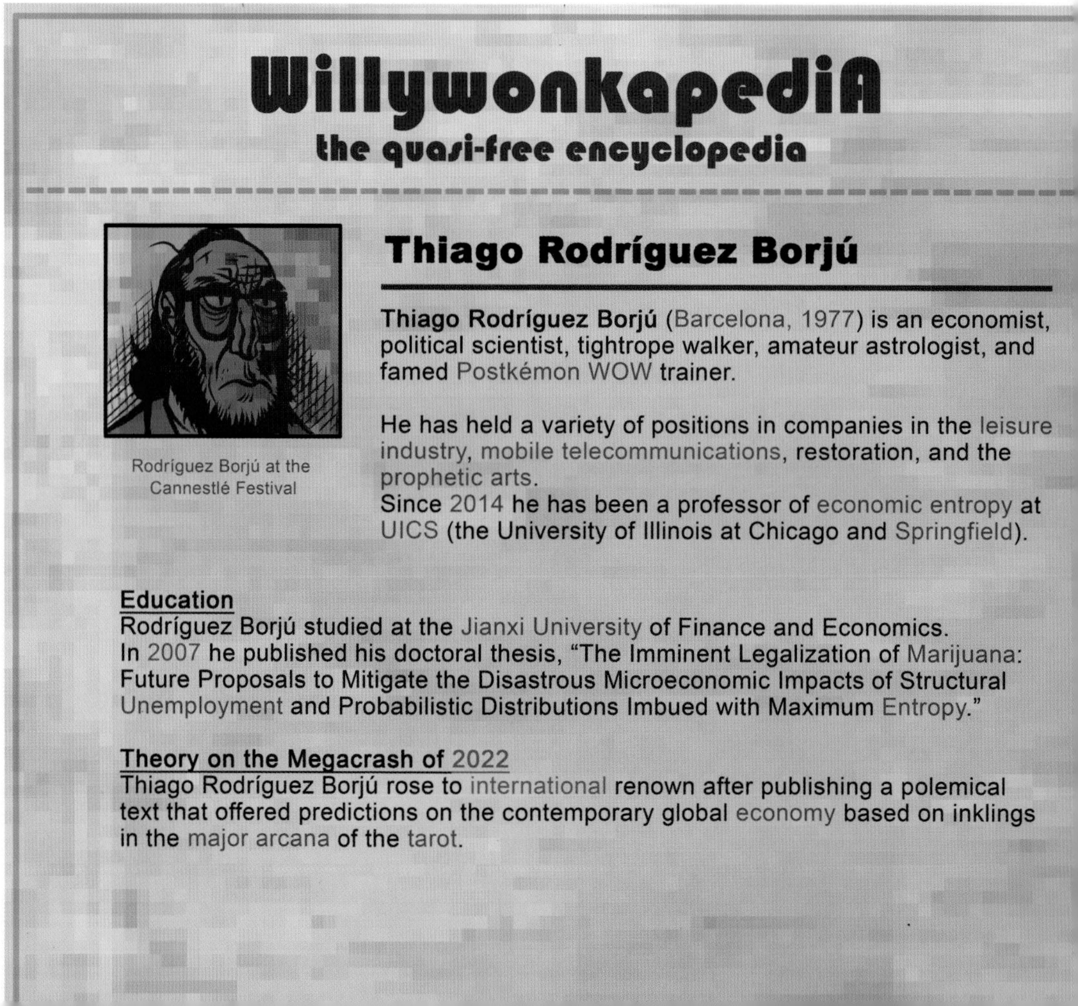

Willywonkapedia

the quasi-free encyclopedia

Thiago Rodríguez Borjú

Rodríguez Borjú at the Cannestlé Festival

Thiago Rodríguez Borjú (Barcelona, 1977) is an economist, political scientist, tightrope walker, amateur astrologist, and famed Postkémon WOW trainer.

He has held a variety of positions in companies in the leisure industry, mobile telecommunications, restoration, and the prophetic arts.
Since 2014 he has been a professor of economic entropy at UICS (the University of Illinois at Chicago and Springfield).

Education

Rodríguez Borjú studied at the Jianxi University of Finance and Economics.
In 2007 he published his doctoral thesis, "The Imminent Legalization of Marijuana: Future Proposals to Mitigate the Disastrous Microeconomic Impacts of Structural Unemployment and Probabilistic Distributions Imbued with Maximum Entropy."

Theory on the Megacrash of 2022

Thiago Rodríguez Borjú rose to international renown after publishing a polemical text that offered predictions on the contemporary global economy based on inklings in the major arcana of the tarot.

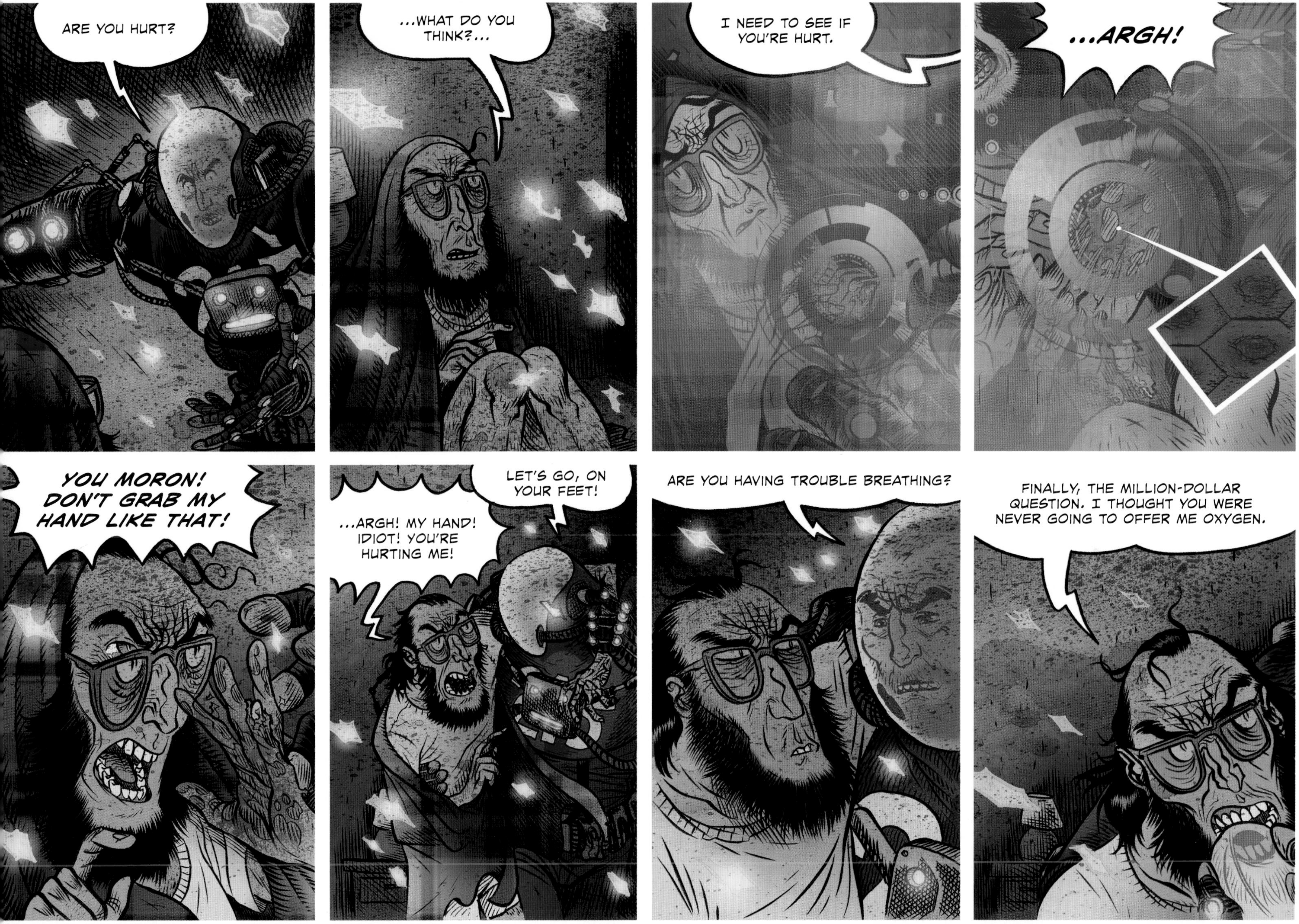
ARE YOU HURT?
...WHAT DO YOU THINK?...
I NEED TO SEE IF YOU'RE HURT.
...ARGH!
YOU MORON! DON'T GRAB MY HAND LIKE THAT!
LET'S GO, ON YOUR FEET!
...ARGH! MY HAND! IDIOT! YOU'RE HURTING ME!
ARE YOU HAVING TROUBLE BREATHING?
FINALLY, THE MILLION-DOLLAR QUESTION. I THOUGHT YOU WERE NEVER GOING TO OFFER ME OXYGEN.

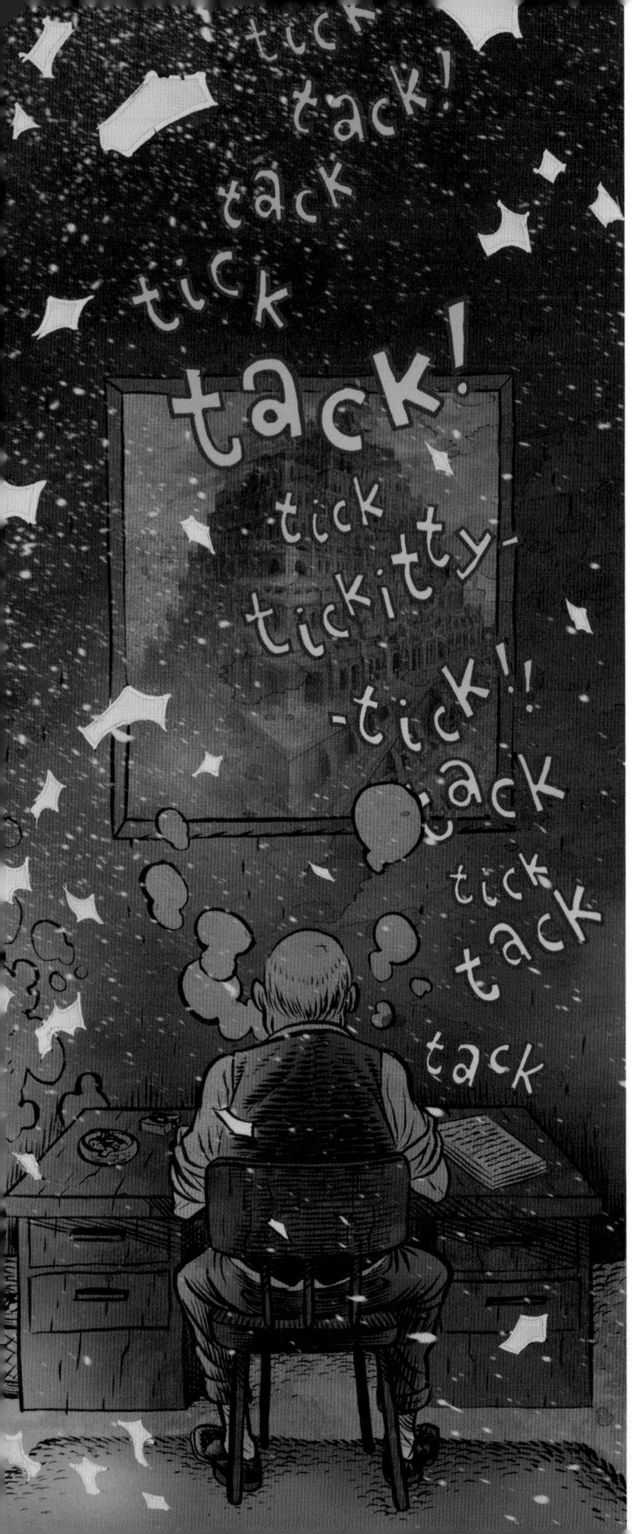
tick
tack!
tack
tick
tack!
tick
tickitty-
-tick!!
tack
tick
tack
tack

Will we succeed in creating
a unit of measure that can assess
with maximum precision and accuracy the
relevance of avant-garde and rear guard
art in moments of great
historical significance?
Will we truly manage it?
And will we be able to universalize
that unit of measure?

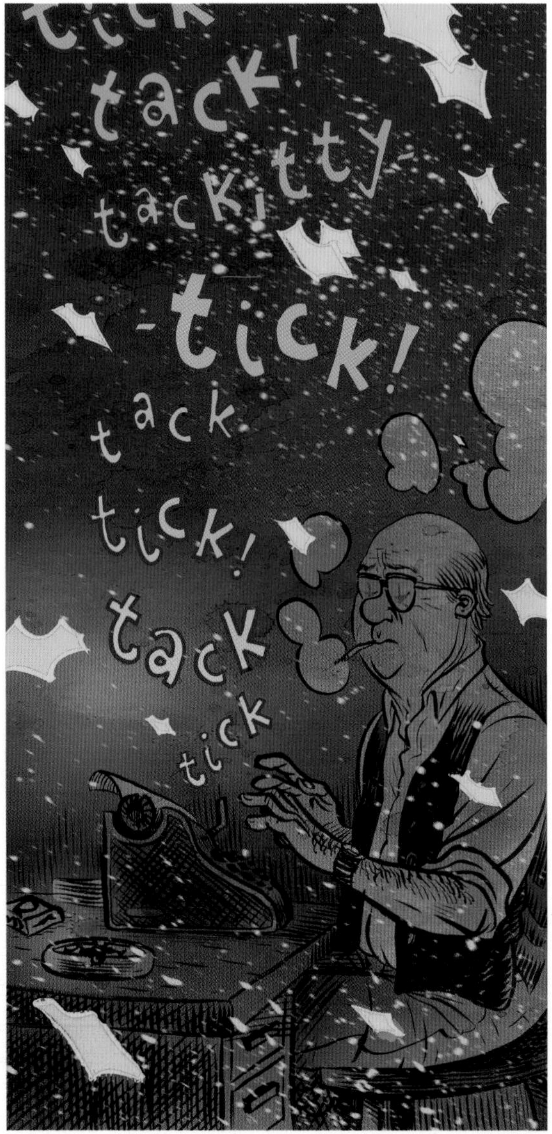
tack!
tackitty-
-tick!
tack
tick!
tack
tick

Homer, the poet, the blind
man who saw visions, who was
both author and character,
wasn't able to change the course
of history with his epic poems,
with his hexameters.

He didn't spark revolutions.

He didn't bring about reforms.

He didn't impede the rise of
Platonism.

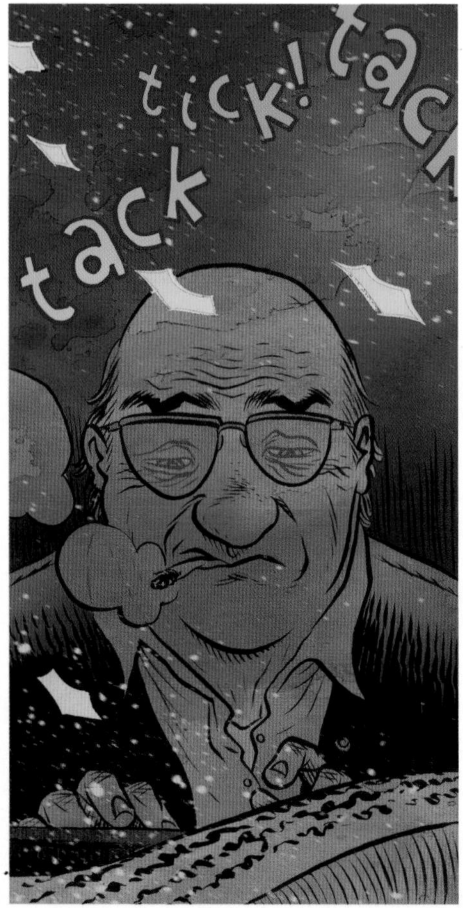
tick!
tack
tack

Art must be able to
demonstrate its usefulness, to
offer consolation to the atheist
and hope to the revolutionary
in the reserves.

**Art must be able to
transform the wor**

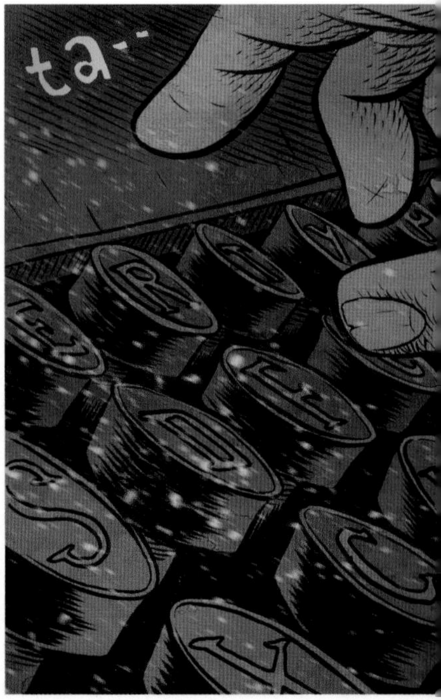
ta-

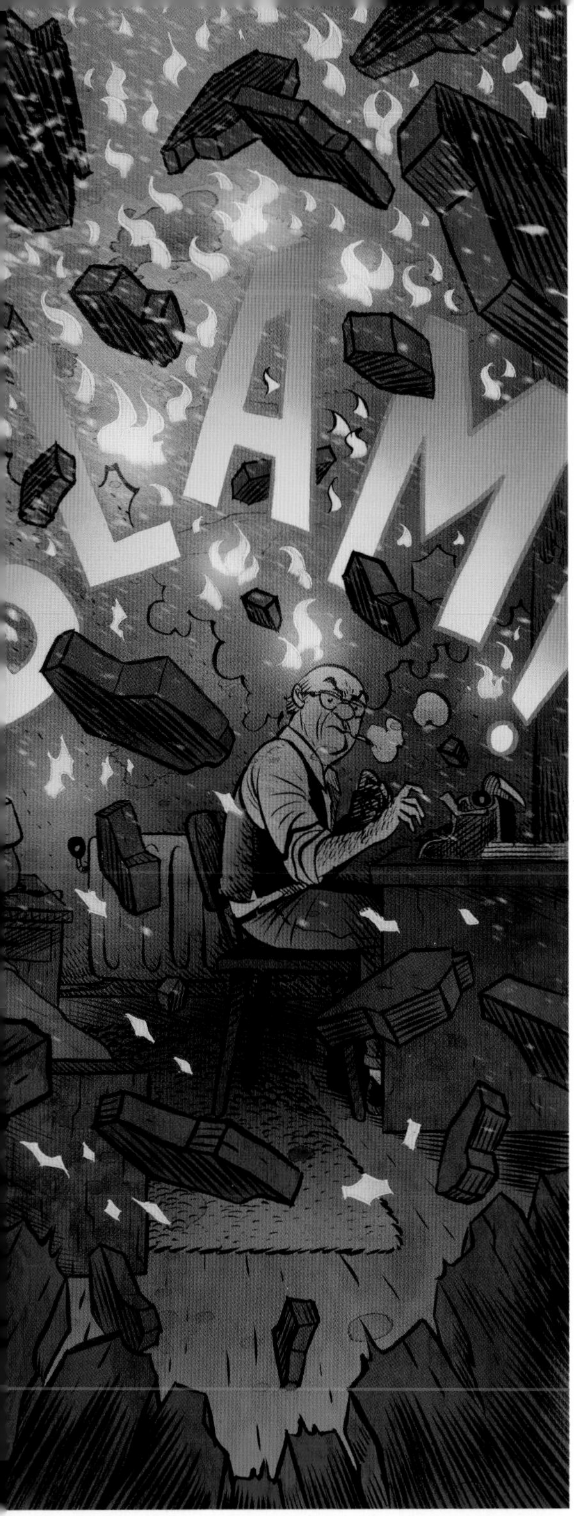

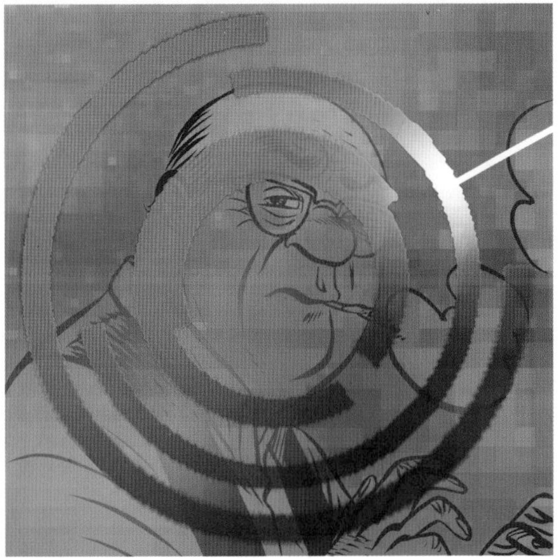

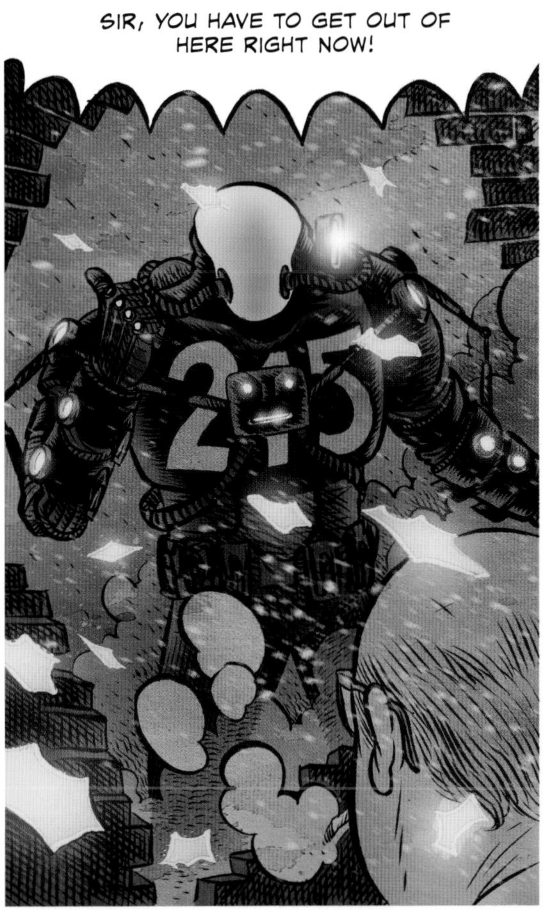
SIR, YOU HAVE TO GET OUT OF HERE RIGHT NOW!

WillywonkapediA
the quasi-free encyclopedia

Theo Alexander Wieseground

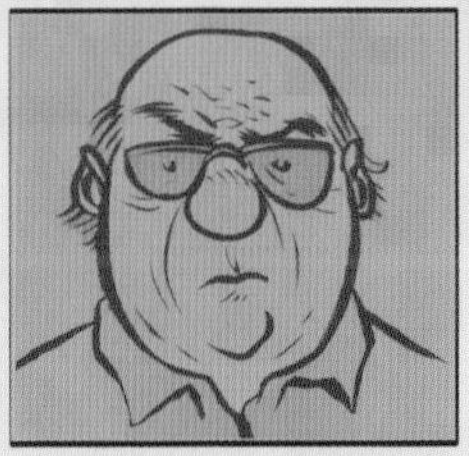

Theo A. Wiesenground at a bowling alley in Kentuckinder

Theo Alexander Wiesenground (Frankfurt am Main, 1965) is a social philosopher and a prolific writer for magazines on fashion, beauty, and cultural consumption trends.

He is considered one of the leading members of the school of non-representability and the Uniformly Accelerated Rectilinear Movement (UARM).

He achieved some level of fame with the publication of "They Don't Represent Us: A Treatise on Art and Politics in Turbulent Times," which won him the Amagrana Essay Prize in 2017, the same year that he claimed, on a well-known microblogging platform, to feel left behind by current events and the technological innovations applied to biotechnology and the footwear industry.

Education

As a boy, the long-suffering Theo A. Wiesenground attended the Hans-Jakobo-Christopher-von-Grimmelshausen-Gymnasium, standing out among his peers as a brilliant

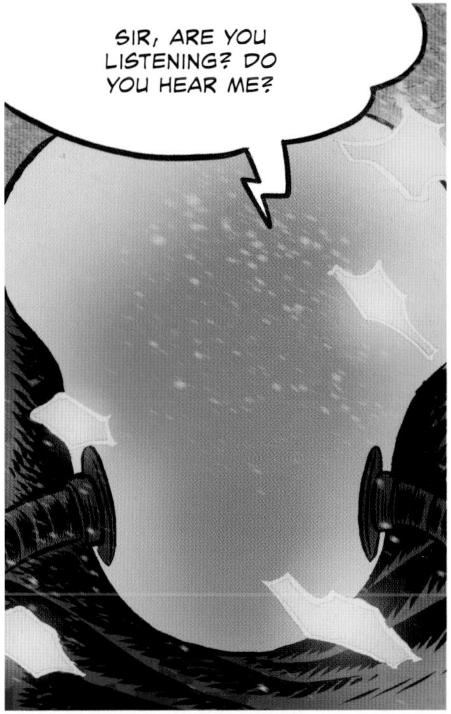
SIR, ARE YOU LISTENING? DO YOU HEAR ME?

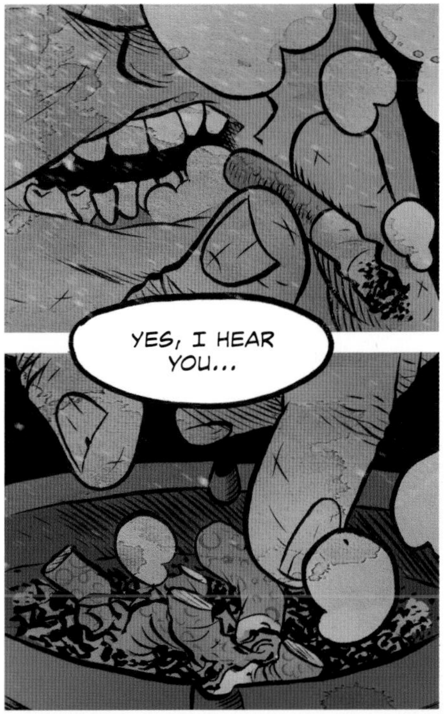
YES, I HEAR YOU...

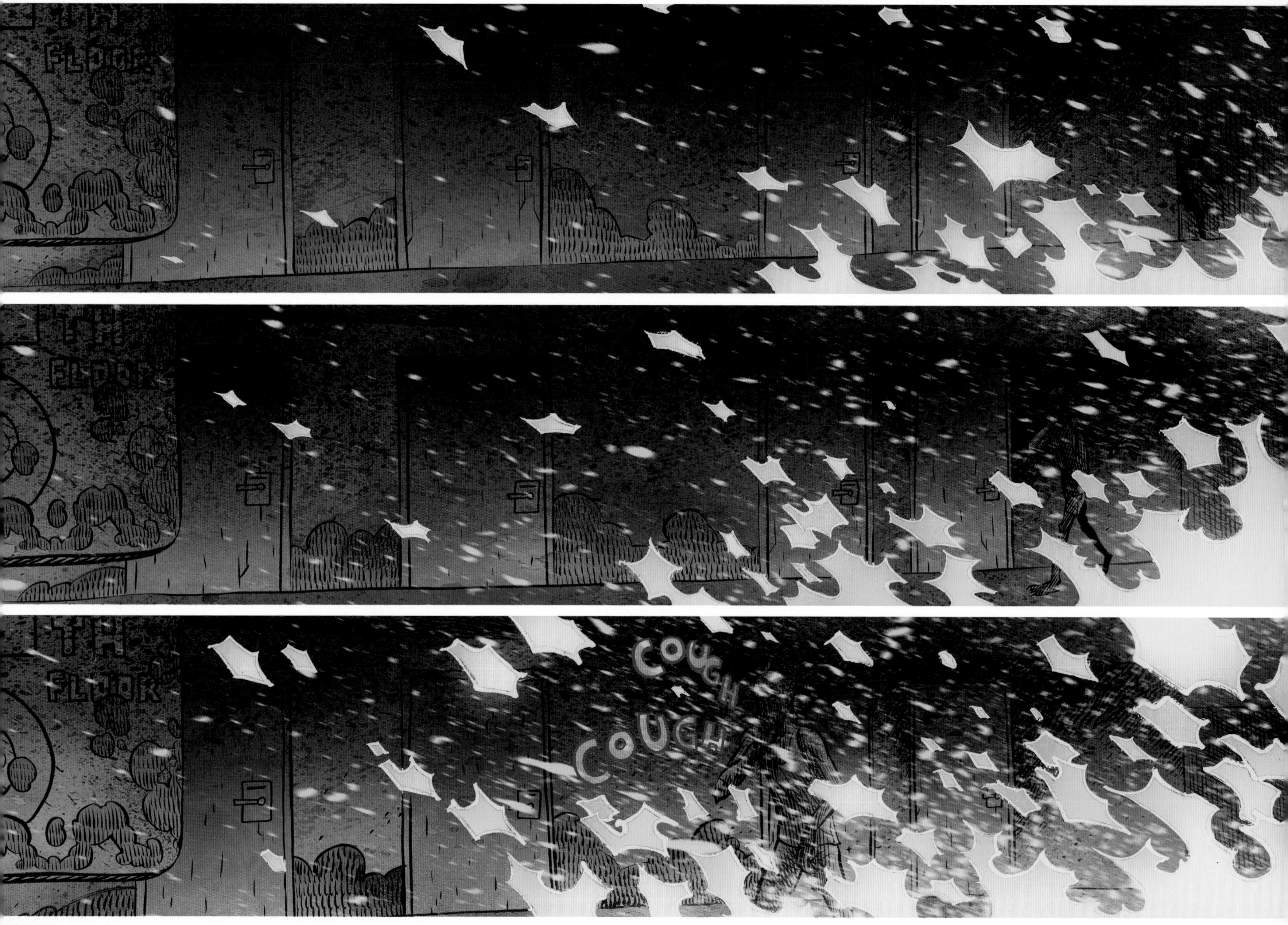
FLOOR
COUGH
COUGH

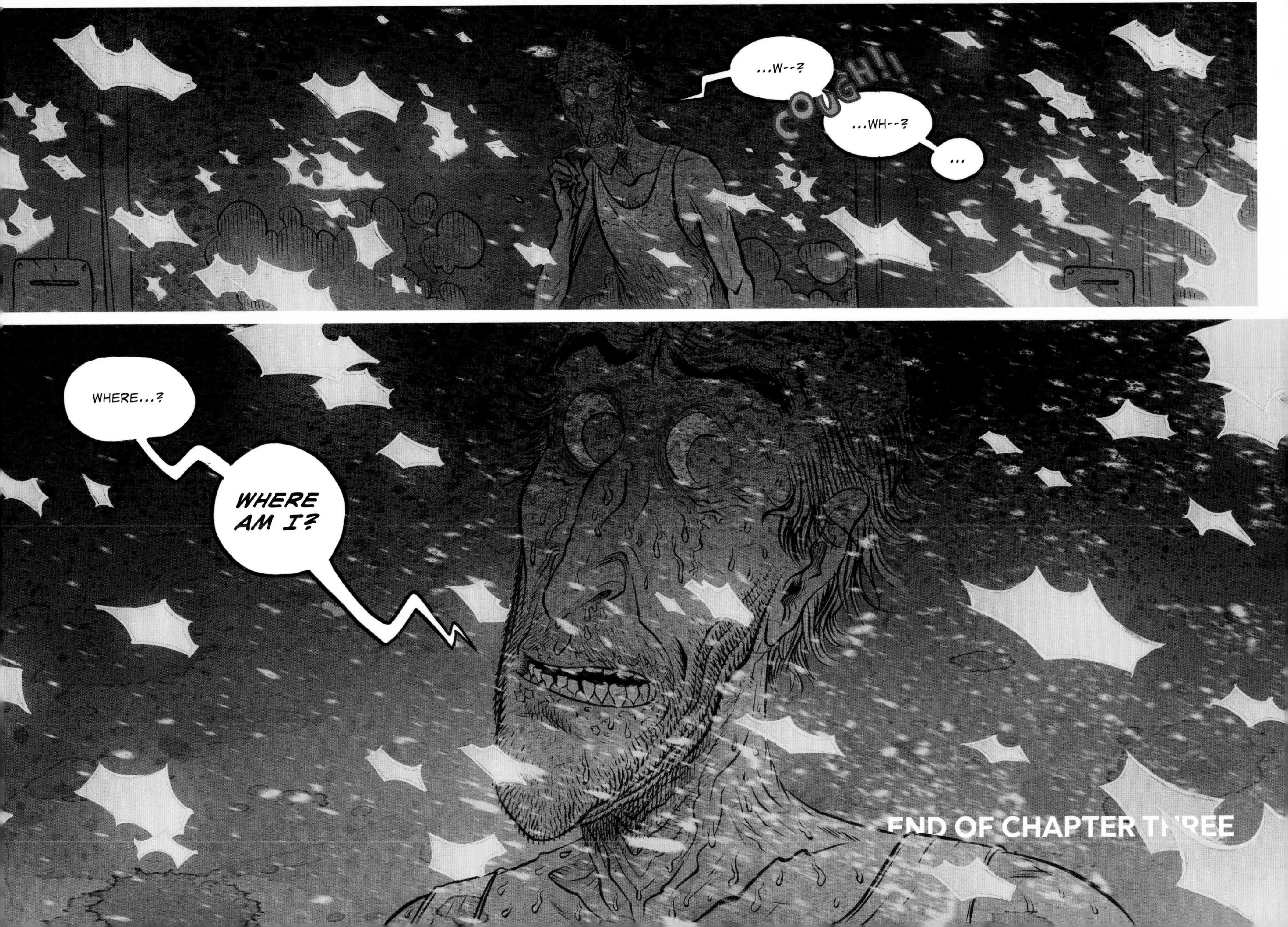
...W--?
COUGH!!
...WH--?
...
WHERE...?
WHERE AM I?
END OF CHAPTER THREE

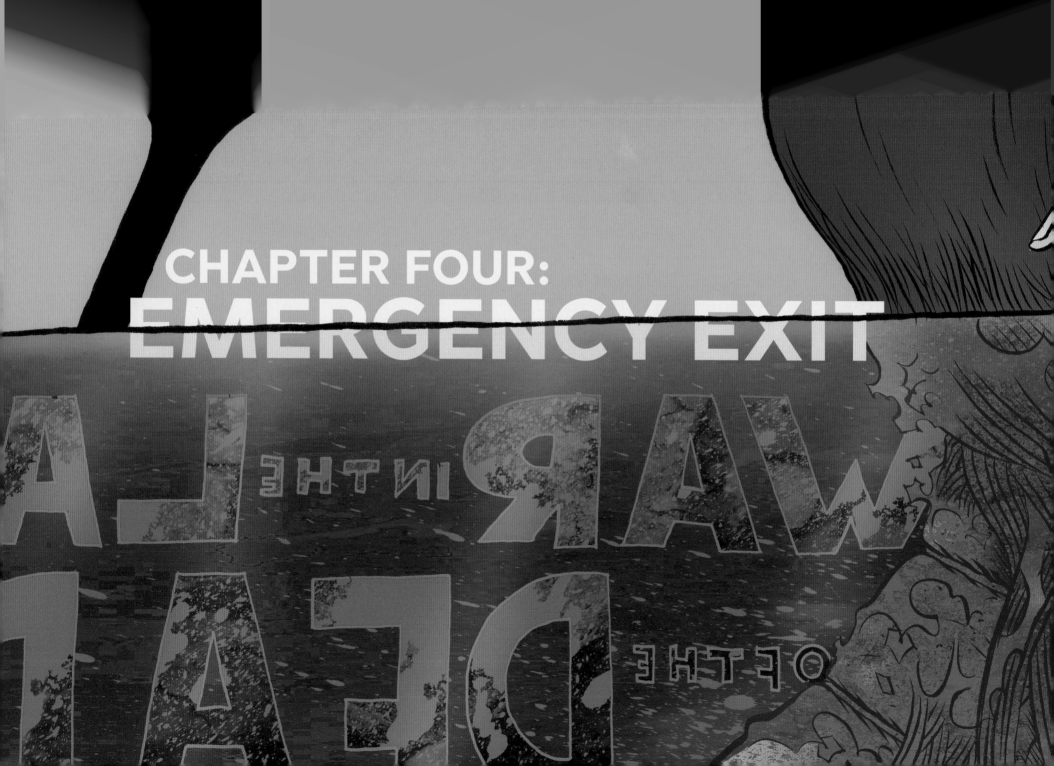

CHAPTER FOUR:
EMERGENCY EXIT

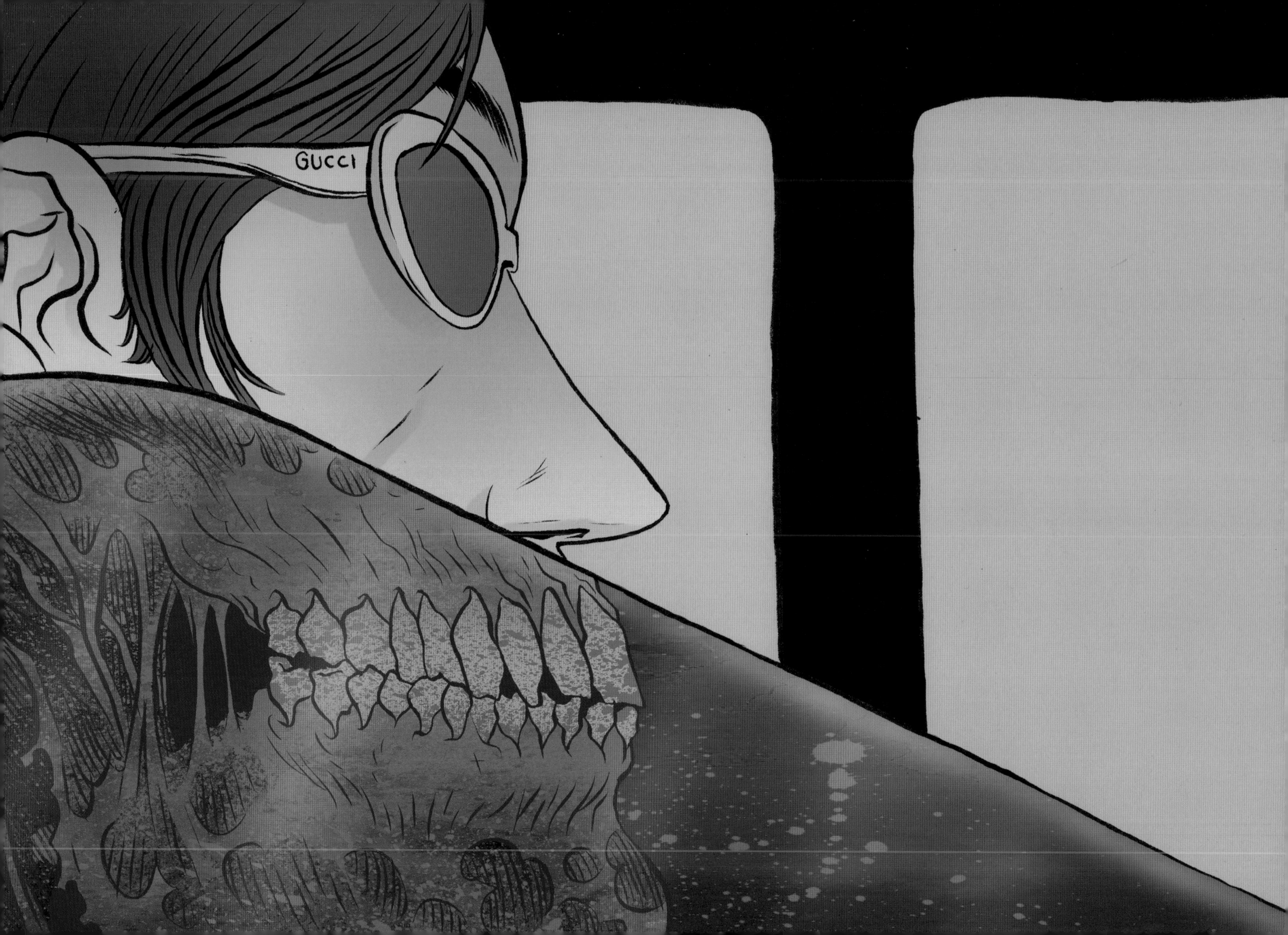
GUCCI

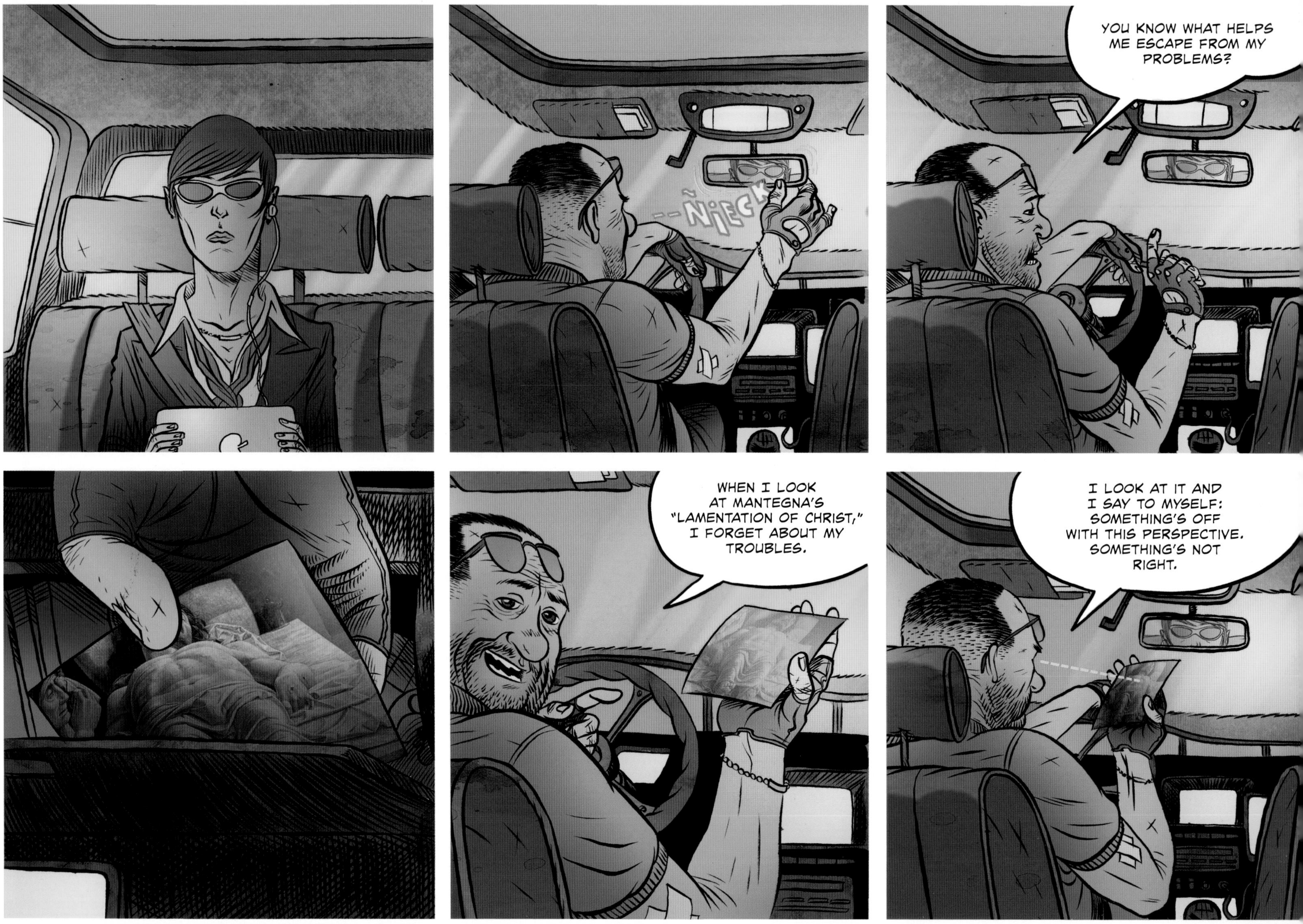
--ÑIECK
YOU KNOW WHAT HELPS ME ESCAPE FROM MY PROBLEMS?
WHEN I LOOK AT MANTEGNA'S "LAMENTATION OF CHRIST," I FORGET ABOUT MY TROUBLES.
I LOOK AT IT AND I SAY TO MYSELF: SOMETHING'S OFF WITH THIS PERSPECTIVE. SOMETHING'S NOT RIGHT.

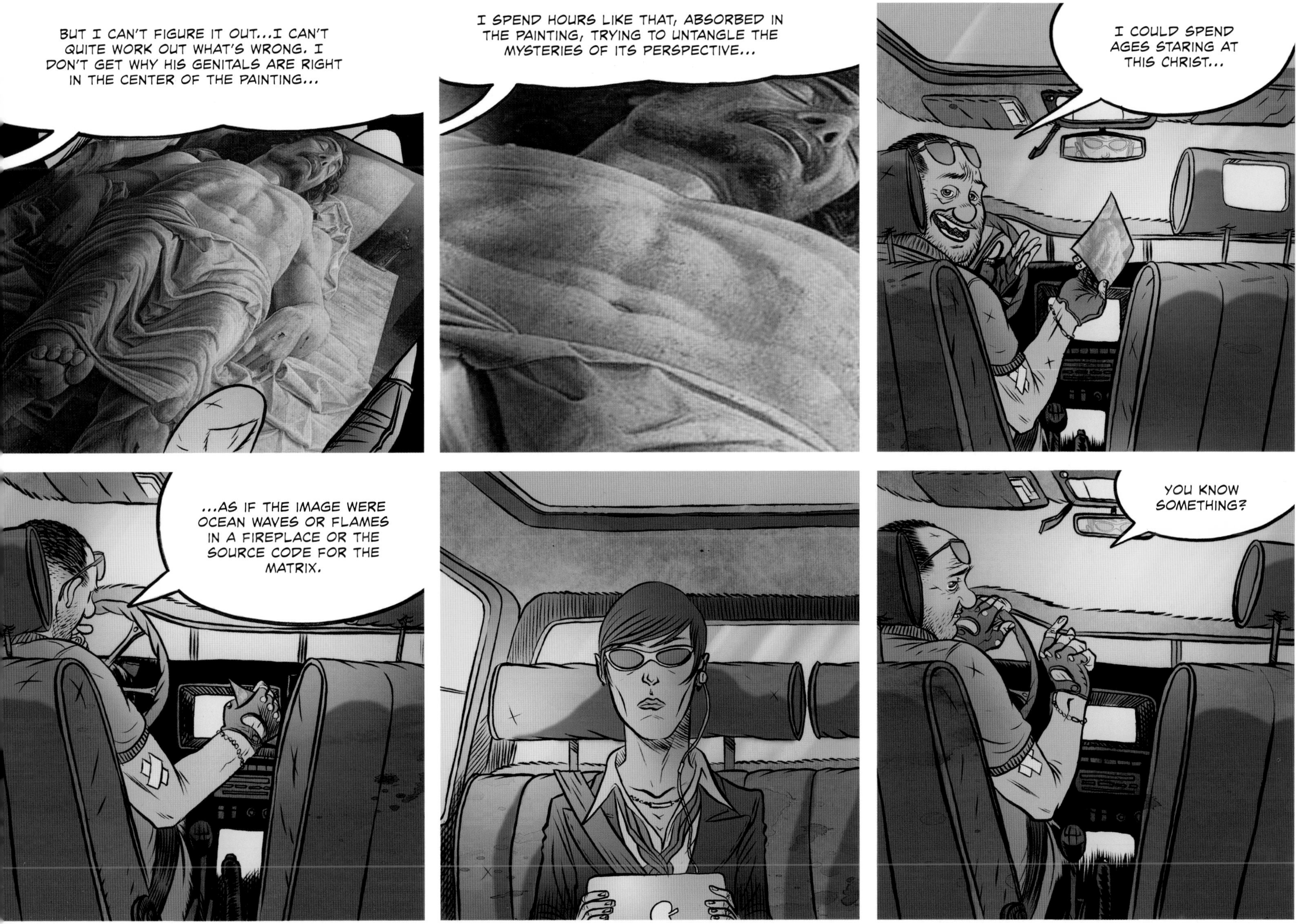
BUT I CAN'T FIGURE IT OUT...I CAN'T QUITE WORK OUT WHAT'S WRONG. I DON'T GET WHY HIS GENITALS ARE RIGHT IN THE CENTER OF THE PAINTING...
I SPEND HOURS LIKE THAT, ABSORBED IN THE PAINTING, TRYING TO UNTANGLE THE MYSTERIES OF ITS PERSPECTIVE...
I COULD SPEND AGES STARING AT THIS CHRIST...
...AS IF THE IMAGE WERE OCEAN WAVES OR FLAMES IN A FIREPLACE OR THE SOURCE CODE FOR THE MATRIX.
YOU KNOW SOMETHING?

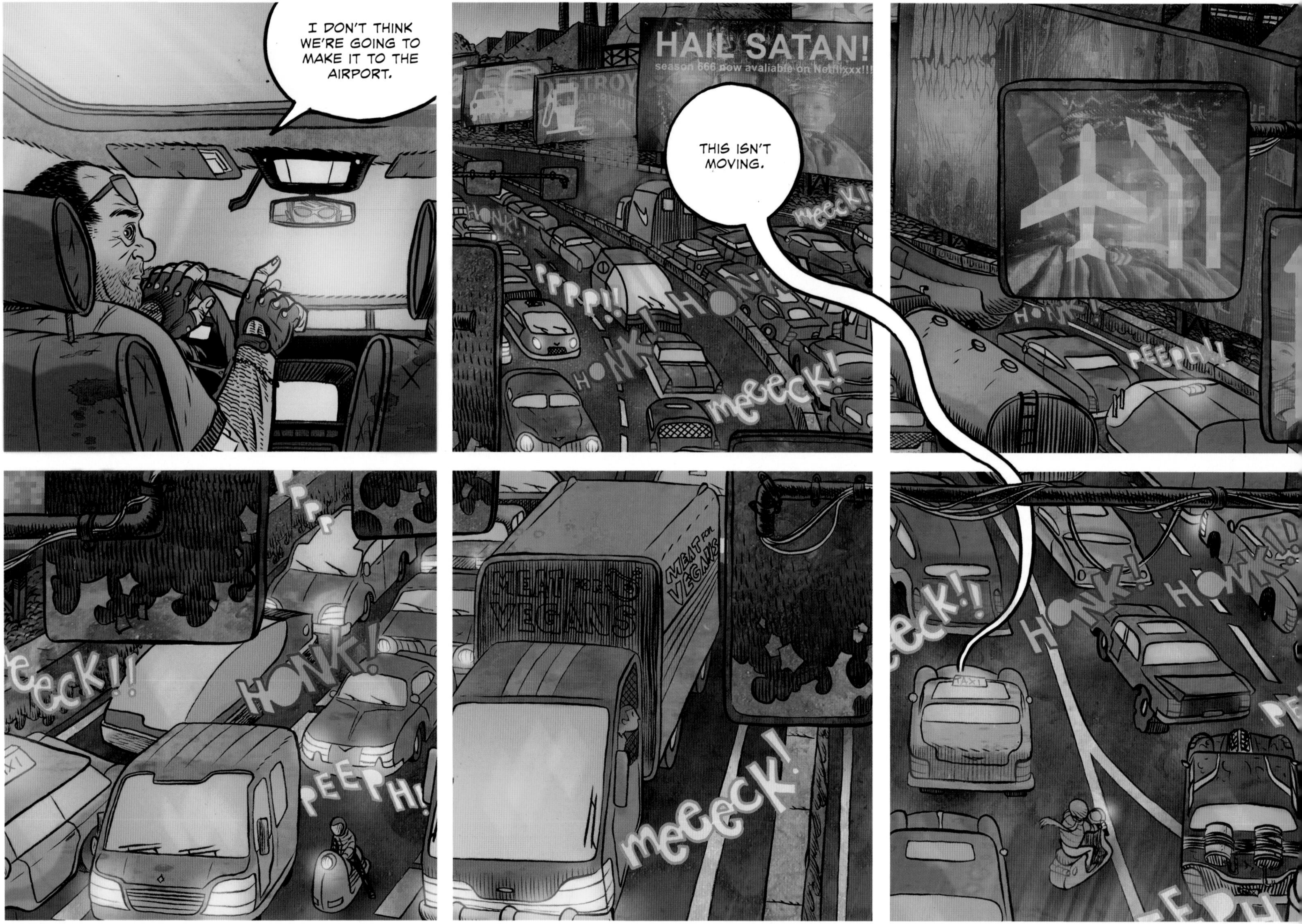

I DON'T THINK WE'RE GOING TO MAKE IT TO THE AIRPORT.
HAIL SATAN!
season 666 now avaliable on Netflixxx!!!
THIS ISN'T MOVING.
HONK!
PPPP!!
HONK!
HONK!
meeeck!
meeeck!
HONK!
PEEPH!!
PPPP
HONK!
eeeck!!
PEEPH!
MEAT FOR VEGANS
MEAT FOR VEGANS
meeeck!
eeck!!
HONK!
HONK!
HONK!
TAXI

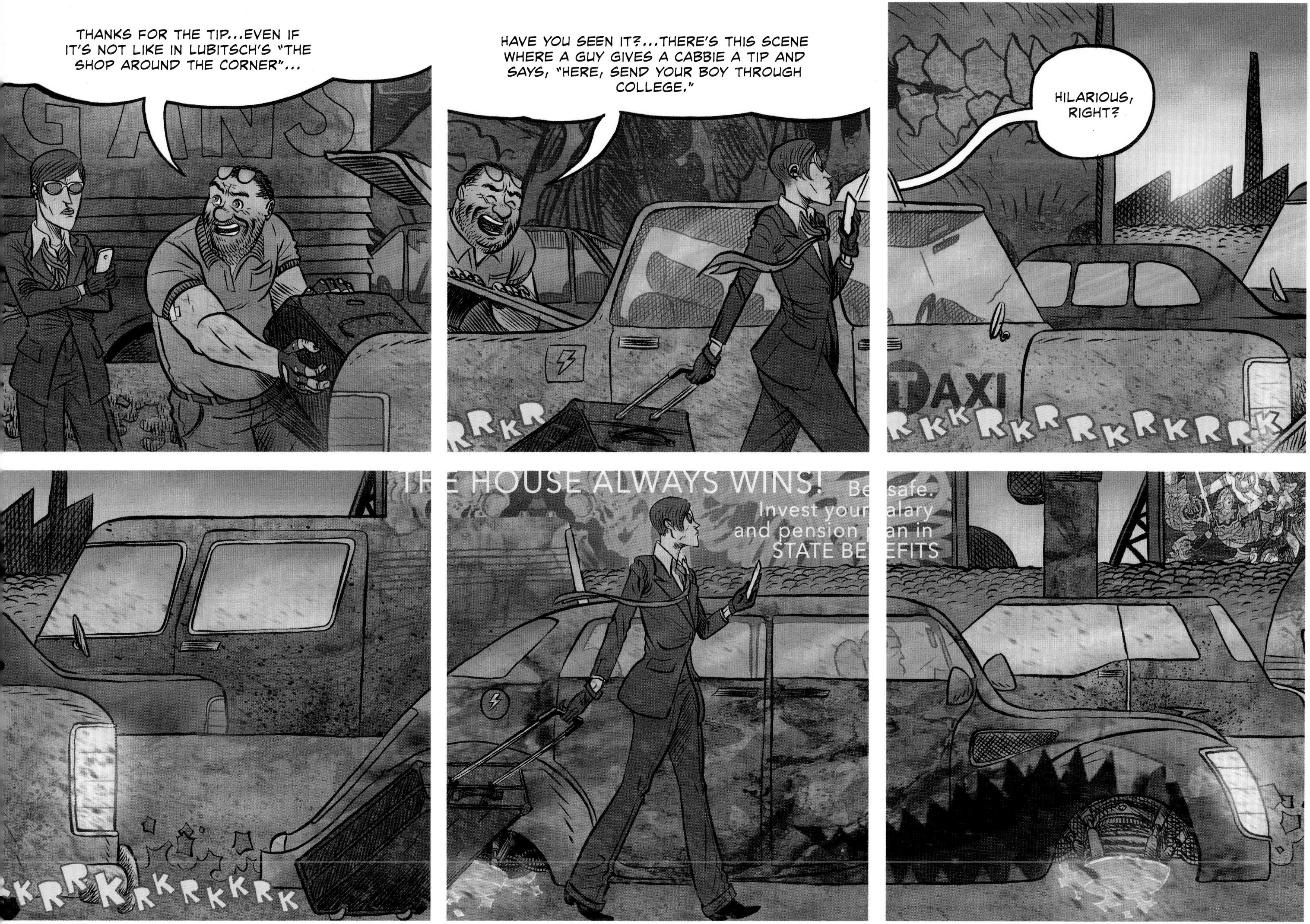
THANKS FOR THE TIP...EVEN IF IT'S NOT LIKE IN LUBITSCH'S "THE SHOP AROUND THE CORNER"...
HAVE YOU SEEN IT?...THERE'S THIS SCENE WHERE A GUY GIVES A CABBIE A TIP AND SAYS, "HERE, SEND YOUR BOY THROUGH COLLEGE."
HILARIOUS, RIGHT?
TAXI
THE HOUSE ALWAYS WINS!

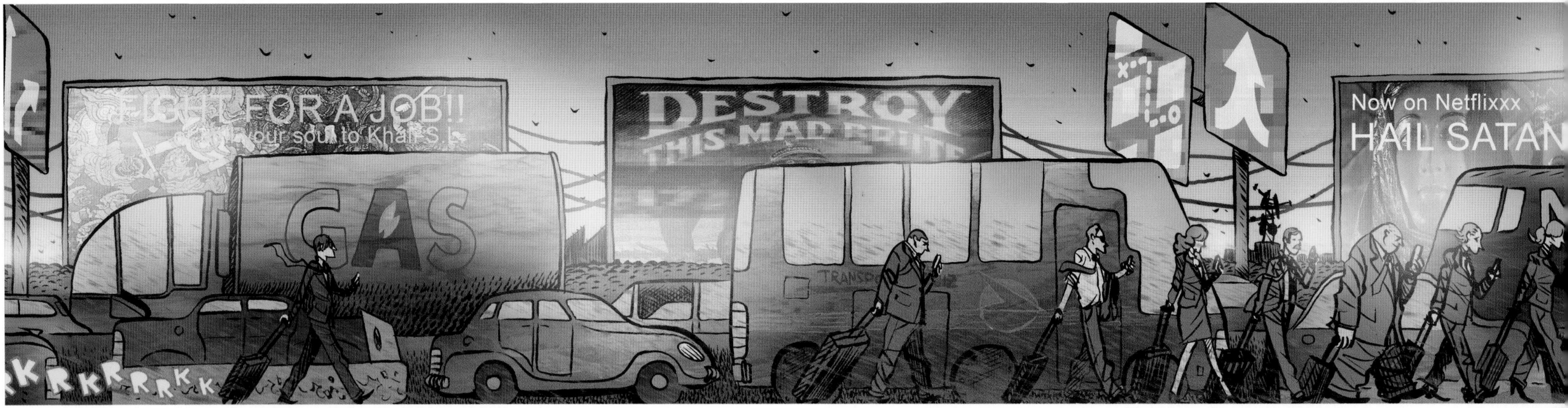

FIGHT FOR A JOB!!
DESTROY
Now on Netflixxx
HAIL SATAN
GAS
RKRKRRRKK

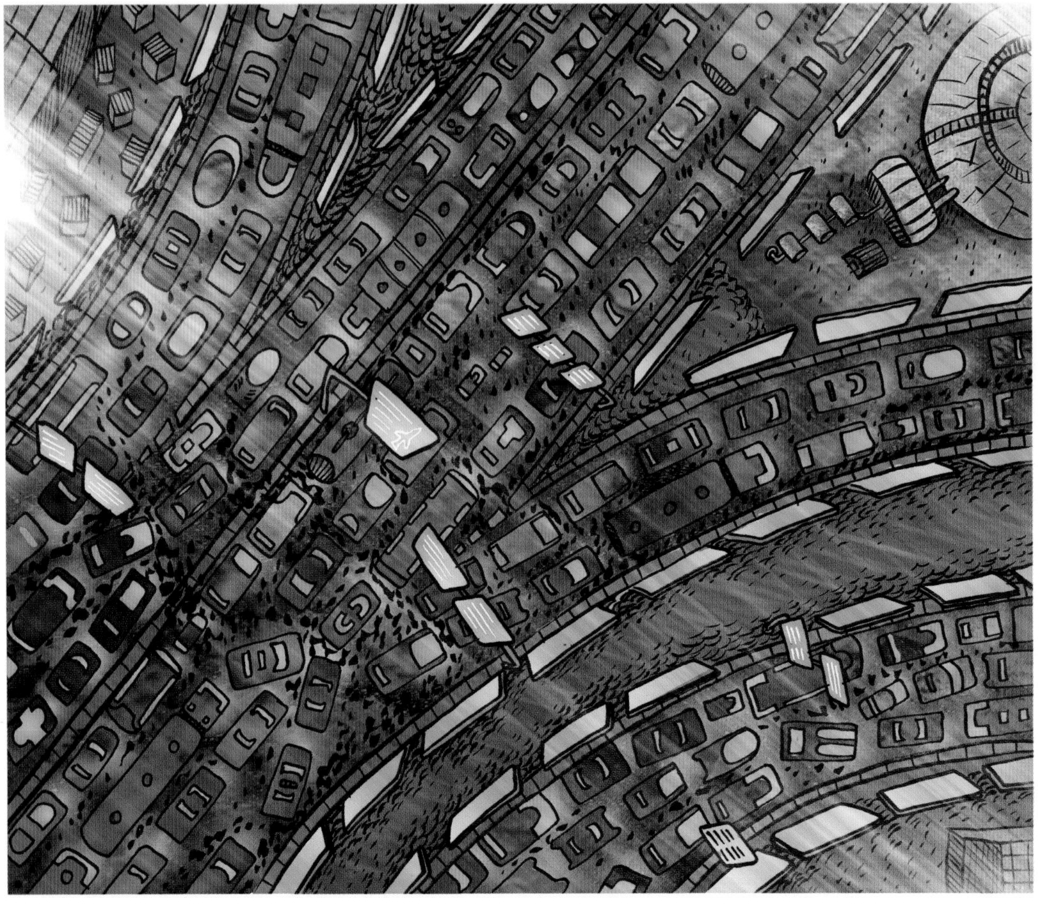

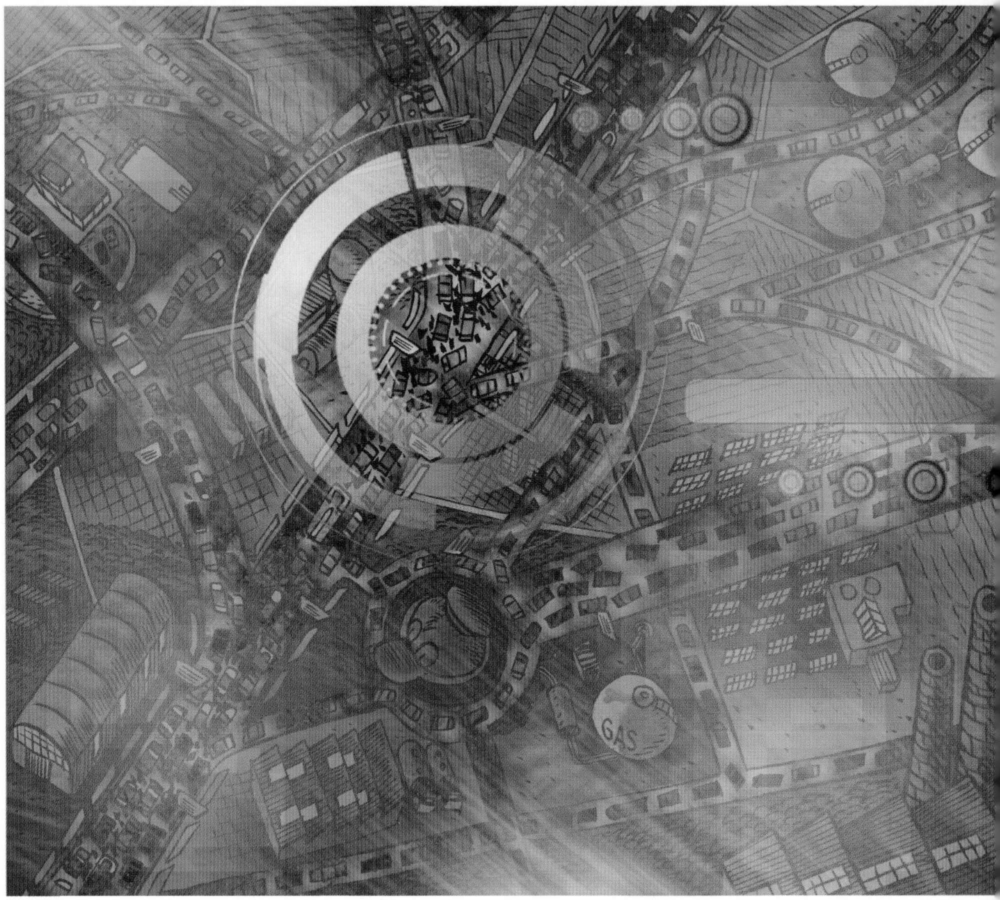

GAS

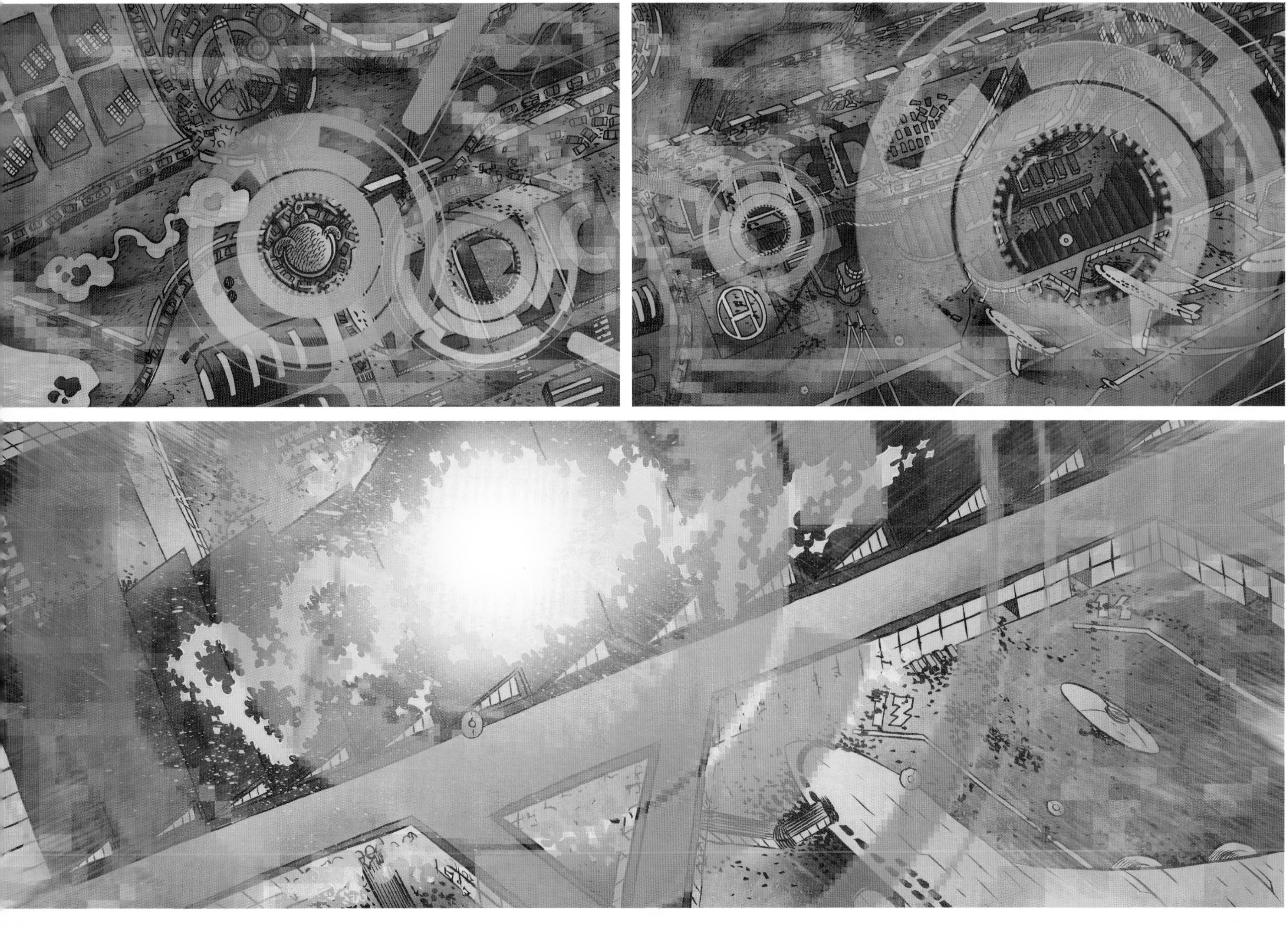

Pages: Home | Site | Tools | Help | Upgrade | Save | Preview | Publish

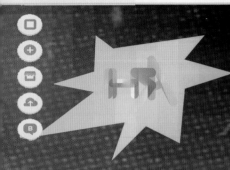

login | user | password

Search

Forgot your password? Don't worry, that's the least of the problems you'll have to face in the near future.

Join (as soon as possible) >

Home | About Us | About the End of the World | Social Network | Collaborate | Members | Volunteers | Communication

Home > About Us > Who Are We?

Who Are We?

- Mission and Values
- Strategic Objectives
- Survivalism Course
- Org Chart
- IHSA in the World
- IHSA vs. NASA
- Criminal Complaints
- Testament 4.0
- Pastimes

Who Are We?

The International Hiking and Survivalism Association (IHSA) is an NGO focused on civil defense and the development of group dynamics to facilitate survival in postapocalyptic scenarios.

It was formed on May 5, 2017, with the aim of providing its members with tools to grapple with the challenges of an increasingly imminent future of devastation and collapse, on both the moral and economic planes.

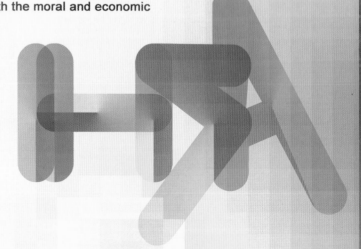

The IHSA has pushed for years to be declared a "public utility" so it can receive government backing to begin the large-scale construction of bunkers, which would constitute major support for a significant population-protection measure.Constructing and maintaining these bunkers would also generate some level of economic recovery for the country in terms of direct and indirect job creation, and would provide psychosocial benefits to the future survivalists of tomorrow.

For more information, call 555 484 989.

Pages: Home Site Tools Help Upgrade Save Preview Publish

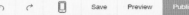

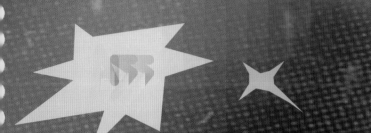

login user password

Search

Forgot your password? Don't worry, that's the least of the problems you'll have to face in the near future.

Join (as soon as possible) >

Home | About Us | About the End of the World | Social Network | Collaborate | Members | Volunteers | Communication

Home > About the End of the World

About the End of the World

- **Leadership and Mass Parapsychology**
- **Solar Flares**
- **Nostradamus & Co**
- **72-Hour Backpack**
- **Hong Kong Flu**
- **Peak Oil**
- **Yellowstone Supervolcano**
- **Public Debt**

About the End of the World

Everything you've always wanted to know about the end of the world (and have never dared to ask for fear of social ostracism or retribution from the various intelligence services prowling around), you will find it here: we offer firsthand information updated in real time by prominent subject matter experts.

The information contained here has been written by accredited professionals from the IHSA, old-school investigative journalists whose hands don't tremble as they down a couple of morning shots, astronomers specializing in meteorites and geomagnetic storms, neo-Darwinian economists, staunch followers of Thomas Malthus, lovers of neologisms, viral marketing gurus, etc., and overseen by the IHSA's International Technical Committee to guarantee the viability of the prophecies we will provide without (in theory) a profit-seeking motive.

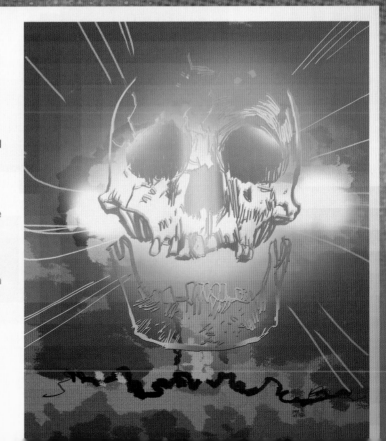

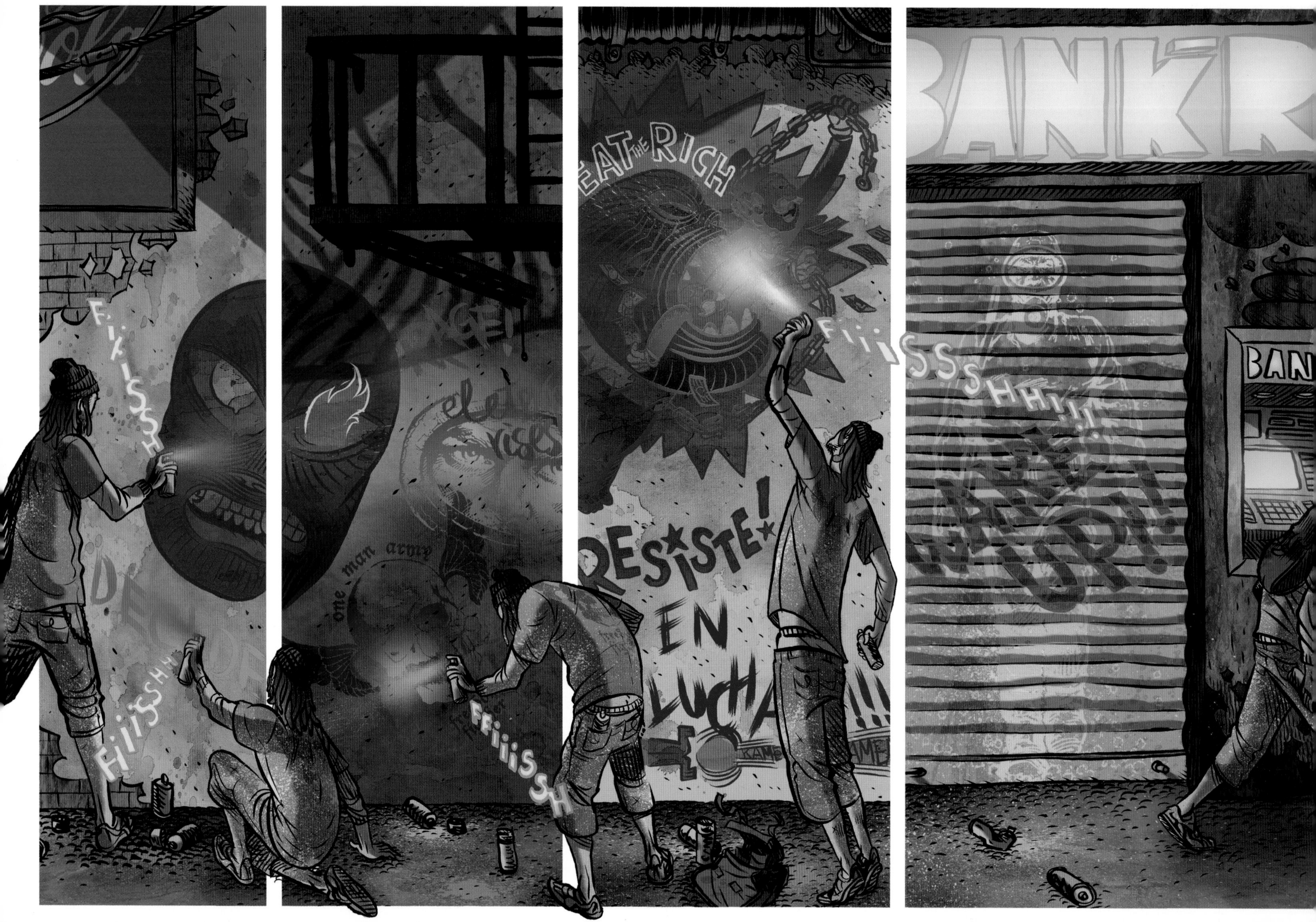
FFIISSH
FIIISSHH
one man army
FFIIISSSH
EAT THE RICH
FIIIISSSSHHH!!!
RESISTE!
EN
LUCHA!!!
BANK
BAN

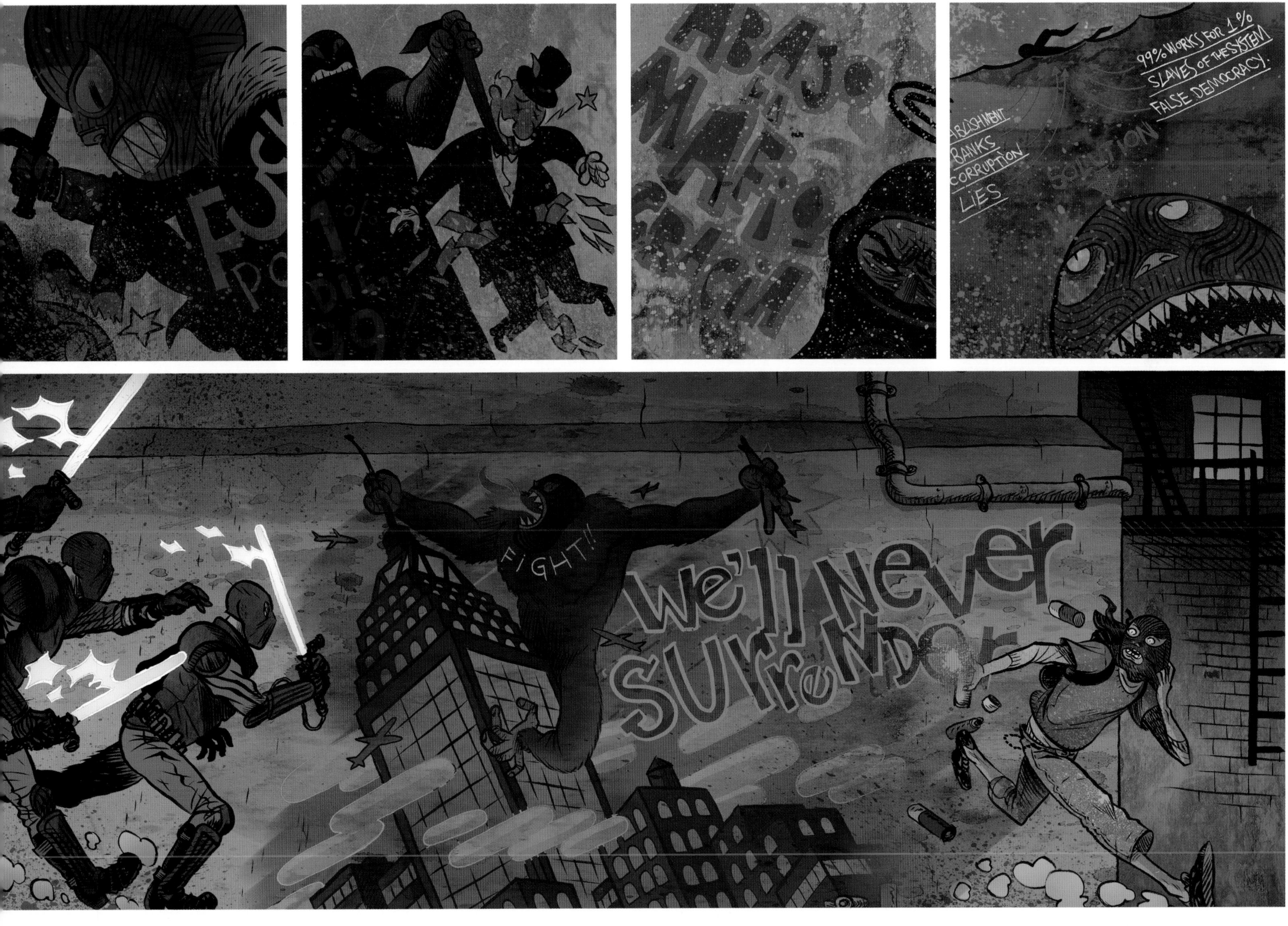
ABAJO
99% WORKS FOR 1%
SLAVES OF THE SYSTEM
FALSE DEMOCRACY.
BANKS
CORRUPTION
LIES
SOLUTION
FIGHT!!
We'll never

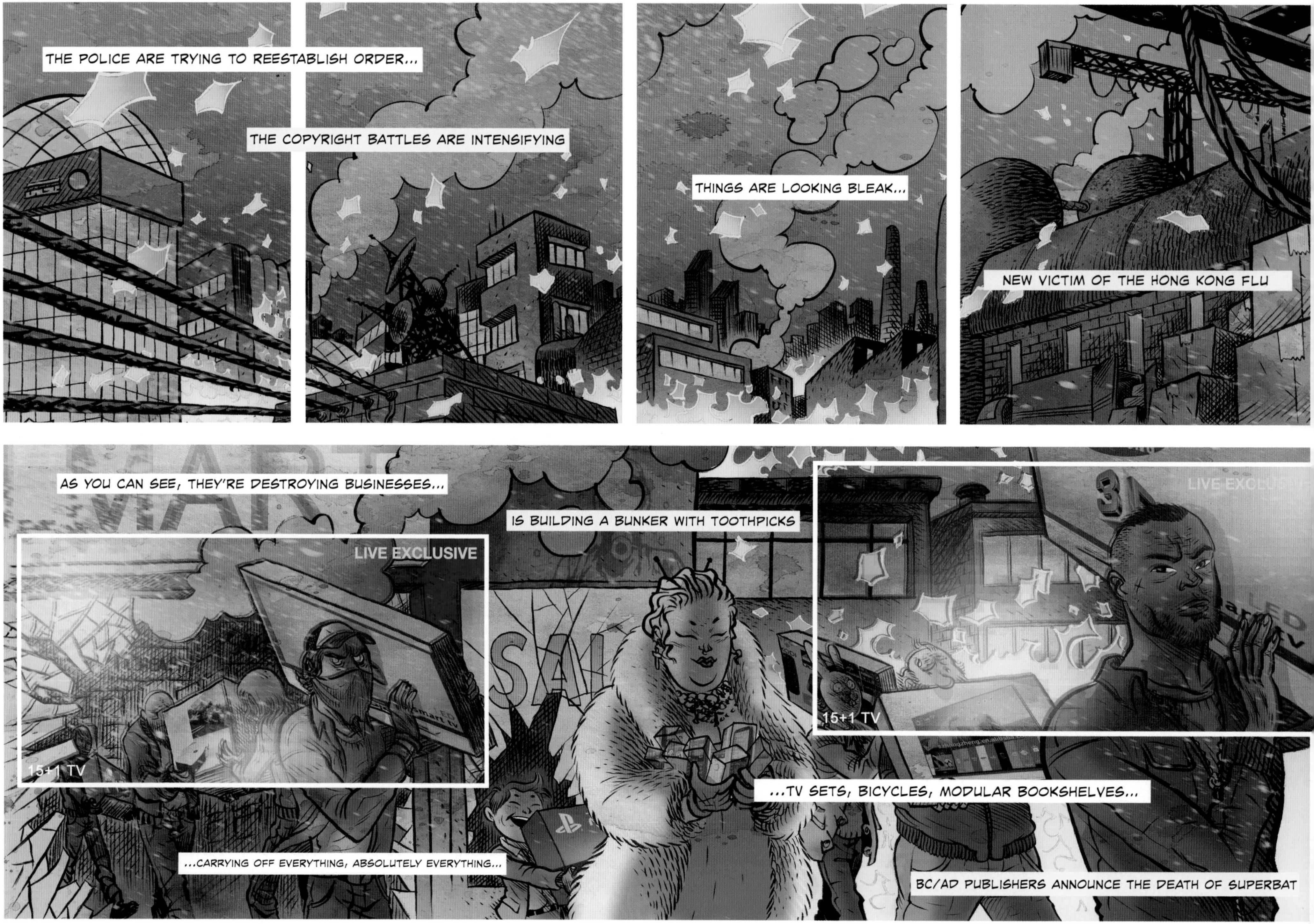
THE POLICE ARE TRYING TO REESTABLISH ORDER...
THE COPYRIGHT BATTLES ARE INTENSIFYING
THINGS ARE LOOKING BLEAK...
NEW VICTIM OF THE HONG KONG FLU
AS YOU CAN SEE, THEY'RE DESTROYING BUSINESSES...
LIVE EXCLUSIVE
15+1 TV
IS BUILDING A BUNKER WITH TOOTHPICKS
LIVE EXCLUSIVE
15+1 TV
...CARRYING OFF EVERYTHING, ABSOLUTELY EVERYTHING...
...TV SETS, BICYCLES, MODULAR BOOKSHELVES...
BC/AD PUBLISHERS ANNOUNCE THE DEATH OF SUPERBAT

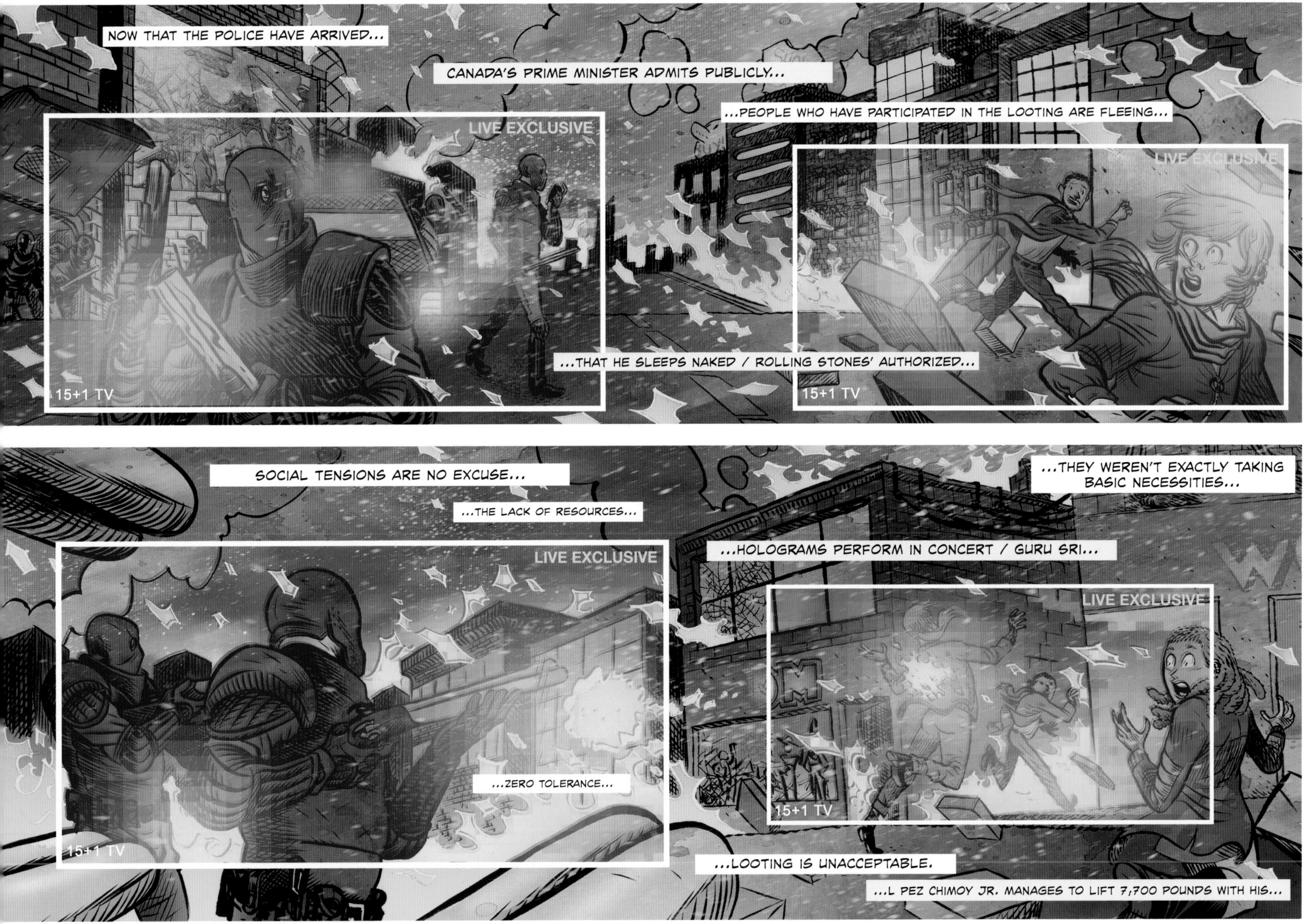
NOW THAT THE POLICE HAVE ARRIVED...
CANADA'S PRIME MINISTER ADMITS PUBLICLY...
LIVE EXCLUSIVE
15+1 TV
...PEOPLE WHO HAVE PARTICIPATED IN THE LOOTING ARE FLEEING...
LIVE EXCLUSIVE
15+1 TV
...THAT HE SLEEPS NAKED / ROLLING STONES' AUTHORIZED...
SOCIAL TENSIONS ARE NO EXCUSE...
...THE LACK OF RESOURCES...
LIVE EXCLUSIVE
...ZERO TOLERANCE...
15+1 TV
...THEY WEREN'T EXACTLY TAKING BASIC NECESSITIES...
...HOLOGRAMS PERFORM IN CONCERT / GURU SRI...
LIVE EXCLUSIVE
15+1 TV
...LOOTING IS UNACCEPTABLE.
...L PEZ CHIMOY JR. MANAGES TO LIFT 7,700 POUNDS WITH HIS...

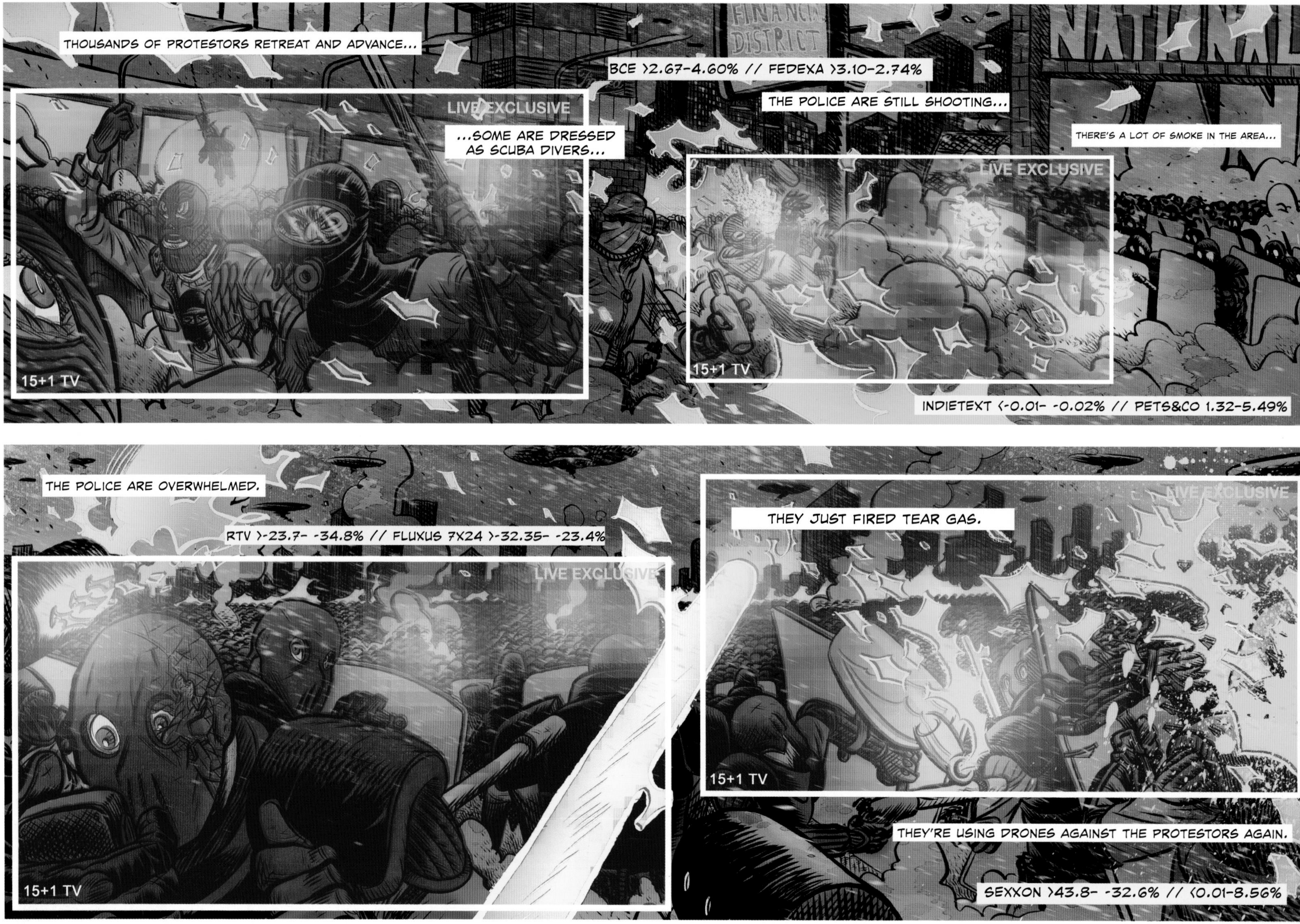
THOUSANDS OF PROTESTORS RETREAT AND ADVANCE...
LIVE EXCLUSIVE
...SOME ARE DRESSED AS SCUBA DIVERS...
15+1 TV
BCE >2.67-4.60% // FEDEXA >3.10-2.74%
THE POLICE ARE STILL SHOOTING...
THERE'S A LOT OF SMOKE IN THE AREA...
LIVE EXCLUSIVE
15+1 TV
INDIETEXT <-0.01- -0.02% // PETS&CO 1.32-5.49%
THE POLICE ARE OVERWHELMED.
RTV >-23.7- -34.8% // FLUXUS 7X24 >-32.35- -23.4%
LIVE EXCLUSIVE
15+1 TV
THEY JUST FIRED TEAR GAS.
LIVE EXCLUSIVE
15+1 TV
THEY'RE USING DRONES AGAINST THE PROTESTORS AGAIN.
SEXXON >43.8- -32.6% // <0.01-8.56%

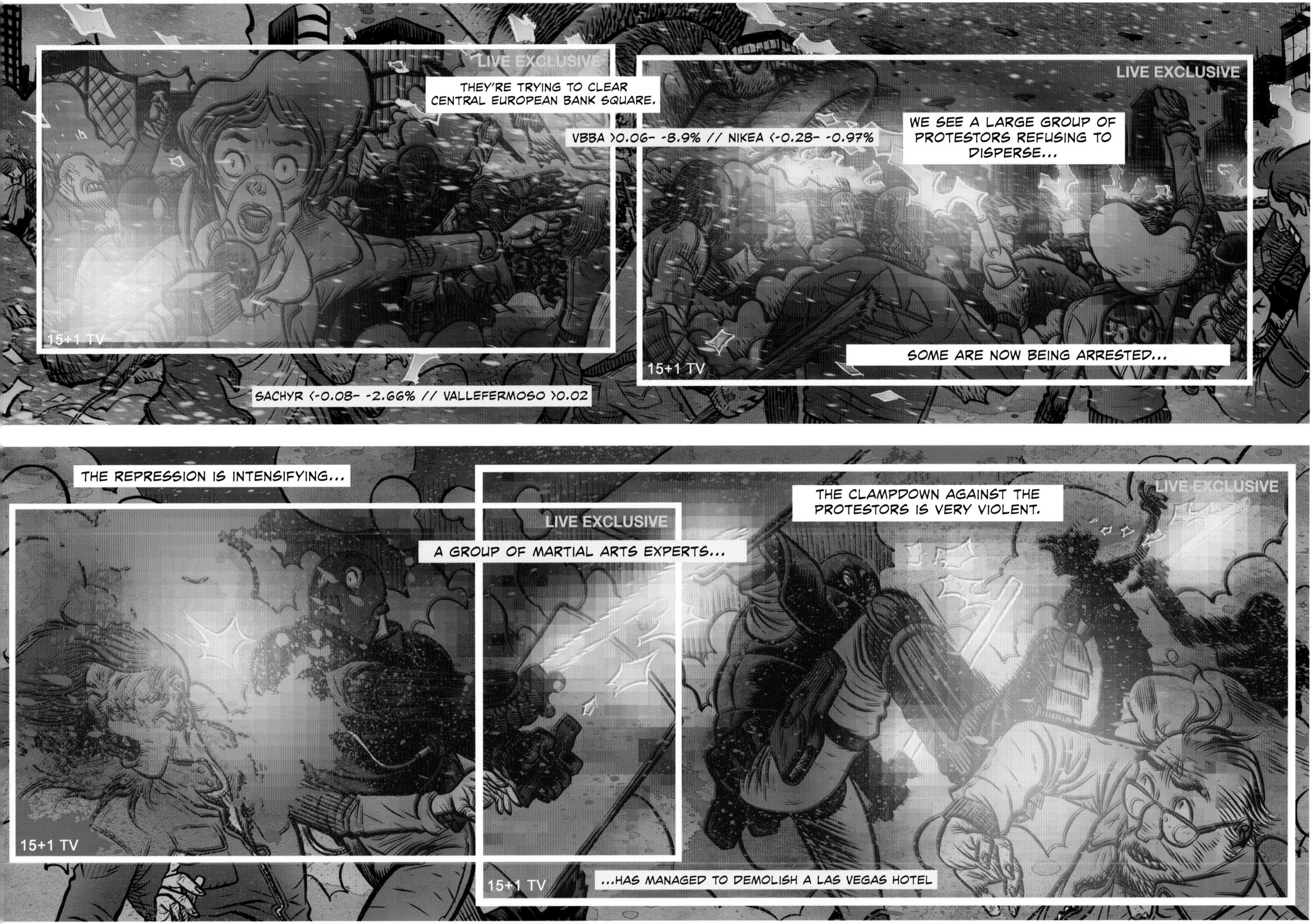
LIVE EXCLUSIVE
THEY'RE TRYING TO CLEAR CENTRAL EUROPEAN BANK SQUARE.
VBBA >0.06- -8.9% // NIKEA <-0.28- -0.97%
15+1 TV
SACHYR <-0.08- -2.66% // VALLEFERMOSO >0.02
LIVE EXCLUSIVE
WE SEE A LARGE GROUP OF PROTESTORS REFUSING TO DISPERSE...
SOME ARE NOW BEING ARRESTED...
15+1 TV
THE REPRESSION IS INTENSIFYING...
LIVE EXCLUSIVE
A GROUP OF MARTIAL ARTS EXPERTS...
15+1 TV
LIVE EXCLUSIVE
THE CLAMPDOWN AGAINST THE PROTESTORS IS VERY VIOLENT.
15+1 TV
...HAS MANAGED TO DEMOLISH A LAS VEGAS HOTEL

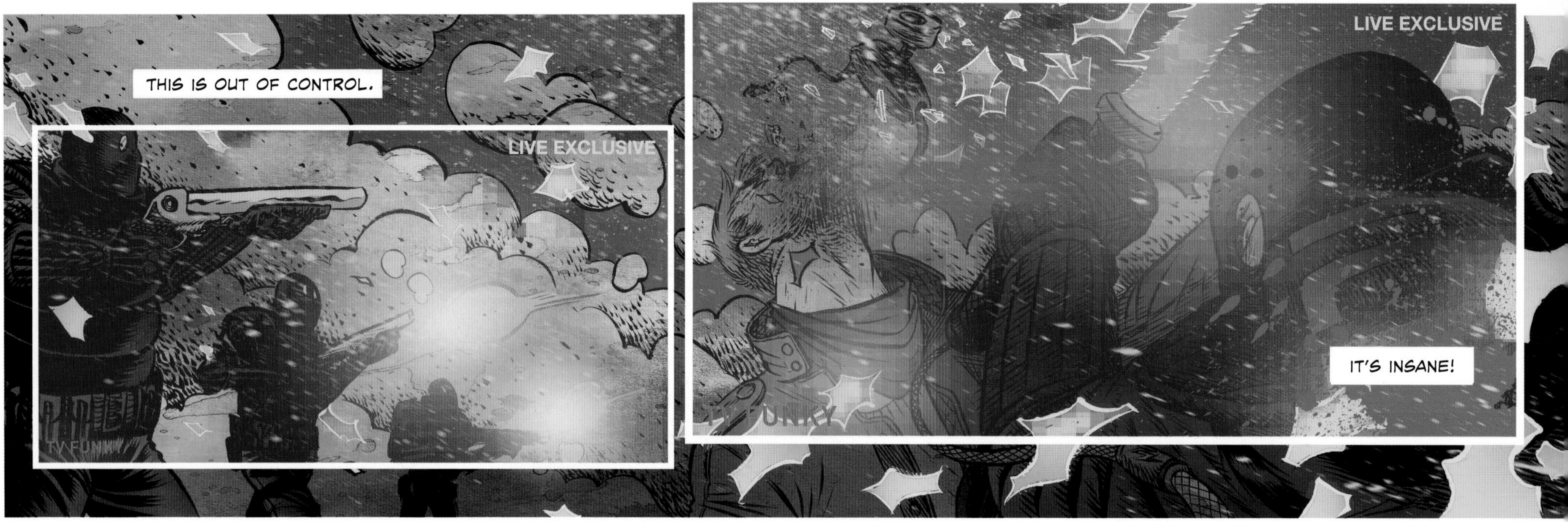
THIS IS OUT OF CONTROL.
LIVE EXCLUSIVE
LIVE EXCLUSIVE
IT'S INSANE!

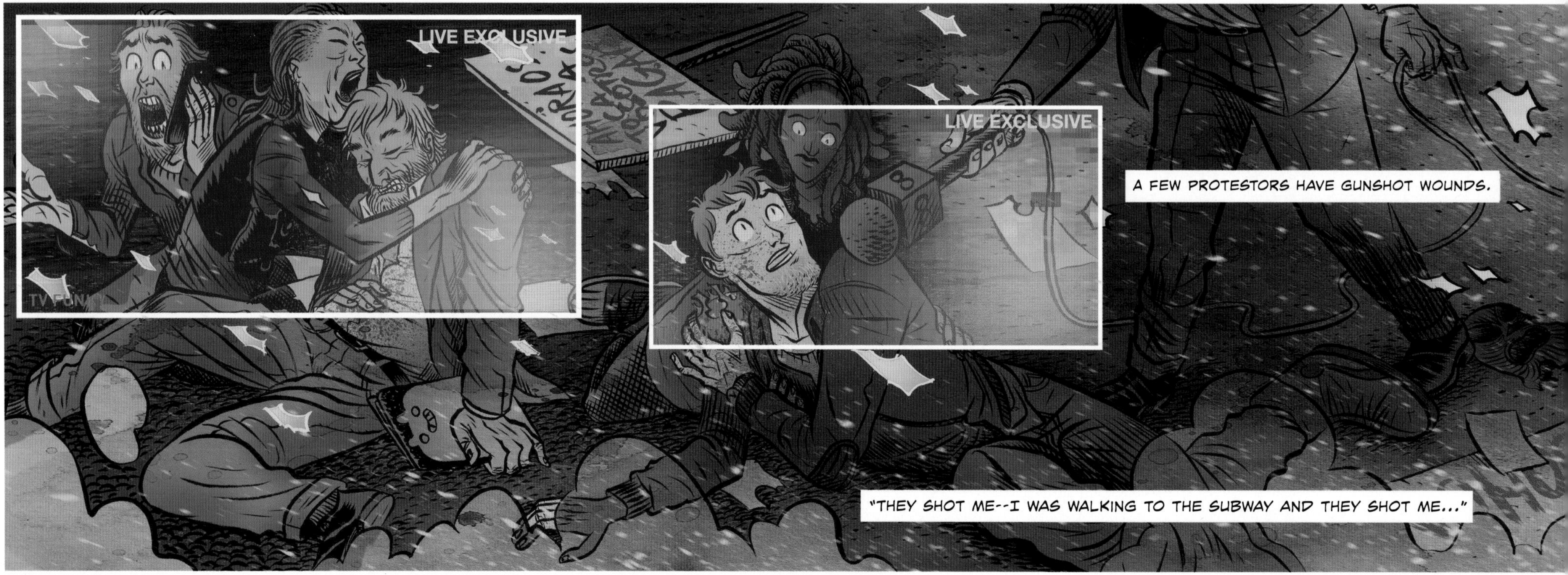
LIVE EXCLUSIVE
LIVE EXCLUSIVE
A FEW PROTESTORS HAVE GUNSHOT WOUNDS.
"THEY SHOT ME--I WAS WALKING TO THE SUBWAY AND THEY SHOT ME..."

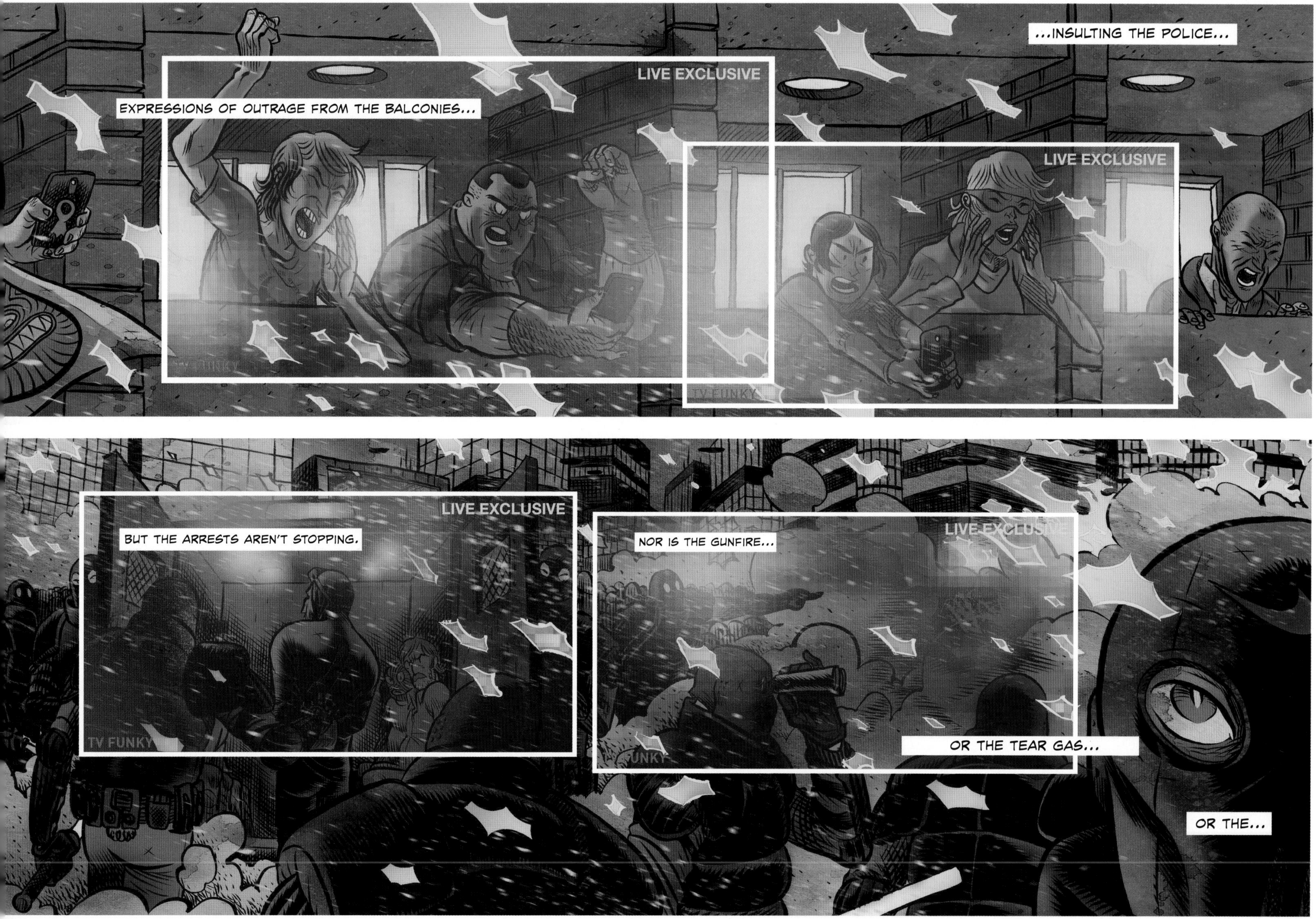
LIVE EXCLUSIVE
EXPRESSIONS OF OUTRAGE FROM THE BALCONIES...
LIVE EXCLUSIVE
...INSULTING THE POLICE...
TV FUNKY
LIVE EXCLUSIVE
BUT THE ARRESTS AREN'T STOPPING.
TV FUNKY
LIVE EXCLUSIVE
NOR IS THE GUNFIRE...
OR THE TEAR GAS...
OR THE...

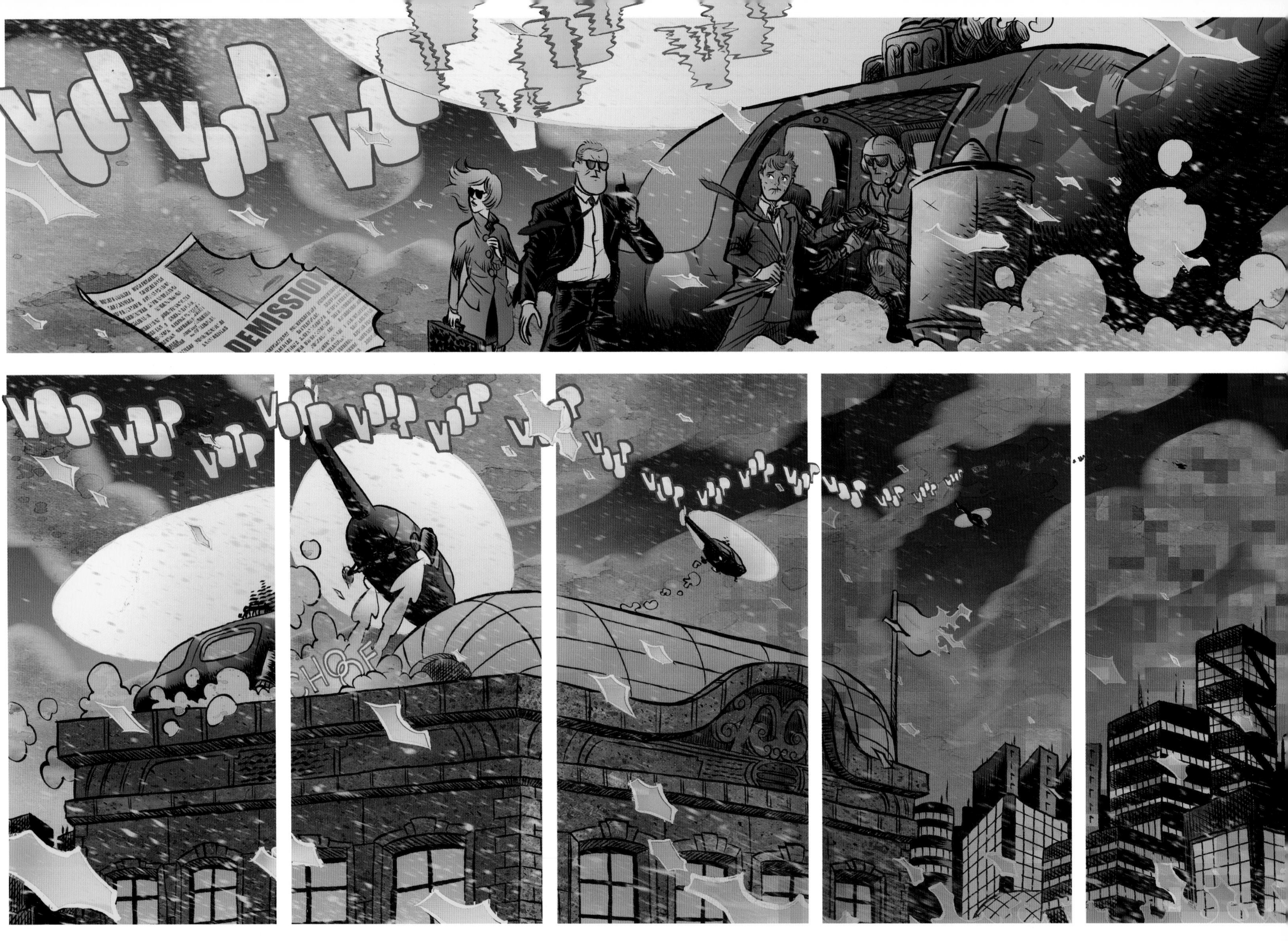
VOOP VOOP VOOP V
DEMISSION
VOOP VOOP VOOP VOOP VOOP VOOP VOOP VOOP
CHOOF
VOOP VOOP VOOP VOOP VOOP VOOP VOOP

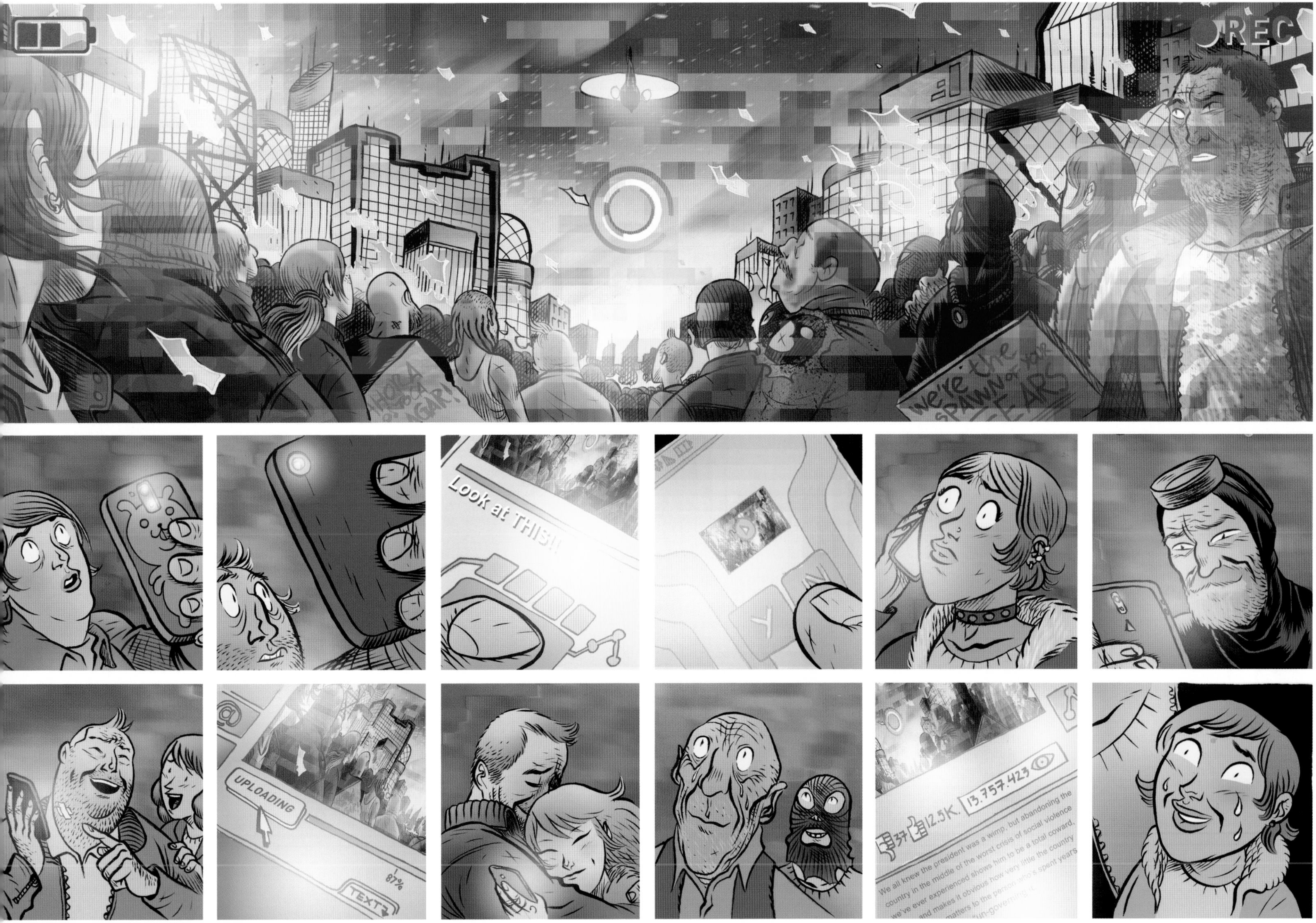
REC
We're the SPAWN of your FEARS
Look at THIS!!
UPLOADING
TEXT
87%
37
12.5K.
13.757.423
We all knew the president was a wimp, but abandoning the country in the middle of the worst crisis of social violence we've ever experienced shows him to be a total coward, and makes it obvious how very little the country matters to the person who's spent years

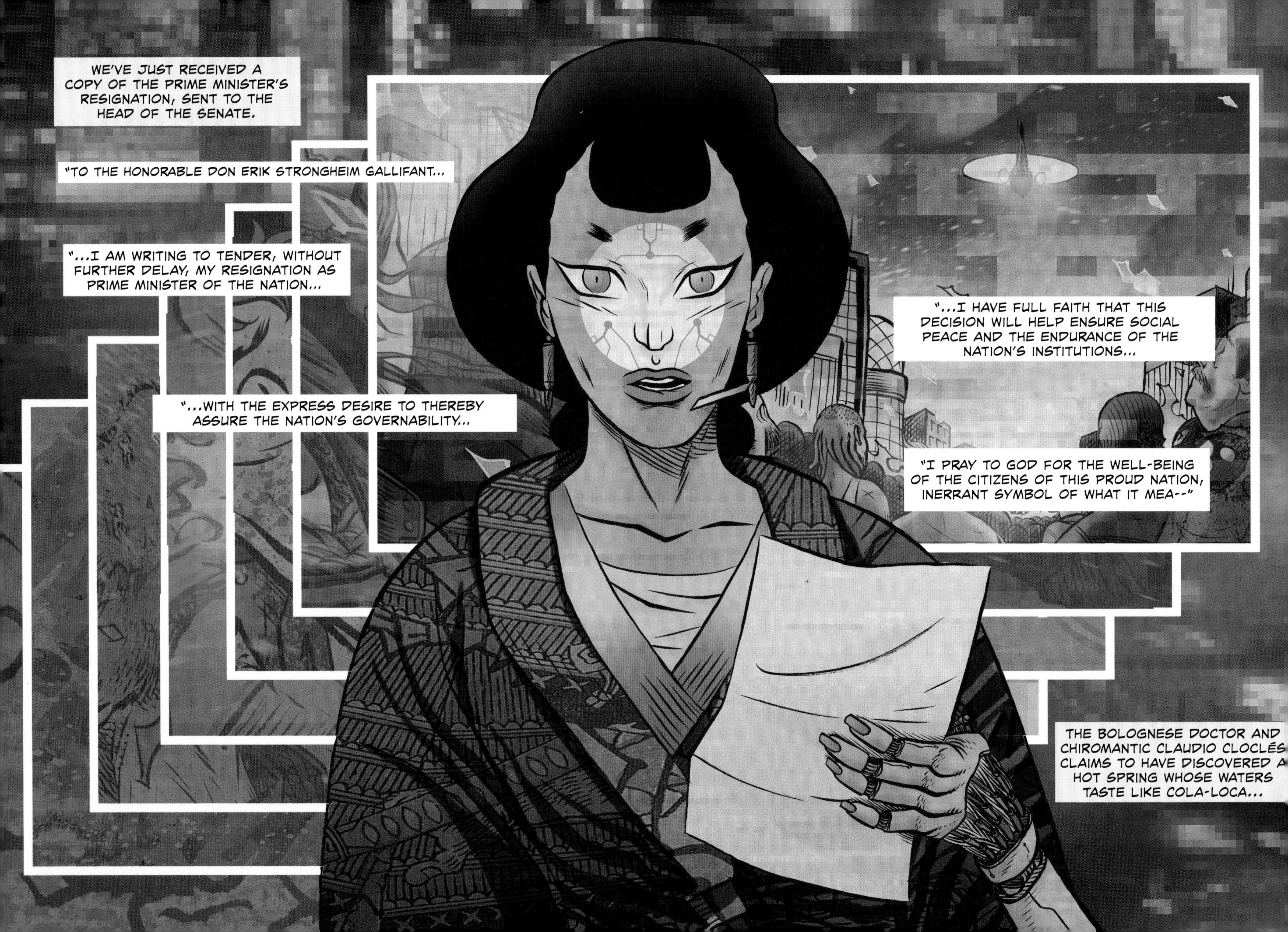
WE'VE JUST RECEIVED A COPY OF THE PRIME MINISTER'S RESIGNATION, SENT TO THE HEAD OF THE SENATE.
"TO THE HONORABLE DON ERIK STRONGHEIM GALLIFANT...
"...I AM WRITING TO TENDER, WITHOUT FURTHER DELAY, MY RESIGNATION AS PRIME MINISTER OF THE NATION...
"...WITH THE EXPRESS DESIRE TO THEREBY ASSURE THE NATION'S GOVERNABILITY...
"...I HAVE FULL FAITH THAT THIS DECISION WILL HELP ENSURE SOCIAL PEACE AND THE ENDURANCE OF THE NATION'S INSTITUTIONS...
"I PRAY TO GOD FOR THE WELL-BEING OF THE CITIZENS OF THIS PROUD NATION, INERRANT SYMBOL OF WHAT IT MEA--"
THE BOLOGNESE DOCTOR AND CHIROMANTIC CLAUDIO CLOCLÉS CLAIMS TO HAVE DISCOVERED A HOT SPRING WHOSE WATERS TASTE LIKE COLA-LOCA...

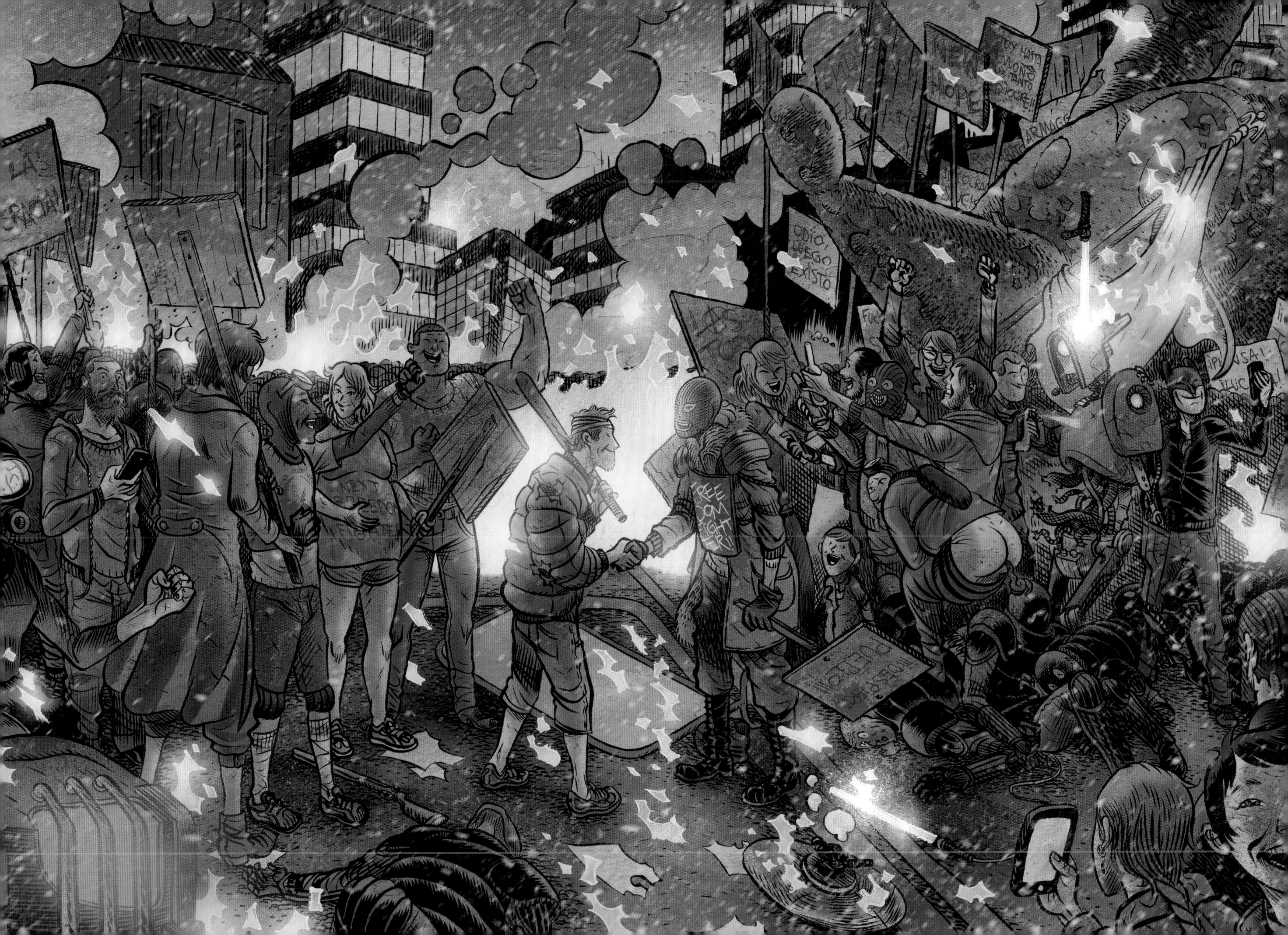
NEW HOPE
ODIO, LUEGO EXISTO
FREEDOM FIGHTER!!

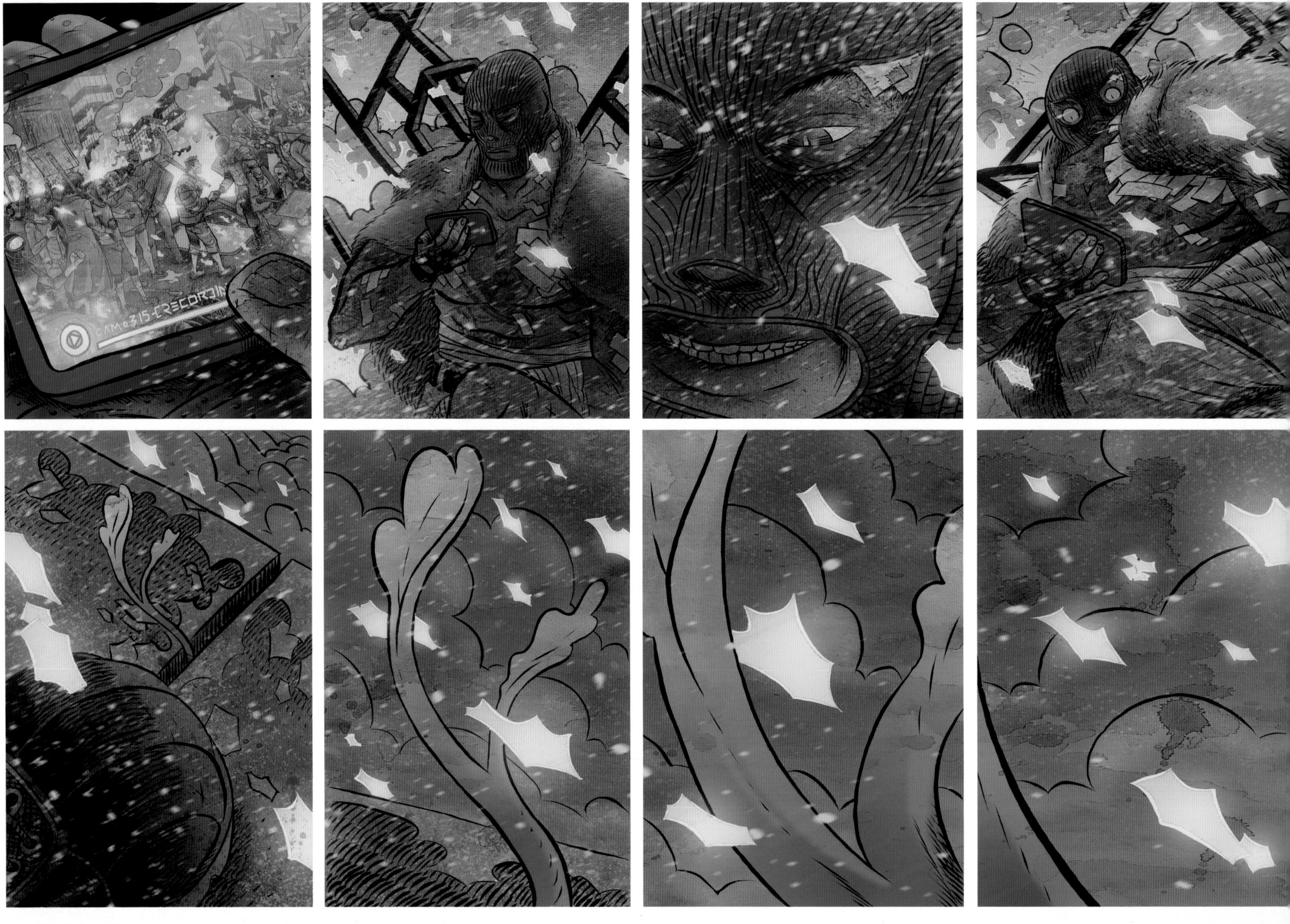
CAM 0315-[RECORDIN

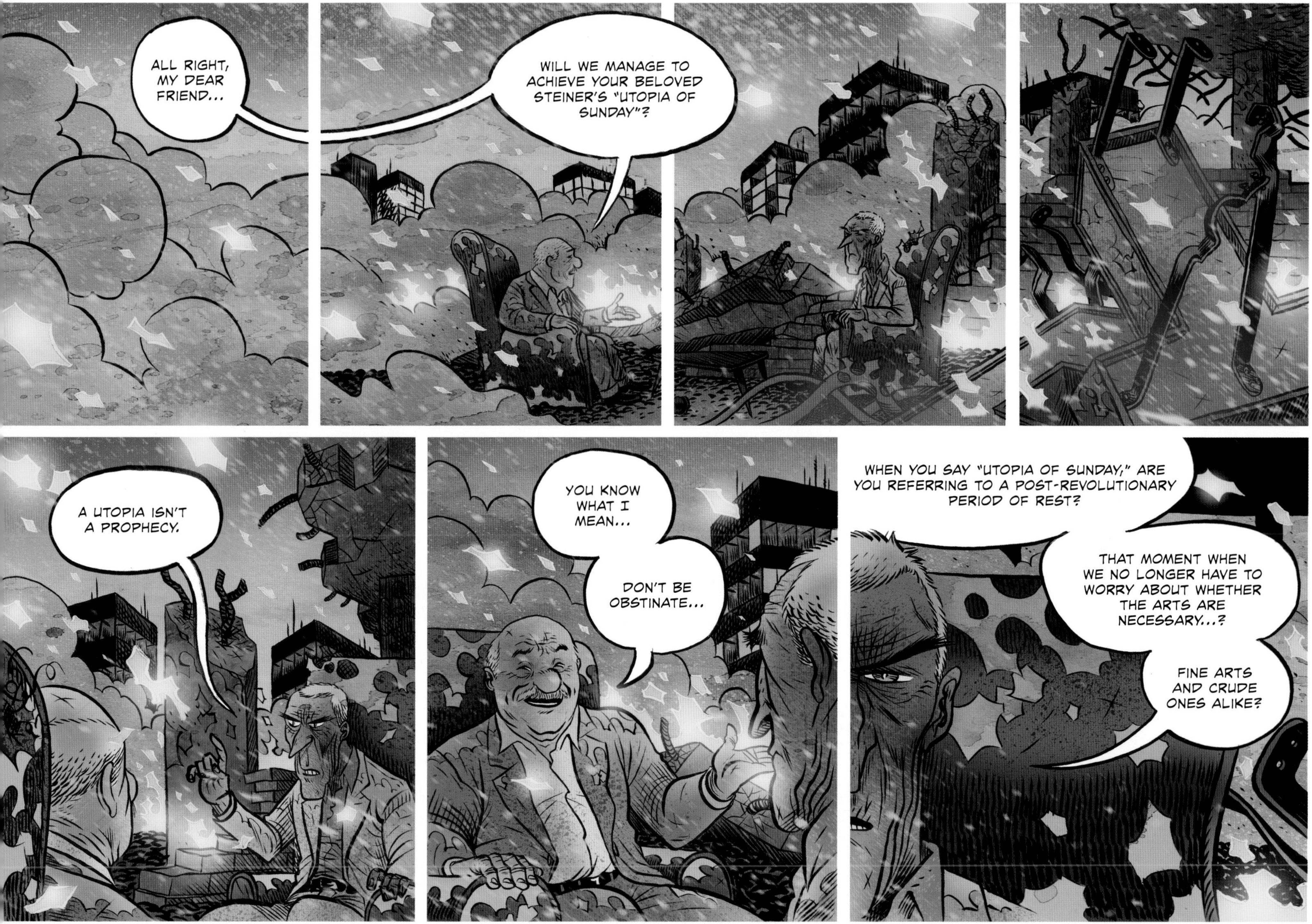
ALL RIGHT, MY DEAR FRIEND...
WILL WE MANAGE TO ACHIEVE YOUR BELOVED STEINER'S "UTOPIA OF SUNDAY"?
A UTOPIA ISN'T A PROPHECY.
YOU KNOW WHAT I MEAN...
DON'T BE OBSTINATE...
WHEN YOU SAY "UTOPIA OF SUNDAY," ARE YOU REFERRING TO A POST-REVOLUTIONARY PERIOD OF REST?
THAT MOMENT WHEN WE NO LONGER HAVE TO WORRY ABOUT WHETHER THE ARTS ARE NECESSARY...?
FINE ARTS AND CRUDE ONES ALIKE?

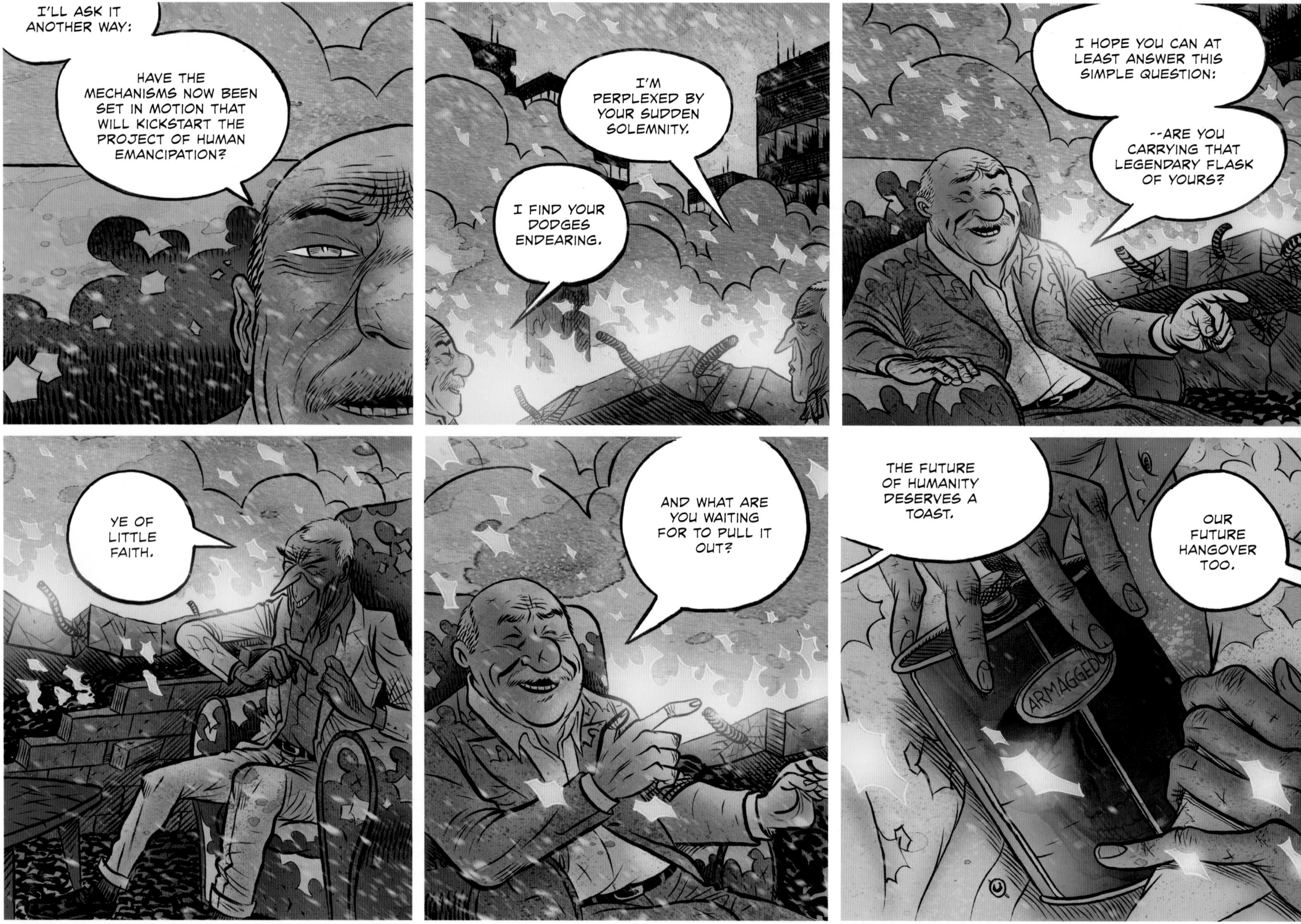
I'LL ASK IT ANOTHER WAY:
HAVE THE MECHANISMS NOW BEEN SET IN MOTION THAT WILL KICKSTART THE PROJECT OF HUMAN EMANCIPATION?
I'M PERPLEXED BY YOUR SUDDEN SOLEMNITY.
I FIND YOUR DODGES ENDEARING.
I HOPE YOU CAN AT LEAST ANSWER THIS SIMPLE QUESTION:
--ARE YOU CARRYING THAT LEGENDARY FLASK OF YOURS?
YE OF LITTLE FAITH.
AND WHAT ARE YOU WAITING FOR TO PULL IT OUT?
THE FUTURE OF HUMANITY DESERVES A TOAST.
OUR FUTURE HANGOVER TOO.
ARMAGGED

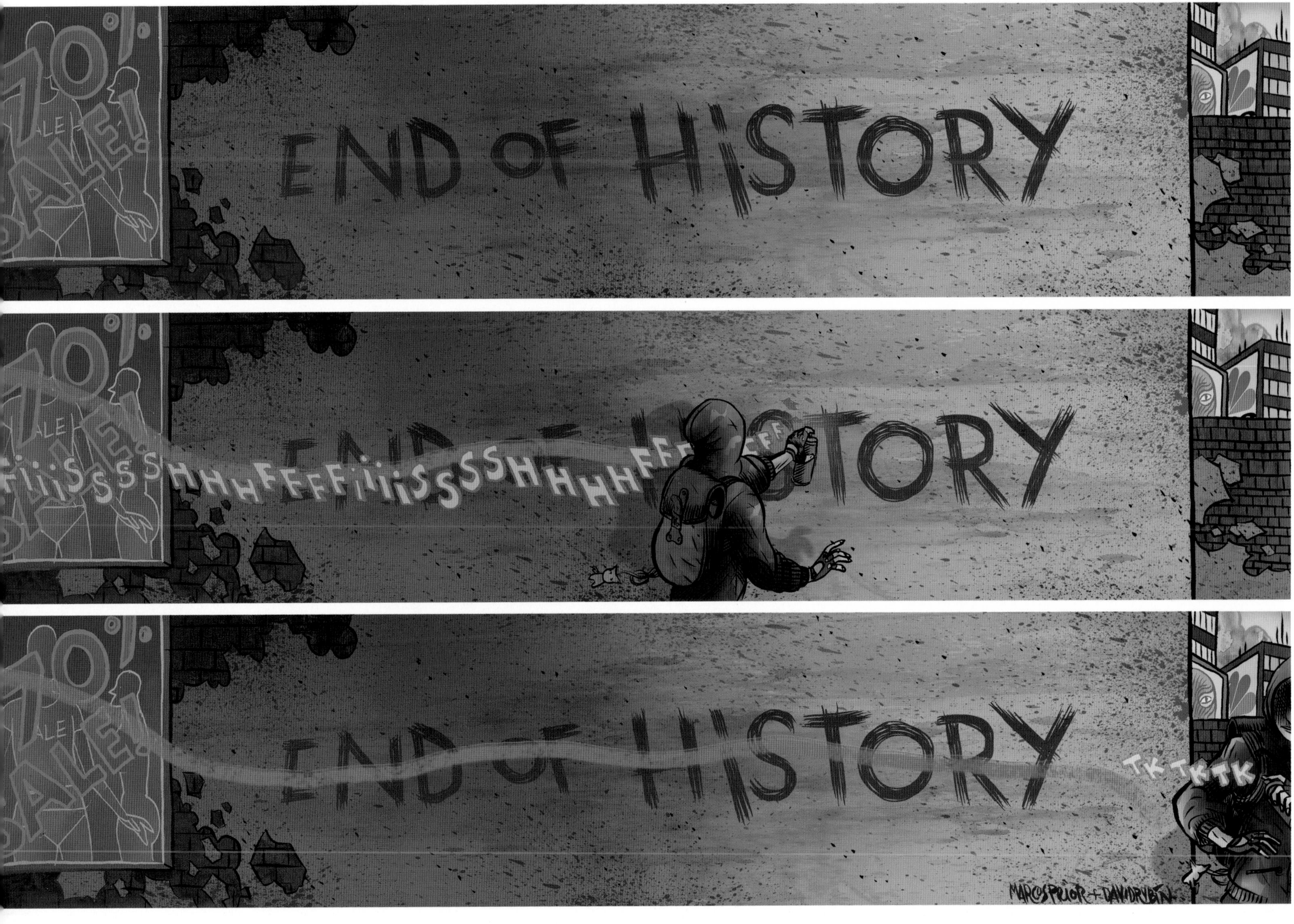
END OF HISTORY
FIIISSSSHHHHFFFFIIIISSSSHHHHFFFF
HISTORY
END OF HISTORY
TK TK TK TK
MARCOS PRIOR + DAVID RUBÍN

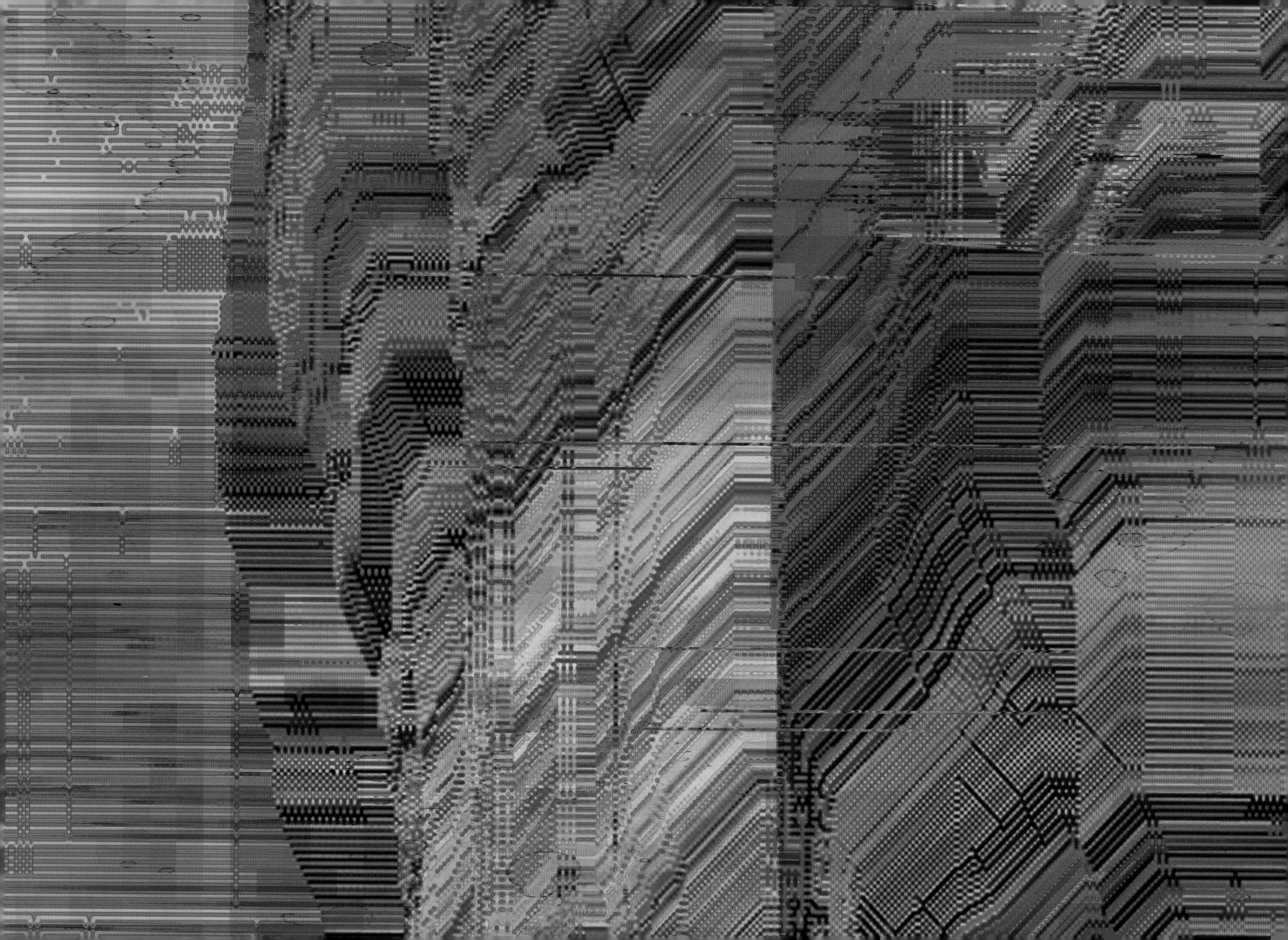

EXTRAS

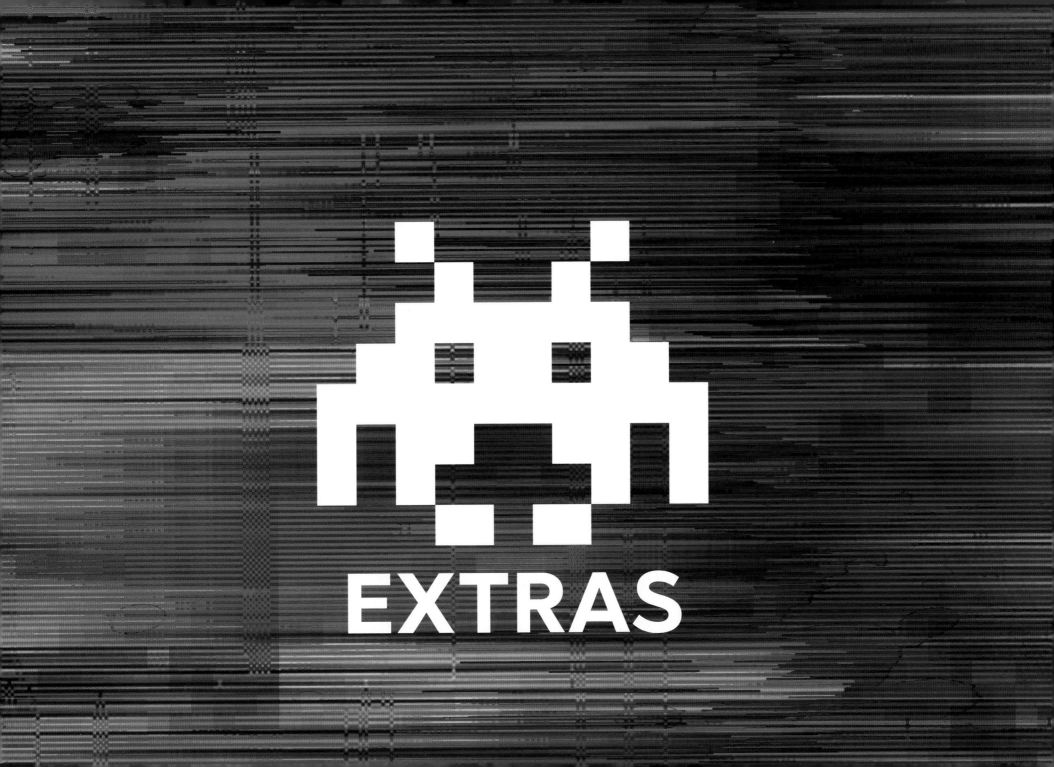

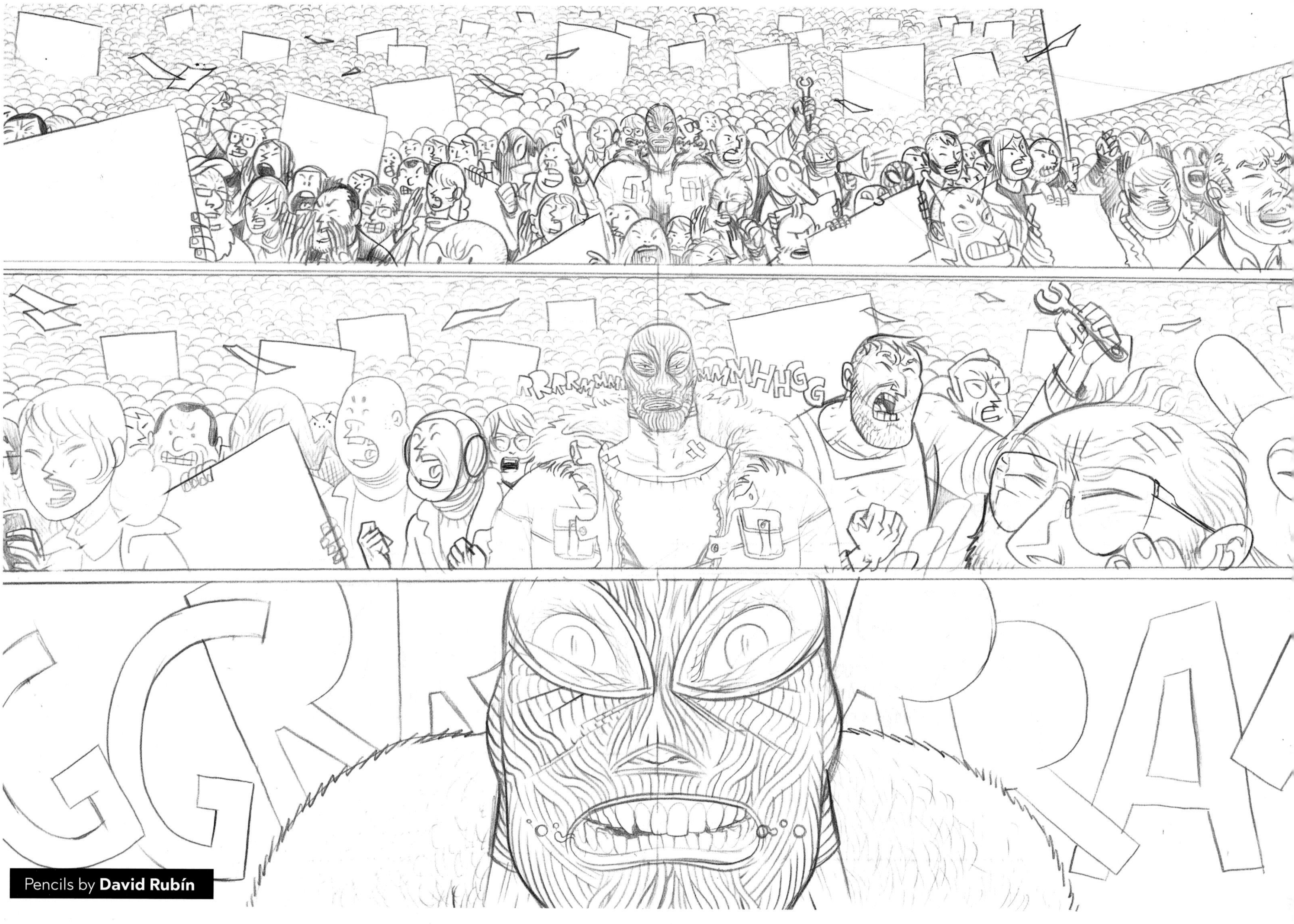
RRRRMMMM
MMMMMHHGG

Pencils by **David Rubín**

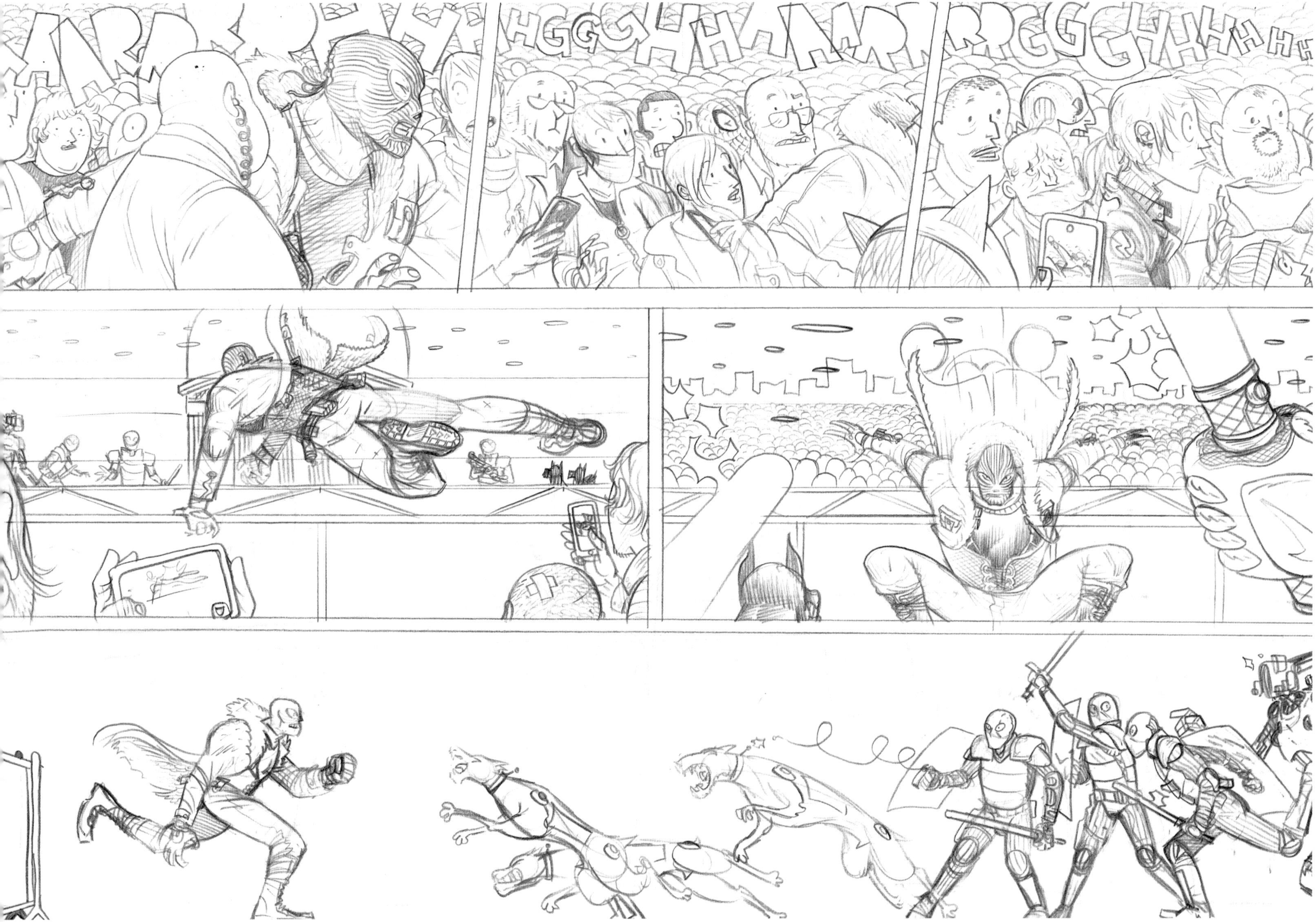
HGGGHH
AARR
RRGGGHHHHH

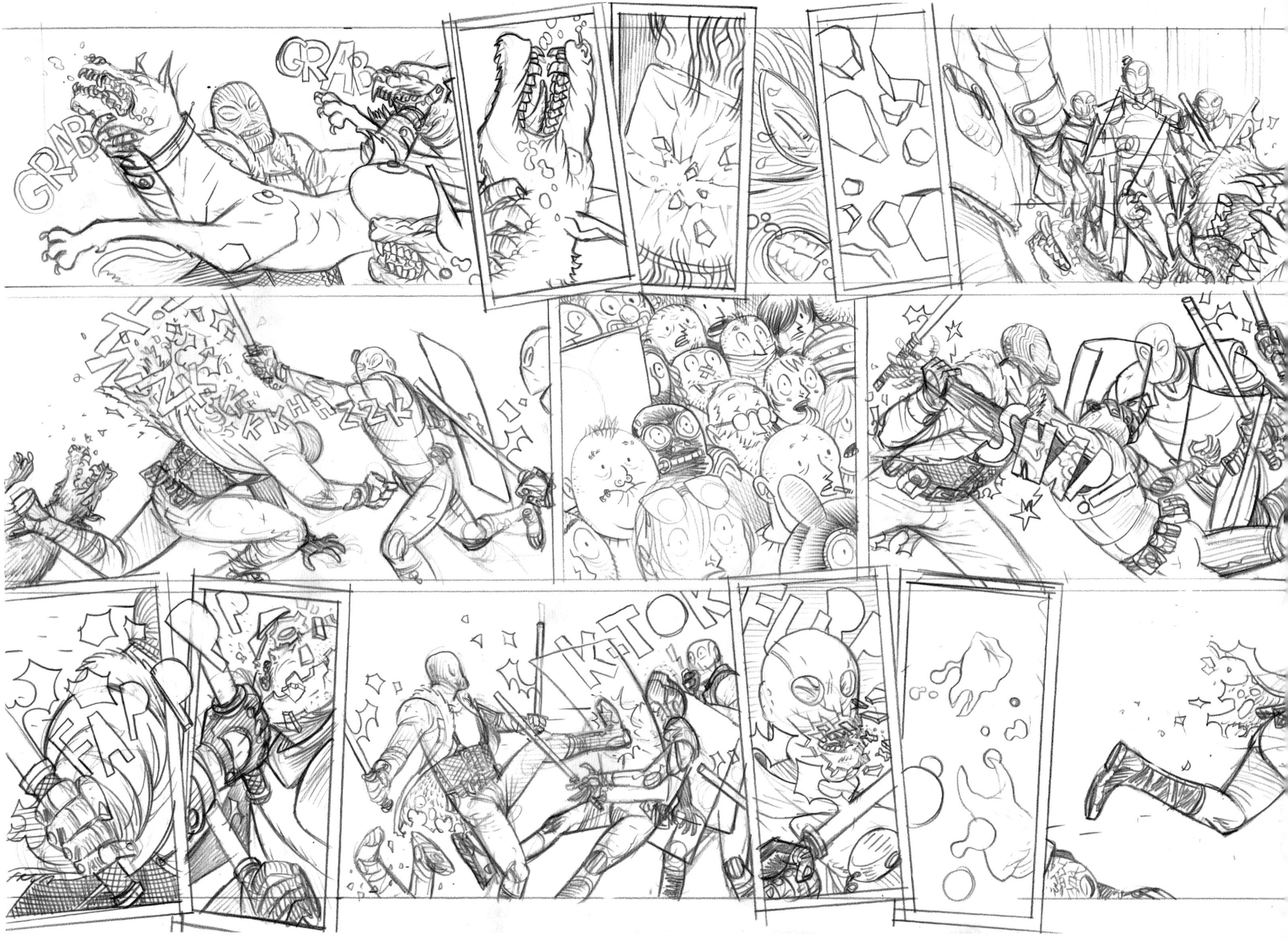
GRAB
GRAB
K-TOK

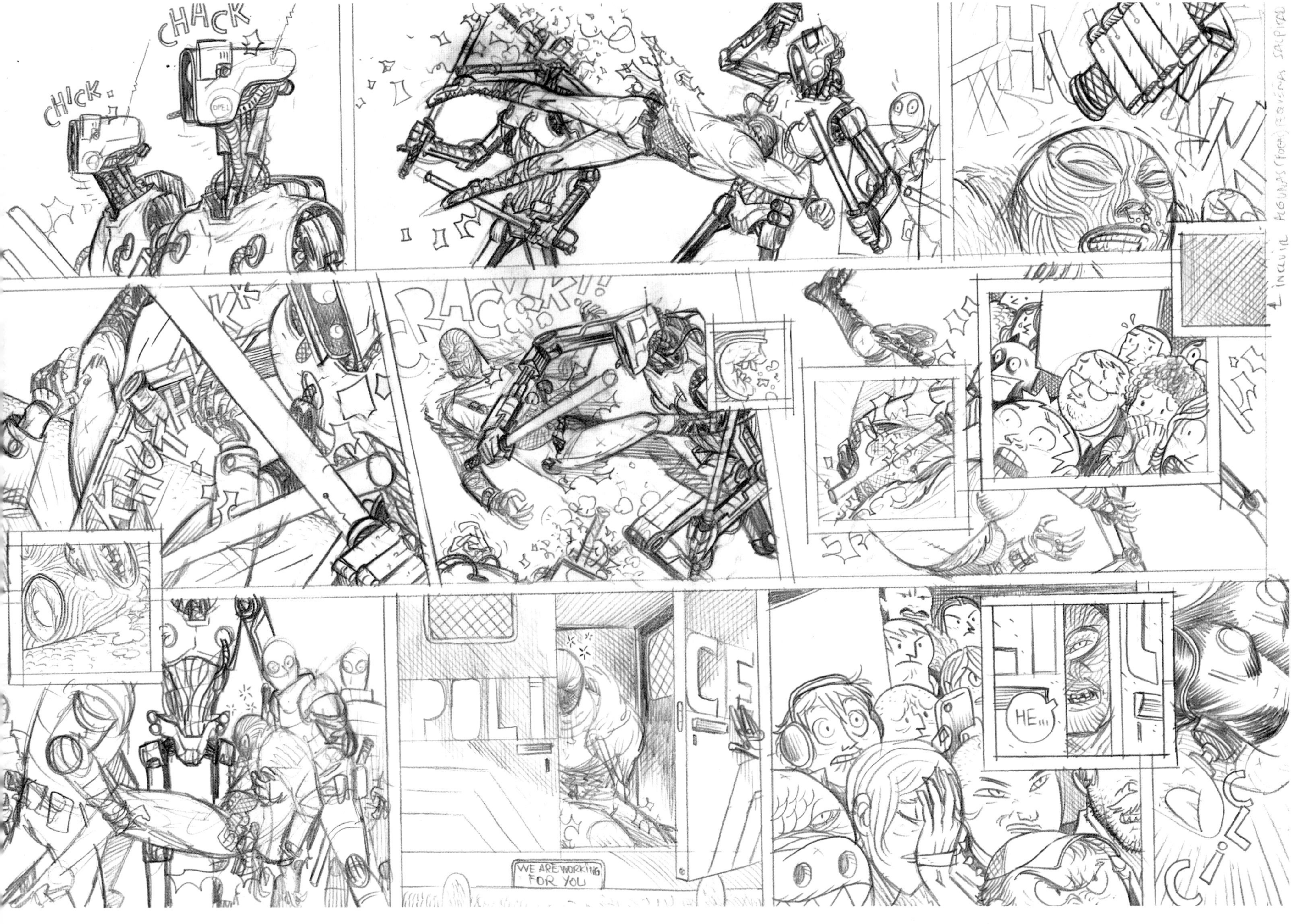
CHICK
CHACK
CRACK
WE ARE WORKING FOR YOU
HE...
INCLUIR ALGUNAS (POCAS) PEQUEÑAS

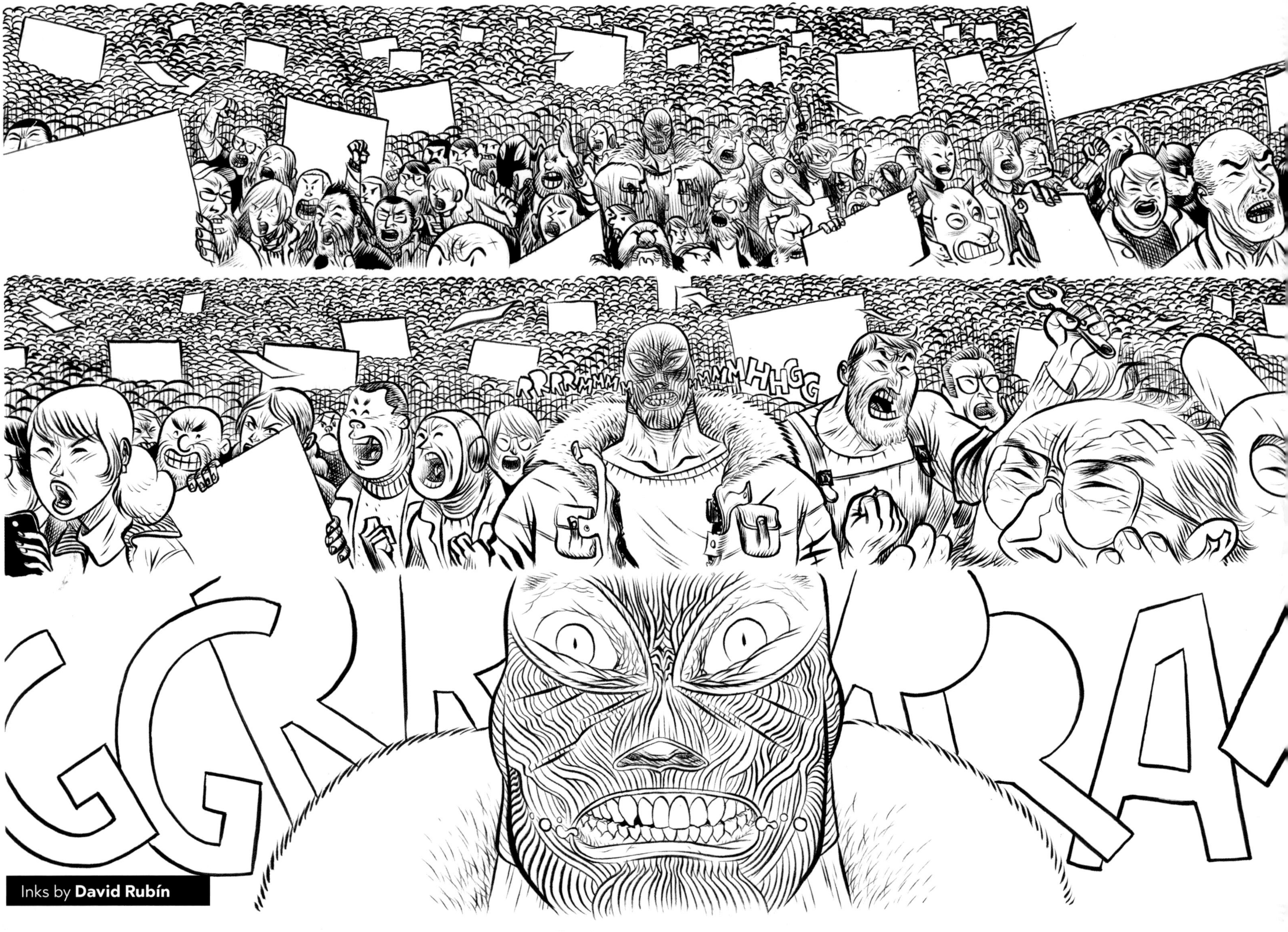
RRRRMMMM
MMMMHHGG
GGR
RA

Inks by **David Rubín**

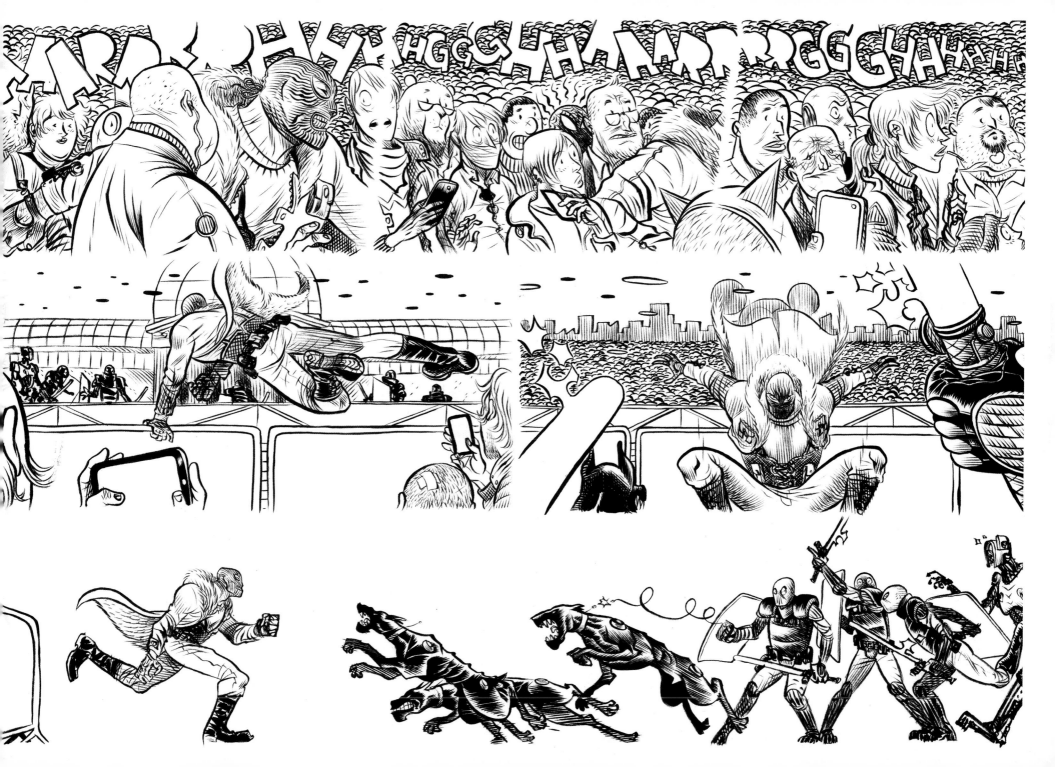

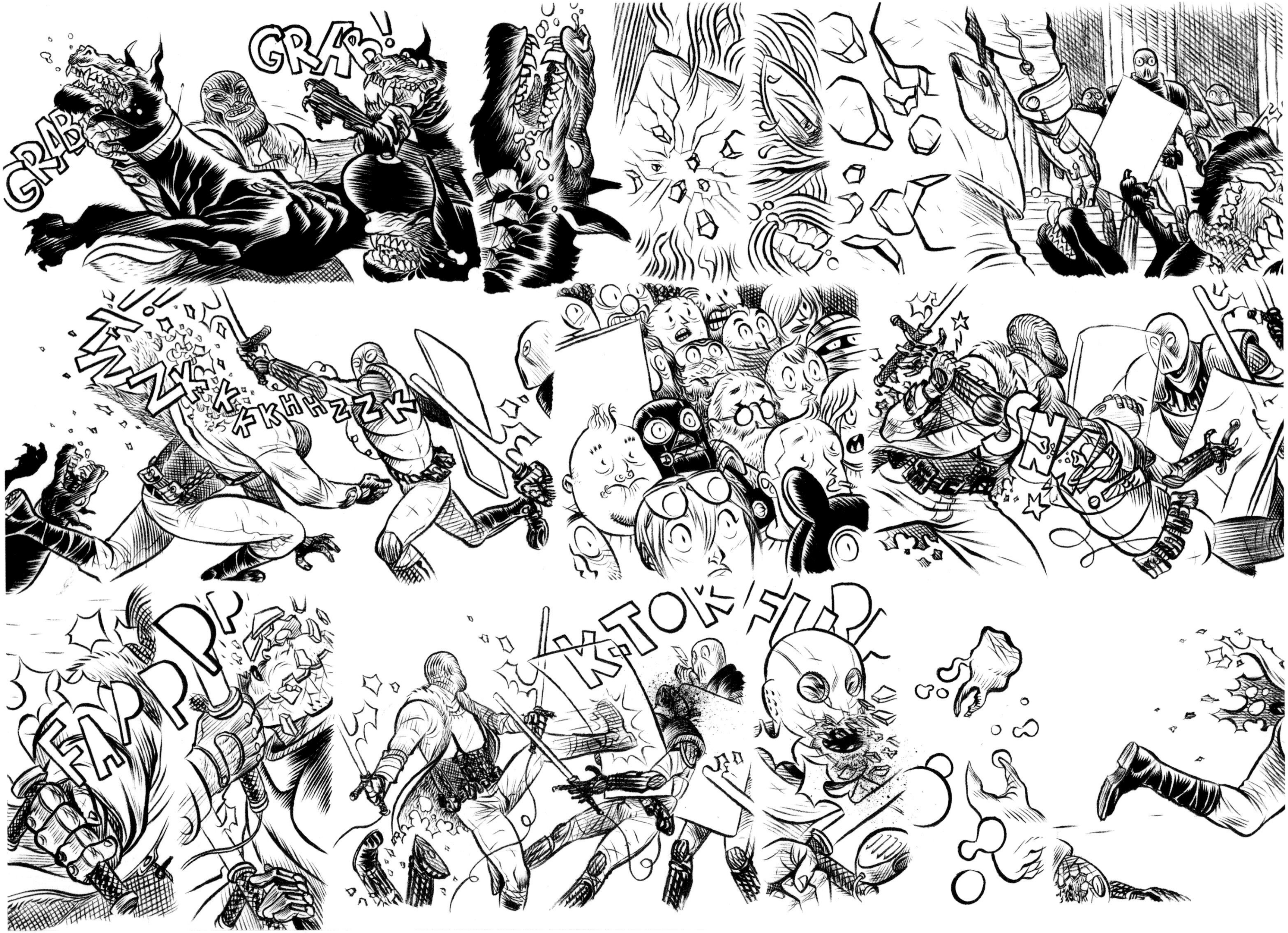
GRABB
GRABB!
FAPPP
KTOK

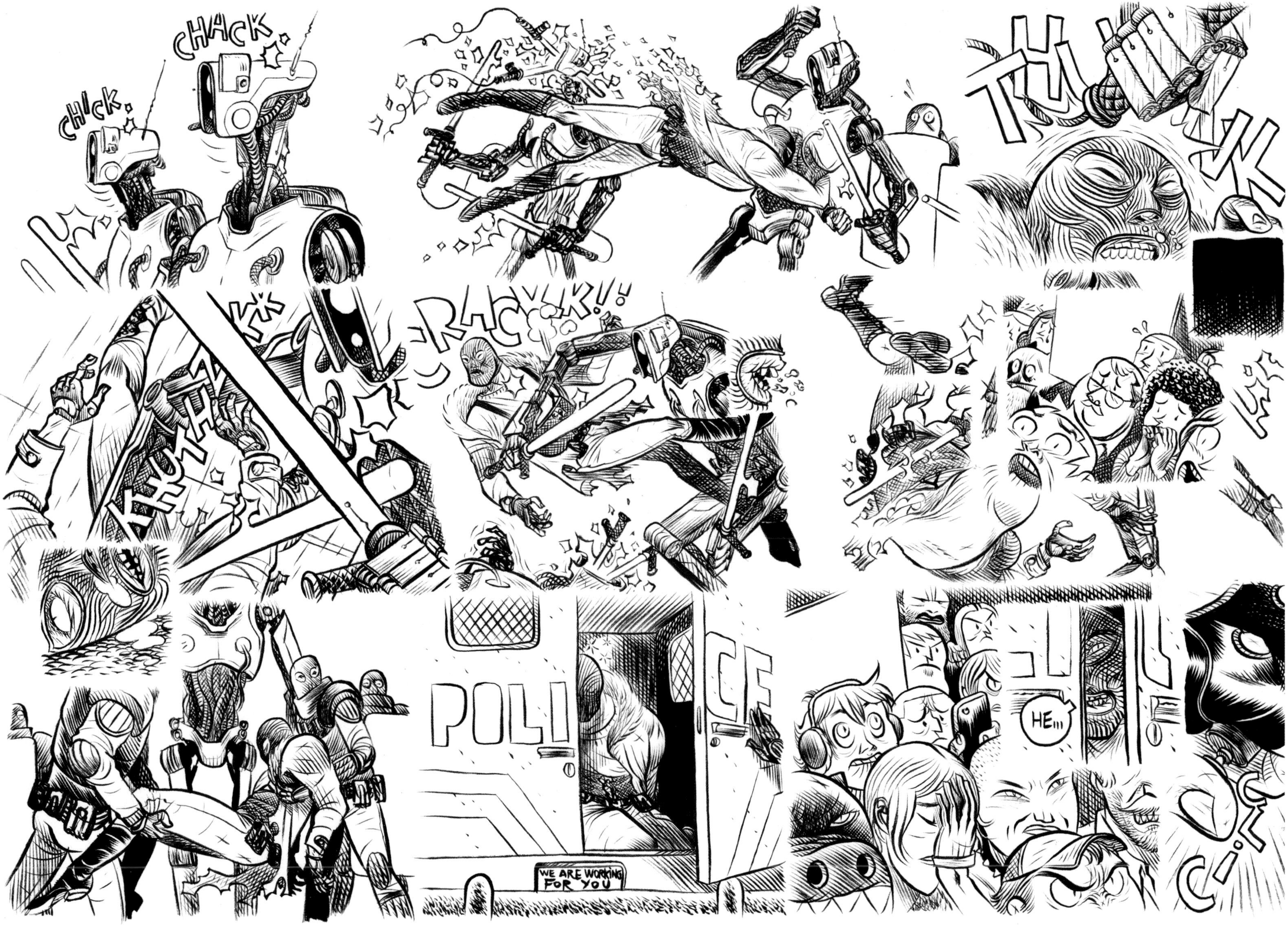
CHICK.
CHACK
POLI
CE
WE ARE WORKING FOR YOU
HE...

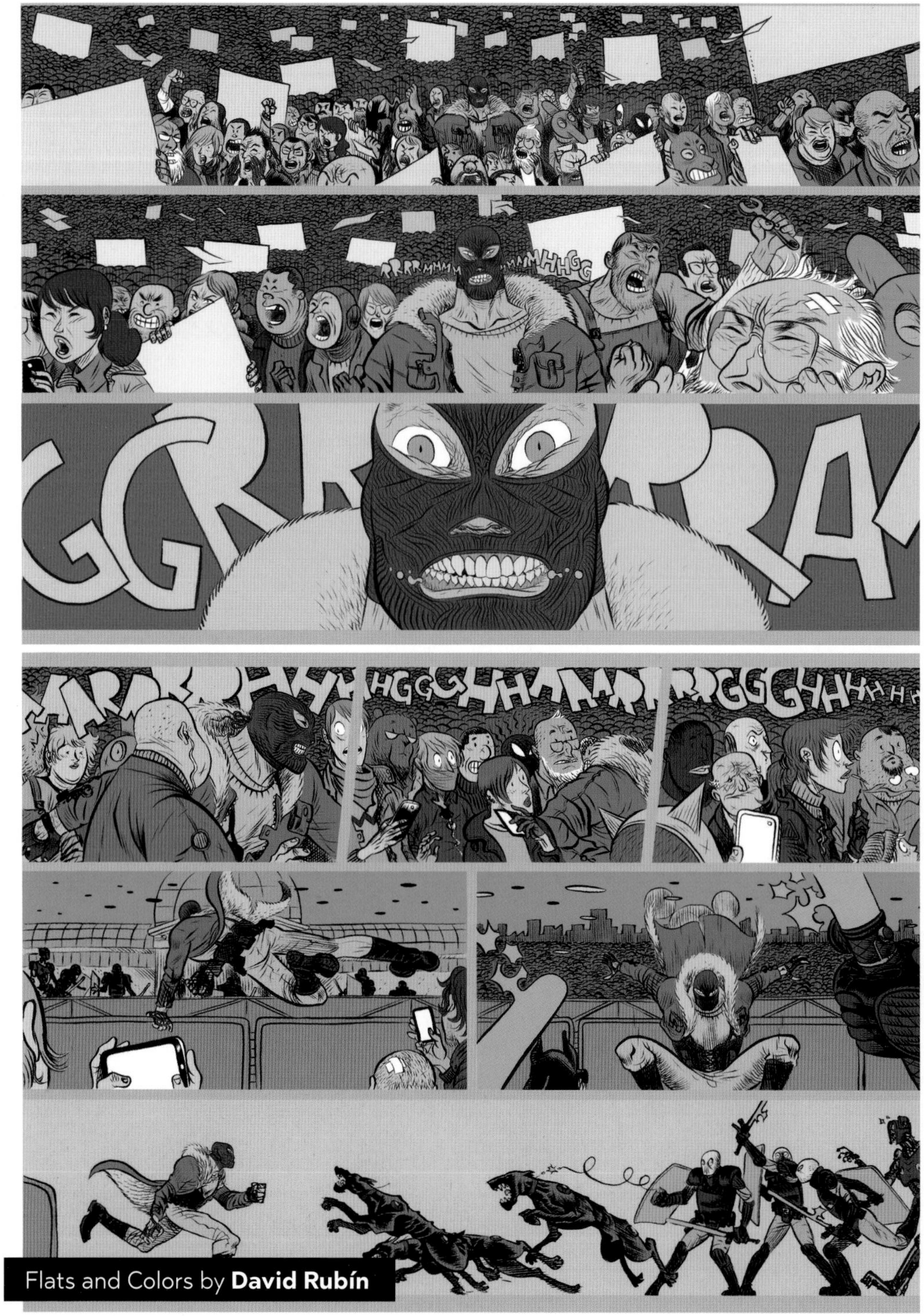

GGRRRRAA

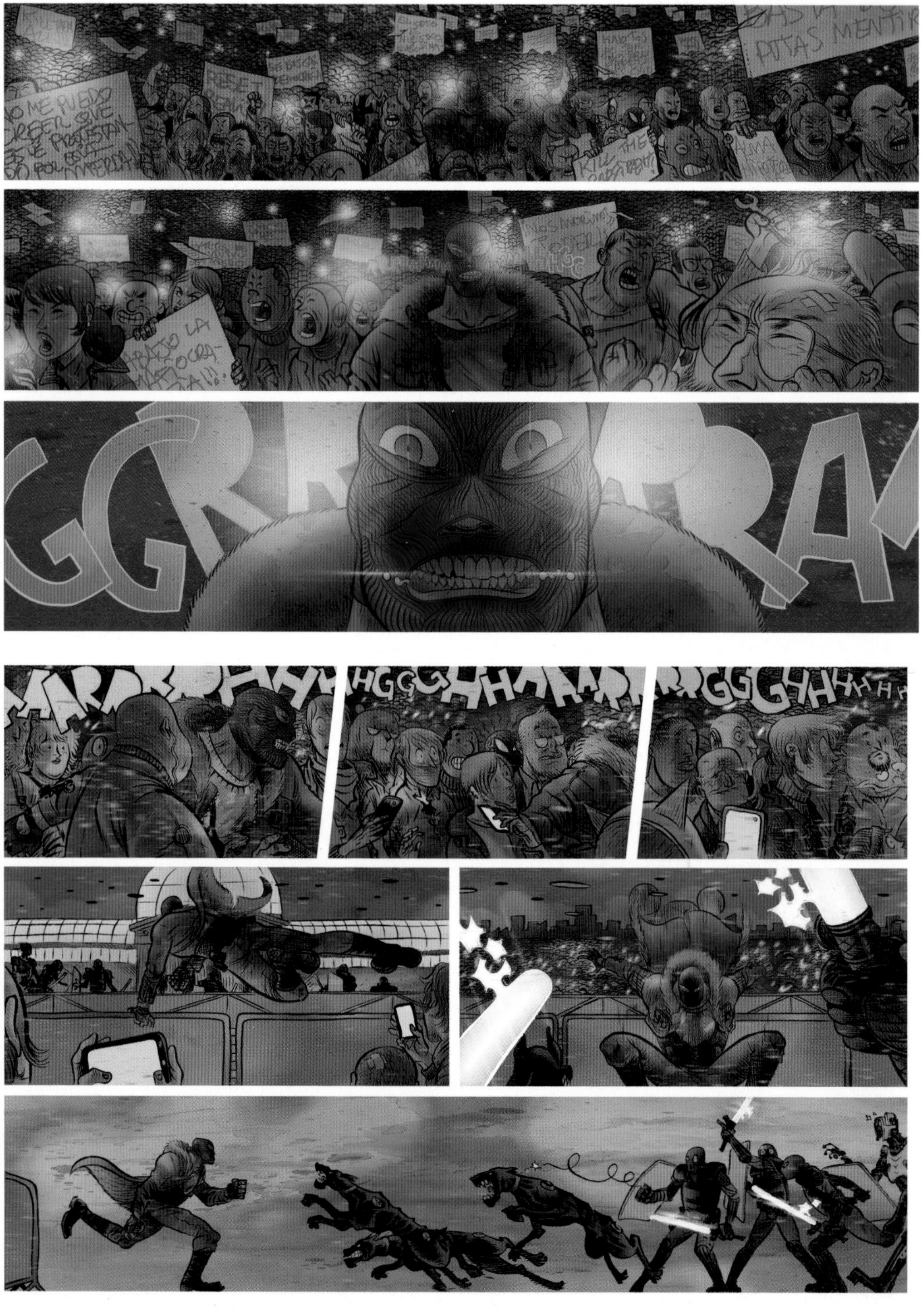

NO ME PUEDO CREER QUE PROTESTANDO POR ESA MIERDA!!
PUTAS MENTIRAS
KILL THE
ABAJO LA
GGRRRRAA

Flats and Colors by **David Rubín**

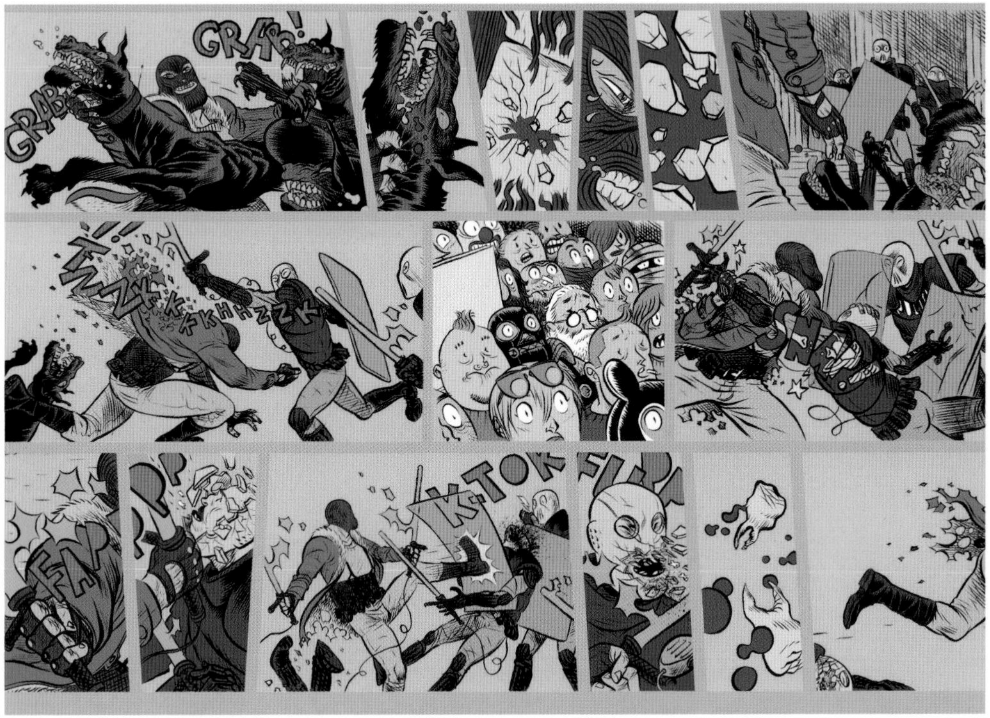
GRAB
GRAB!
FAP

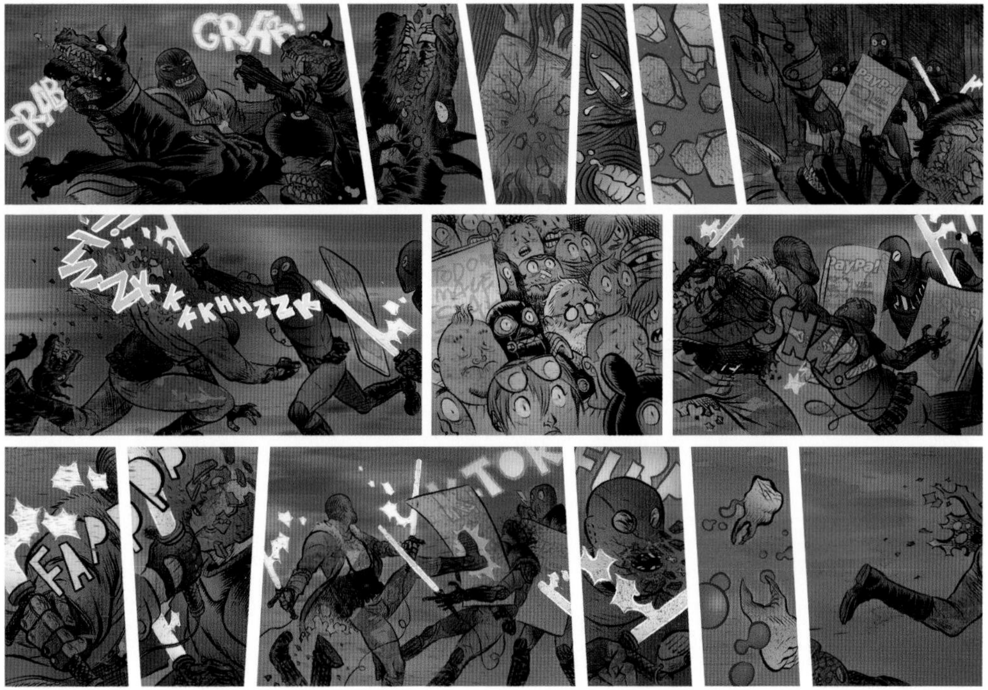
GRAB
PayPal

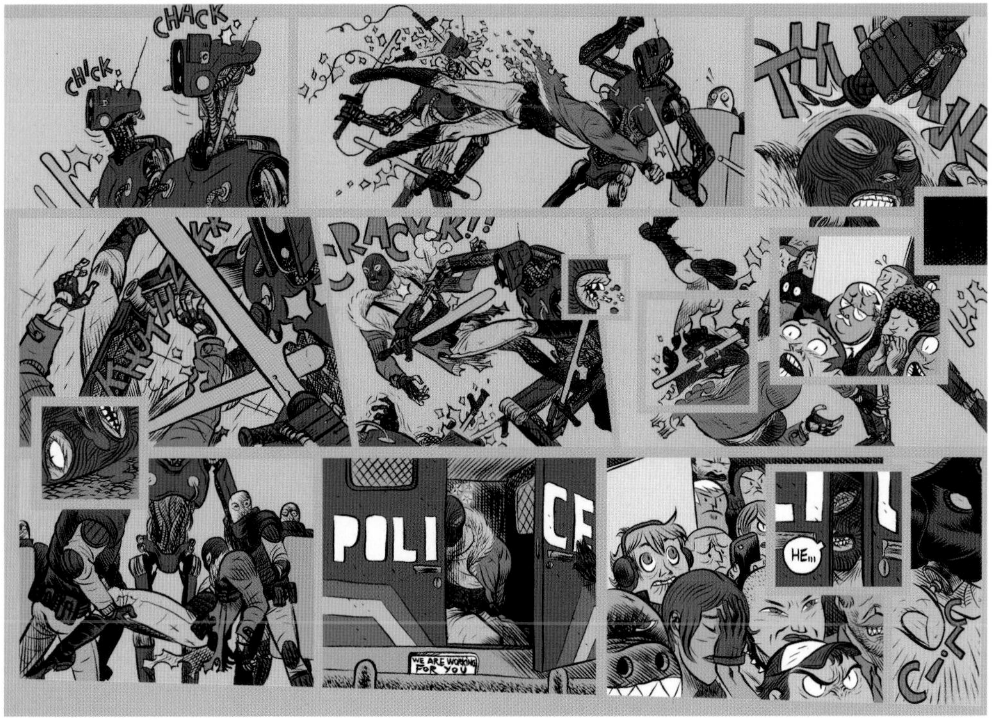
CHACK
CHACK
POLI
CE
WE ARE WORKING FOR YOU
HE,,,

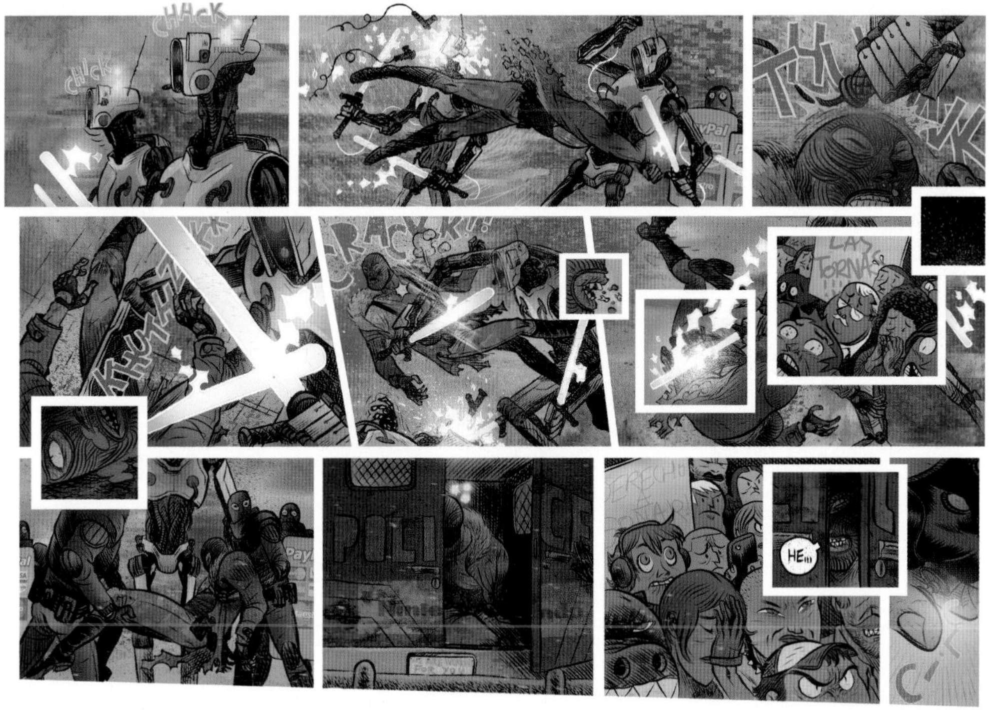
CHACK
HE,,,

MARCOS PRIOR

DAVID RUBÍN

Marcos Prior was born in Barcelona, Spain in 1975. Since then, he has made illustrations for publishers such as Cruïlla/SM, Editions Rockdelux, and Sol 90. He has also contributed storyboards for advertising campaigns such as Ogilvy Bassat, Vinizius Young & Rubicam, McCann, Shackleton Group, and Adding-Targis. He is the visionary cartoonist behind *Necropolis* (Astiberri) and *The Year of the 4 Emperors* (Diábolo Ediciones). He's collaborated with illustrator Danide on *Potlatch* (Norma Editorial) and *Fagocitosis* (Glénat).

His most recent book published in Spain was *Bunker Catalog* (Astiberri) with artist Jordi Pastor.

David Rubín was born in Ourense, Spain in 1977. He studied graphic design and launched into the world of comics, animation, and illustration. He is the creator of the two volume epic *The Hero* (Dark Horse Comics) and the artist behind the adaptation of the epic poem *Beowulf* (Image), in collaboration with Santiago Garcia. Rubín illustrated two spin off books based on Paul Pope's *Battling Boy*, focusing on the character of Aurora West, titled *The Rise of Aurora West* and *The Fall of the House of West* (First Second). Other titles include *The Fiction* with writer Curt Pires (BOOM! Studios) and *Ether* with writer Matt Kindt (Dark Horse Comics).

Marcos Prior Photo by **Jordi Pastor**

David Rubín Photo by **Mr. Satán**

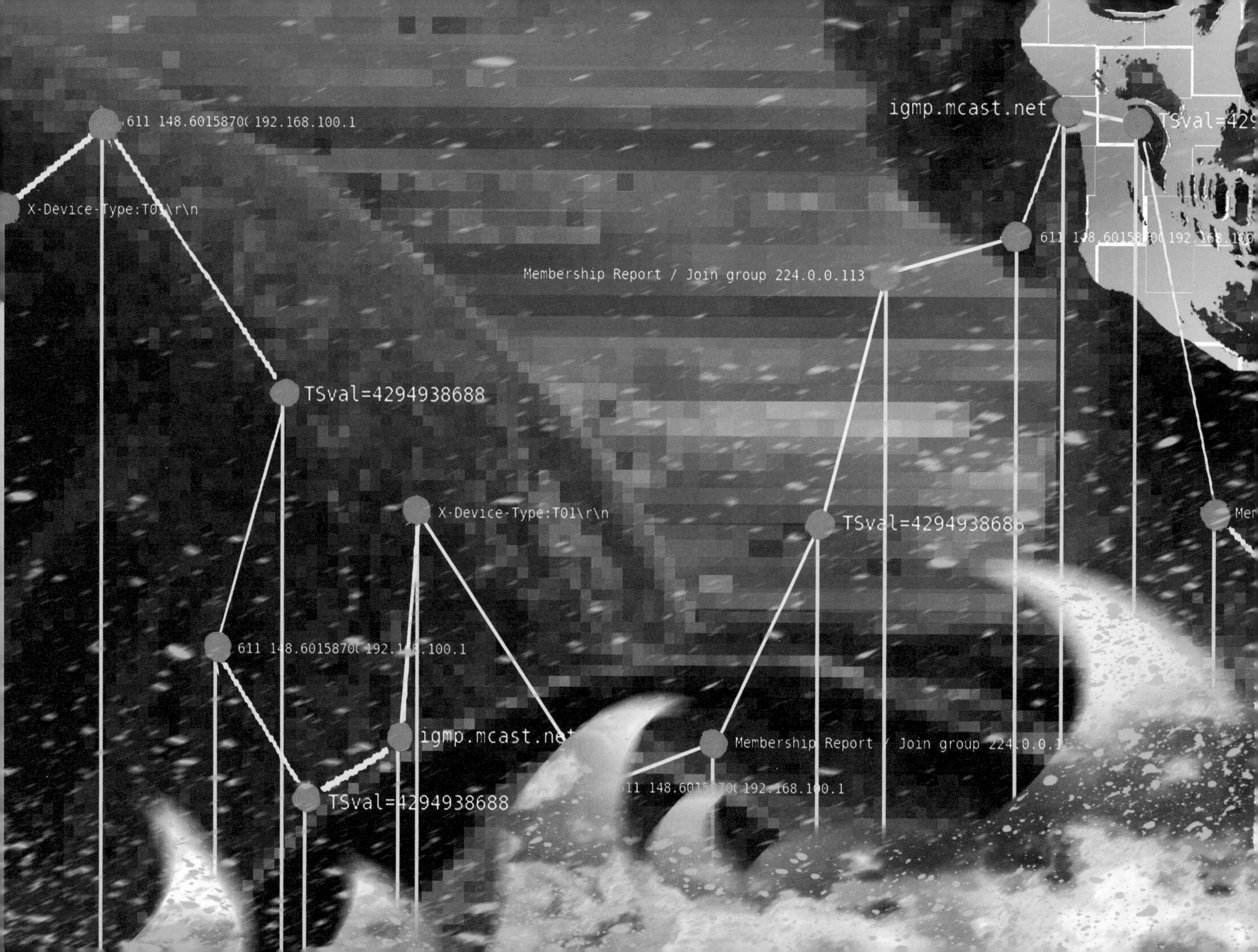

611 148.6015870 192.168.100.1
X-Device-Type:T01\r\n
TSval=4294938688
X-Device-Type:T01\r\n
611 148.6015870 192.168.100.1
igmp.mcast.net
TSval=4294938688
igmp.mcast.net
Membership Report / Join group 224.0.0.113
TSval=4294938688
Membership Report / Join group 224.0.0.1
611 148.6015870 192.168.100.1